Spelling
Dictionary

DAVID FIRNBERG

CASSELL

ACKNOWLEDGEMENTS

Cliff Parfit of the National Association for Remedial Education and
teacher adviser to the ILEA gave helpful advice on the project at all stages.

We were able to prepare this dictionary and set the final version in type –
all with the aid of a computer system developed by Hamish Carmichael.
His skill in devising the system and in adapting it to our special needs was
of great value and we are grateful for his contribution. Our thanks are also
due to two major British companies, ICL and Plessey, for the provision of
computer facilities and for much technical assistance.

Adele Barclay prepared the American spelling entries; and Christopher
White helped us with the usage of 'who' and 'whom'.

We are also grateful to Colston Sanger for several suggestions which
have been incorporated in the introductory pages of the revised edition of
the dictionary.

Cassell
Wellington House
125 Strand
London WC2R 0BB

British Library Cataloguing in Publication Data
A catalogue entry for this book is available
from the British Library

ISBN 0-304-34589-X

Printed and bound in Great Britain by
Biddles Ltd, Guildford and King's Lynn

ABOUT THIS DICTIONARY

This dictionary is not just an English dictionary with the definitions missing; the words in it have been chosen especially because they may not be easy to spell. For this reason some common words will not be found in it.

However, to have included all the words in the language which are difficult to spell would have made the dictionary too long, so we decided to limit ourselves to words likely to be used by the general reader or writer. This meant that only the commonest legal, medical and musical terms could be included. Very few proper names are given, and foreign words are included only if they have passed into common use. Thus 'chauffeur' and 'debut' are included, but not 'habitué' or 'parvenu'. A few common slang words have also been given.

This dictionary does not set out to define words. But when there is similarity in the spelling or sound of words, a brief definition is given in brackets: for example:

    complement (to add to)
    compliment (praise)
    principal (chief)
    principle (moral code)

HOW TO USE THIS DICTIONARY

Layout

The entries in this dictionary are arranged in two ways. Root words are listed in strict alphabetical order. Under each root word will be found its derived form. To make finding a word as clear and easy as possible, the derived forms are given in full. They are arranged alphabetically after their root word, except that plurals follow immediately after the singular.

ROOT WORD	fun	ROOT WORD	divine (God-like)
DERIVED FORMS	funnier	DERIVED FORMS	divinely
	funnily		divinity
	funny		divinities (*pl.*)

It has not been possible to include every derived form but, when a derived form in common usage is not given, you can make it by adding to the unchanged root the ending that you want. For instance, when you can form the past form of verbs by adding 'd' or 'ed' to the root, this does not appear in the dictionary.

One problem in English is the inconsistent way that these past forms are made. Many words ending in a vowel and single consonant double the consonant when an ending such as 'ed', 'ing' or 'er' is added; for example, 'jog, jogging', 'besot, besotted'. But others do not follow this pattern; for example, 'benefit, benefited', 'budget, budgeted'. This dictionary will enable you to learn the patterns each word follows.

In the case of adjectives the basic form is given but the forms in 'er' and 'est' have been omitted whenever they can be made by simply adding the endings to the root. Even when the root changes, only the 'er' or comparative form is given because the 'est' or superlative form behaves in the same way. For example, 'blunt' is given, but not 'blunter' or 'bluntest'; 'creamy' and 'creamier' are given, but not 'creamiest'.

Plurals

Plurals are given in all cases where the root word is changed to make the plural:

> gallery
> > galleries (*pl.*)

They are not given when they are formed by adding 's' to the root.

Possessives

The possessive forms of nouns give many people trouble. They do not know where to put the apostrophe. This edition of *Cassell's Spelling Dictionary* includes many examples of possessives. You should find an example to guide you wherever you open the book. In addition, tricky examples are always given, for example, under 'brother':

> brother-in-law
> > brothers-in-law (*pl.*)
> > brother-in-law's (of the brother-in-law)
> > brothers-in-law's (of the brothers-in-law)

There are further notes on forming the possessive and using the apostrophe on page viii.

Spelling adopted

Although many dictionaries have been consulted during the compilation of this one, the Oxford series of dictionaries was adopted as the authority for British spelling and the Webster series for American spellings.

Both these sources sometimes recognise several alternative spellings for the same word. Where more than one spelling exists, the alternatives are given.

bale, bail (out of aeroplane)

American spellings

In writing you may need to be aware of words with different British or American spelling. Where the American spelling is commonly different from the British, the American variant is given and printed like this:

epaulette
epaulet

Sometimes only a derived word is spelled differently:

abstract
abstraction
abstractor
abstracter

Sometimes the root and all the derived forms are different:

aesthete
esthete
aesthetic
esthetic
aesthetical
esthetical
aestheticism
estheticism

In cases where an American variant exists but the British spelling is acceptable to Americans, then only the British version is given.

-ise or -ize?

In British usage verbs and their associated forms ending in '-ise' can also be spelt '-ize'. Some people opt for one form and some for the other.

Americans always use '-ize', except in a few cases which are listed below. If you prefer '-ize', follow the American spellings of these words. Where a word is given ending in '-ise' and no American spelling is given, be careful: the Americans spell these words with '-ise' too, e.g.:

advertise	advise	afranchise
apprise	arise	braise
chastise	circumcise	comprise
compromise	concise	demise
despise	devise	disfranchise
disguise	emprise	enfranchise
enterprise	excise	exercise
expertise	franchise	guise
improvise	incise	merchandise
misadvise	misprise	mortise
precise	premise	prise
reprise	revise	supervise
surmise	surprise	televise
	treatise	

Foreign words

When a foreign word has been taken into common usage, American and British spellings sometimes differ. The two versions are shown in the usual way. However, if it is only a matter of accents – British 'abbé', American 'abbe' – then only the British version is given. Sometimes only the plural is affected:

château
    châteaux, *châteaus* (*pl.*)

COMMON SPELLING RULES (AND EXCEPTIONS)

English spelling is notoriously inconsistent. Here are some rules of thumb, with examples – and exceptions.

1. 'i before e, except after c.' This rule works well in most cases – 'believe', 'chief', 'diesel', 'friend', 'receive' – but watch out for exceptions such as 'counterfeit', 'either', 'neither', 'weird', 'sleight' and proper names such as 'Keith' and 'Sheila'.

2. In compound words such as 'almighty', 'fulfil', 'until', 'welfare', the double 'll' of 'all', 'full' and 'fill', 'till' and 'well' becomes a single 'l'. Exceptions include 'farewell', 'fullness', 'illness' and 'wellbeing'.

3. Verbs whose roots end in a vowel + single consonant + 'e', e.g. 'bake', 'chase', drop the 'e' when 'ed', 'ing' or 'er' is added: 'baker', 'chasing'. As always, there are exceptions, such as 'ageing'.

4. The silent 'e' is also dropped before a vowel in compound words but retained before a consonant, for example:

valueless	valuable
pursue	pursuing

Some exceptions are 'argument', 'awful', 'duly', 'truly' and 'wholly'.

5. Nouns ending in 'y' form their plurals by substituting 'ies' for 'y', except where 'y' is preceded by a vowel, for example:

ambiguity	ambiguities
category	categories
penny	pennies
BUT	
array	arrays
key	keys
chimney	chimneys

6. Many words have alternative spellings, either of which is correct. The important thing is to be consistent in your use of a particular spelling. Examples are:

abridgment	abridgement
disk	disc
despatch	dispatch
hullo	hallo (or hello)
inquire	enquire
loth	loath
mediaeval	medieval
ratable	rateable
spelt	spelled
Welsh rabbit	Welsh rarebit

How to use the apostrophe

Possessives

The apostrophe is used mainly to indicate possession or relationship as, for example, in:

the child's mother (the mother of the child)
the boys' school (the school of the boys)

Most people hesitate for a moment when forming the possessive of names ending in 's'. The usual practice with short names is to add another 's' as well as the apostrophe – 'St James's Street'. But with longer names the final 's' is often omitted; 'Mr Jenkins' office' is perfectly acceptable.

Whether an apostrophe is needed in phrases such as 'a week's holiday' or 'six weeks' work' is really a matter of style. Grammarians would say that it depends on whether 'six weeks' is regarded as a descriptive genitive or an adjectival phrase, for example: 'three minutes' rest' or 'the three-minute rule'.

Possessive pronouns

Possessive pronouns do not have an apostrophe:

mine, his, hers, its, ours, yours, theirs, whose

The exception is 'one's'.

Be careful of 'it's' which has the same form as the corresponding possessive adjective. It never has an apostrophe. ('It's' is short for 'it is' and should be used only in sentences such as 'It's raining today.')

The apostrophe to show omission

The 'It's raining' example shows this use of the apostrophe. It is used to show that something has been left out of a word. An extreme example is 'fo'c's'le' which is a shortening of 'forecastle'. You will also find the apostrophe used in this way in verse where the poet uses it to shorten words to fit the metre.

Plurals

The apostrophe is also used occasionally to indicate the plural of a word or symbol that does not ordinarily have a plural, for example:

There are two m's and two t's in committee.

If the meaning is clear without the apostrophe, then you can leave it out: '1830s' rather than '1830's', 'MPs' rather than 'MP's' which could be taken as a possessive.

SOURCES OF CONFUSION

To lay or lie

lay (laid, lying) – to place, set or arrange something (this verb always has an object)

> I laid the table before I left home.
> They were still laying the carpet at four o'clock.
> He had laid the matter before the committee.

lie (lay, lying, lain) – to be in a horizontal position (as in bed) or to take that position

> I lie down on my bed every afternoon.
> The book was lying on the table.
> The dog had lain in the same position all day.
> The apples lay in the long grass.

lie (lied, lying) – to tell untruths

> Do not lie to me.
> I lied to you about the money.
> The accused is lying about his actions.

To raise or rise

Similar confusion affects the meaning of these two words, although luckily their actual forms do not lead to confusion.
   Like 'lay', 'raise' always has an object.

raise – to lift

> I raise my hand in a salute.
> The Customs officer opened the suitcase by raising the lid.
> She raised herself in bed.

rise – to get up, get higher

> In May the sun rises at four o'clock.
> Get up, the sun has risen.
> The water in the river is rising.
> The star slowly rose above the horizon.

Who or whom

The rule is that 'who' is the subject and 'whom' the object:

> The man who came to dinner is my cousin.
> The man whom I invited to dinner was late.

However, 'whom' is rarely used in spoken English. We say: 'Who did you meet there?' and 'Who did you hear that from?' 'The person it belongs to' sounds more natural than 'the person to whom it belongs'.
   In general, 'whom' is rarely used without a preceding preposition, as in 'to whom', 'from whom', 'by whom', 'with whom', 'of whom':

> The author of whom I had heard a great deal was at the dinner.

Note that 'whose' is sometimes used instead of 'of whom':

> Whose is this coat?

aback
abacus
  abacuses (*pl.*)
  abaci (*pl.*)
abandon
  abandoned
  abandoning
  abandonment
abase (to humiliate)
  abasement
  abasing
abash (to embarrass)
abate (to decrease)
  abatement
  abating
abattoir
abbé (priest)
abbess (*fem.*)
  abbesses (*pl.*)
  abbess's (of the abbess)
  abbesses'
      (of the abbesses)
abbey (building)
abbot
  abbot's (of the abbot)
  abbots' (of the abbots)
abbreviate
  abbreviating
  abbreviation
abdicate
  abdicating
  abdication
abdomen
  abdominal
abduct
  abduction
  abductor
aberration
abet (to encourage)

abets
abetted
abetter
abetting
abettor (legal)
abeyance
abhor (to hate)
  abhorred
  abhorrence
  abhorrent
  abhorring
  abhors
abide
  abidance
  abiding
  abode
ability
  abilities (*pl.*)
abject (miserable)
  abjection
  abjectly
abjure
  abjuration
  abjuring
ablative (*grammar*)
ablaze
able
  able-bodied
  ably
ablution (washing)
abnegate
  abnegating
  abnegation
abnormal
  abnormality
  abnormalities (*pl.*)
  abnormally
  abnormity
  abnormities (*pl.*)
aboard
abode (dwelling)
abolish
  abolishes
  abolition
  abolitionary

abominable
  abominably
abominate
  abominating
  abomination
aboriginal
  aboriginally
  aborigine
abort
  abortion
  abortionist
  abortive
abound
about
  about-face
above
  above-board
abracadabra
abrade (to scrape)
  abrading
abrasion
  abrasive
abreast
abridge
  abridgement
  abridging
  abridgment
abroad
abrogate
  abrogating
  abrogation
abrupt
abscess
  abscesses (*pl.*)
abscissa (geometry)
  abscissas, abscissae (*pl.*)
abscond
absent
  absence
  absented
  absentee
  absenteeism
  absently
  absent-minded
  absents (he, she)

absinth
absinthe
absolute
  absolutely
absolve
  absolution
  absolving
absorb (to take into)
  absorbency
  absorbent
  absorption
  absorptive
abstain
  abstainer
  abstention
abstemious
  abstemiously
abstinence
  abstinent
abstract
  abstraction
  abstractor
  abstracter
abstruse
  abstrusely
  abstruseness
absurd
  absurdity
  absurdities (*pl.*)
  absurdly
abundance
  abundant
  abundantly
abuse
  abusing
  abusive
  abusively
abut
  abutment
  abuts
  abutted
  abutting
abysmal
  abysmally
abyss

abysses (*pl.*)
acacia
academy
  academies (*pl.*)
  academia
  academic
  academical
  academically
  academician
  academies'
    (of the academies)
  academy's
    (of the academy)
accede
  acceding
  accession
accelerate
  accelerating
  acceleration
  accelerator
accent
  accent's (of the accent)
  accents' (of the accents)
accentuate
  accentuating
  accentuation
accept
  acceptability
  acceptable
  acceptance
access (approach)
  accesses (*pl.*)
  accessibility
  accessible
  accessibly
accession (*from* accede)
accessory, accessary
  accessories (*pl.*)
accidence (*grammar*)
accident
  accidents (*pl.*)
  accidental
  accidentally
acclaim
  acclamation

acclimatise
  acclimatize
  acclimatisation
  acclimatization
  acclimatising
  acclimatizing
accolade
accommodate
  accommodating
  accommodation
accompany
  accompanied
  accompanies
  accompaniment
  accompanist
  accompanist's
    (of the accompanist)
  accompanists'
    (of the accompanists)
  accompanying
accomplice
    (partner in crime)
accomplish
  accomplished
  accomplishes
  accomplishment
accord
  accordance
  according
  accordion
    (musical instrument)
accost
account
  accountability
  accountable
  accountancy
  accountant
  accountant's
    (of the accountant)
  accountants'
    (of the accountants)
accoutrements
  accouterments
accredit
  accreditation

accredited
accrediting
accretion
accrue
  accrual
  accruing
accumulate
  accumulating
  accumulation
  accumulator
accurate
  accuracy
  accurately
accursed, accurst
accusative (*grammar*)
accuse
  accusation
  accusatory
  accuser
  accusing
accustom
  accustomed
ace
acerbate (to embitter)
  acerbating
  acerbic
  acerbity (bitterness)
acetate
  acetic (acid)
acetylene
ache
  aching
achieve
  achievable
  achievement
  achieving
achromatic
acid
  acidic
  acidified
  acidify
  acidifying
  acidity
acidosis
acknowledge

acknowledgement
acknowledging
acknowledgment
acme (top)
acne (pimple)
acolyte (attendant)
aconite (plant, drug)
acorn
acoustic
  acoustical
  acoustically
  acoustics
acquaint
  acquaintance
  acquaintanceship
acquiesce
  acquiescence
  acquiescent
  acquiescing
acquire
  acquirement
  acquiring
  acquisition
  acquisitive
acquit (to pardon)
  acquits
  acquittal
  acquitted
  acquitting
acre
  acreage
acrid
  acridity
acrimonious
  acrimoniously
  acrimony
acrobat
  acrobatic
  acrobatically
acronym
acrophobia
    (dread of heights)
acropolis
across
acrostic

acrylic
act
  actable
  acting
action
  actionable
activate
  activating
  activation
active
  actively
  activism
  activist
  activity
  activities (*pl.*)
actor
  actor's (of the actor)
  actors' (of the actors)
actress
  actresses (*pl.*)
  actress's (of the actress)
  actresses'
      (of the actresses)
actual
  actuality
  actualities (*pl.*)
  actually
actuary
  actuaries (*pl.*)
  actuarial
  actuaries'
      (of the actuaries)
  actuary's
      (of the actuary)
actuate
  actuating
  actuation
acumen
acupuncture
acute
  acuity
  acutely
  acuteness
adage (proverb)
adagio

3

adagios (*pl.*)
adamant
adapt (to make suitable)
 adaptability
 adaptable
 adaptation
 adaption
 adaptive
 adaptor (device)
 adapter (person)
add
addendum
 addenda (*pl.*)
adder (snake)
addict
 addiction
 addictive
addition
 additional
 additionally
 additive
addle
 addled
 addling
address
 addresses (*pl.*)
 addressed
 addressee
 addresses
adduce
 adducing
adenoid
 adenoidal
adept (clever)
adequate
 adequacy
 adequately
adhere
 adherence
 adherent
 adhering
 adhesion
 adhesive
ad hoc
adieu

adieus, adieux (*pl.*)
ad infinitum
adipose (fat)
 adiposity
adjacent
 adjacency
 adjacencies (*pl.*)
 adjacently
adjective (*grammar*)
 adjectival
 adjectivally
adjoin (to be next to)
 adjoining
adjourn (to postpone)
 adjournment
adjudicate
 adjudicating
 adjudication
 adjudicator
adjunct
adjust
 adjustable
 adjuster
 adjustment
adjutant (officer)
adjuvant (helpful)
ad-lib (to improvise)
 ad-libbed
 ad-libbing
 ad-libs
adman
 admen (*pl.*)
administer (an oath)
 administered
 administering
administrate
     (to manage)
 administrating
 administration
 administrative
 administrator
admiral
 admiral's
     (of the admiral)

admirals'
     (of the admirals)
 admiralty
admire
 admirable
 admirably
 admiration
 admirer
 admiring
admission
 admissibility
 admissible
 admissibly
admit
 admits
 admittance
 admitted
 admitting
admixture
admonish
 admonished
 admonishes
admonition
 admonitory
ad nauseam
ado (fuss)
adolescent
 adolescents (*pl.*)
 adolescence
 adolescent's
     (of the adolescent)
 adolescents'
     (of the adolescents)
adopt
 adopter
 adoption
 adoptive
adore
 adorable
 adorably
 adoration
 adorer
 adoring
adorn
 adornment

adrenalin
adrift
adroit (clever)
adsorb (on surface)
  adsorbent
  adsorption
adulate (to flatter)
  adulating
  adulation
adult (grown up)
adulterate
    (to make less pure)
  adulterant
  adulterating
  adulteration
adultery
  adulterer
  adulterer's
      (of the adulterer)
  adulterers'
      (of the adulterers)
  adulteress (fem.)
  adulteresses (pl.)
  adulteress's
      (of the adulteress)
  adulteresses'
      (of the adulteresses)
  adulterous
  adulterously
advance
  advancement
  advancing
advantage
  advantageous
  advantageously
advent (arrival)
Advent
  (time before Christmas)
adventitious (accidental)
  adventitiously
adventure
  adventurer
  adventuring
  adventurous
  adventurously

adverb
  adverbial
adversary (enemy)
  adversaries (pl.)
  adversary's
      (of the adversary)
  adversaries'
      (of the adversaries)
adverse (unfavourable)
  adversely
adversity (misfortune)
advertise
  advertisement
  advertiser
  advertising
advice (suggestion)
advise (to give advice)
  advisability
  advisable
  advisedly (deliberately)
  adviser, advisor
  advising
  advisory
advocate (lawyer)
  advocate's
      (of the advocate)
  advocates'
      (of the advocates)
advocate (to recommend)
  advocacy
  advocating
  advocation
aegis
  aegises (pl.)
aeon
aerate
  aerating
  aeration
  aerator
aerial (in the air)
  aerially
aerial (radio)
aerobatics
aerodrome
  airdrome

aerodynamics
aerofoil
  airfoil
aeronaut
  aeronaut's
      (of the aeronaut)
  aeronauts'
      (of the aeronauts)
  aeronautical
  aeronautics
aeroplane
  airplane
aerosol
aerospace
aesthete
  esthete
  aesthetic
  esthetic
  aesthetically
  esthetically
  aestheticism
  estheticism
afar (distant)
affable
  affability
  affably
affair
affect (to influence)
  affectation (pretence)
affection (love)
  affectionate
  affectionately
affidavit
affiliate
  affiliating
  affiliation
affinity
  affinities (pl.)
affirm
  affirmation
  affirmative
  affirmatively
affix
afflict
  affliction

affluent
affluence
afford
afforest
afforestation
affray
affrays (*pl.*)
affront
aficionado
afield
afloat
aforesaid
afraid
afresh
Afrikaans
after
aftermath
afternoon
afterthought
afterwards
again
against
agape
agate
age
aged
ageing
ageless
agelessness
aging
agency
agencies (*pl.*)
agency's
(of the agency)
agencies'
(of the agencies)
agenda
agent
agglomerate
agglomeration
aggrandise
aggrandize
aggrandisement
aggrandizement
aggrandising

aggrandizing
aggravate
aggravating
aggravation
aggregate (total)
aggregation
aggregate
(used in concrete)
aggression
aggressive
aggressively
aggressiveness
aggressor
aggrieve
aghast
agile
agilely
agility
agitate
agitating
agitation
agitator
aglow
agnostic
agnosticism
ago
agog
agony
agonies (*pl.*)
agonise
agonize
agonising
agonizing
agoraphobia
(dread of open spaces)
agrarian
agree
agreeable
agreeably
agreed
agreeing
agreement
agriculture
agricultural
agriculturist

agriculturalist
aground
ague
ahead
ahoy
aid
aide (helper)
aiding
aide-de-camp
aides-de-camp (*pl.*)
ail (to be ill)
ailing
ailment
aileron
aim
aimless
aimlessly
aimlessness
air
airborne
air-conditioned
aircraft
aircraftman
airfield
air force
air hostess
air hostesses (*pl.*)
airing
airless
airlessness
airlift
air line
airline
airlock
airmail
airman
airmen (*pl.*)
airplane (*see* aeroplane)
airport
air raid
airspace
airtight
airworthiness
airworthy
airy

airily
airiness
airy-fairy
aisle (church gangway)
ajar
akimbo
akin
alabaster
à la carte
alacrity
à la mode
alarm
  alarmist
alas
albatross
  albatrosses (pl.)
albeit
albino
  albinos (pl.)
  albinism
album
albumen (white of egg)
albumin (protein)
alchemy
  alchemist
alcohol
  alcoholic
  alcoholism
alcove
alderman
  aldermen (pl.)
  aldermanic
  aldermanry
  alderman's
      (of the alderman)
  aldermanship
  aldermen's
      (of the aldermen)
ale (beer)
alert
  alertly
  alertness
alfresco
alga
  algae (pl.)

algebra
  algebraic
  algebraical
  algebraically
alias
  aliases (pl.)
alibi
  alibis (pl.)
alien
  alienable
  alienate
  alienating
  alienation
  alienator
alight (to get down)
alight (lit up, on fire)
align, aline
  alignment, alinement
alike
aliment (food)
  alimentary canal
alimony
alive
alkali
  alkalis (pl.)
  alkalies (pl.)
  alkaline
  alkalinity
all-American
allay (to reduce, lessen)
allege
  allegation
  alleged
  allegedly
  alleging
allegiance (loyalty)
allegory (story)
  allegories (pl.)
  allegorical
  allegorically
allegro (in music)
  allegretto
alleluia, halleluiah,
              hallelujah
allergy (reaction)

allergies (pl.)
allergic
alleviate
  alleviating
  alleviation
alley
  alleys (pl.)
alliance
alligator
  alligator's
      (of the alligator)
  alligators'
      (of the alligators)
alliteration
allocate
  allocating
  allocation
allocution (speech)
allot
  allotment
  allots
  allotted
  allotting
allow
  allowable
  allowance
alloy
  alloys (pl.)
all right
allude (to mention)
  alluding
allure (to tempt)
  allured
  allurement
  alluring
allusion (from allude)
alluvial
ally
  allies (pl.)
  alliance
  allied
  allies' (of the allies)
  allying
  ally's (of the ally)
alma mater

7

almanac
almighty
almond
almoner
almost
alms (charity)
aloe (plant)
aloft
alone
along
aloof
  aloofly
  aloofness
aloud
alp
  alpine
alpaca
alphabet
  alphabetical
  alphabetically
already
also
  also-ran
altar (in church)
alter (to change)
  alterable
  alteration
  altered
  altering
altercate (to quarrel)
  altercating
  altercation
alternate
  alternating
  alternation
  alternator
alternative
  alternatively
although
altimeter
altitude
alto
  altos (pl.)
altogether
altruism

altruist
altruistic
altruistically
alum
aluminium
aluminum
always
amalgam
  amalgamate
  amalgamating
  amalgamation
amanuensis
  amanuenses (pl.)
amass
amateur
  amateurish
  amateurishly
  amateurishness
  amateurism
amaze
  amazement
  amazing
ambassador
  ambassadorial
  ambassador's
    (of the ambassador)
  ambassadors'
    (of the ambassadors)
  ambassadress (*fem.*)
  ambassadresses (pl.)
  ambassadress's
    (of the ambassadress)
  ambassadresses'
  (of the ambassadresses)
amber
ambi- (both)
  ambidextrous
  ambience
  ambient
  ambiguity
  ambiguous
  ambiguously
ambit (extent)
ambition
  ambitious

ambitiously
ambivalence
  ambivalent
amble
  ambling
ambulance
  ambulant (able to walk)
ambush
  ambushes (pl.)
ameliorate
  ameliorating
  amelioration
amen
amenable
  amenably
amend (to correct)
  amendment
amenity
  amenities (pl.)
American
  Americana
  Americanise
  Americanize
  Americanising
  Americanizing
  Americanism
amethyst
amiable (good tempered)
  amiability
  amiably
amicable (friendly)
  amicability
  amicably
amid
  amidships
  amidst
amiss
amity
ammeter
ammonia
ammunition
amnesia (loss of memory)
amnesty (pardon)
  amnesties (pl.)
amoeba

amoebas, amoebae (*pl.*)
amoebic
amok, amuck
among
amongst
amoral (not moral)
amorally
amorous (loving)
amorously
amorousness
amorphous
amortise
amortize
amortising
amortizing
amortisation
amortization
amount
amour
ampere
ammeter
amperage
ampersand (and sign)
amphetamine
amphibia
amphibian
amphibious
amphitheatre
amphitheater
ample
amplitude
amply
amplify
amplification
amplified
amplifier
amplifies
amplifying
ampoule
ampul
amputate
amputating
amputation
amputee
amuck, amok

amulet
amuse
amusement
amusing
anachronism
anachronistic
anaemia
anaemic
anaesthetic
anesthetic
anaesthesia
anesthesia
anaesthetisation
anesthetization
anaesthetise
anesthetize
anaesthetising
anesthetizing
anaesthetist
anesthetist
anagram
anal (*from* anus)
analgesic (pain-killer)
analgesia
analogous
analog (computer)
analogical
analogue
analogy
analogies (*pl.*)
analyse
analyze
analysing
analyzing
analysis
analyses (*pl.*)
analyst
analyst's
(of the analyst)
analysts'
(of the analysts)
analytic
analytical
analytically
anarchist

anarchic
anarchical
anarchism
anarchist's
(of the anarchist)
anarchists'
(of the anarchists)
anarchy
anathema
anathemas (*pl.*)
anatomy
anatomical
anatomic
anatomically
anatomise
anatomize
anatomised
anatomized
anatomising
anatomizing
anatomist
ancestor
ancestor's
(of the ancestor)
ancestors'
(of the ancestors)
ancestral
ancestress
ancestresses (*pl.*)
ancestress's
(of the ancestress)
ancestresses'
(of the ancestresses)
ancestry
anchor
anchorage
anchored
anchoring
anchovy
anchovies (*pl.*)
ancient
ancillary
anecdote
anecdotal
anemometer (wind gauge)

anemone (flower)
aneroid
aneurysm
anew
angel
  angelic
  angelical
  angelically
  angel's (of the angel)
  angels' (of the angels)
anger
  angered
  angering
  angrier
  angrily
  angry
angina
angle (corner)
angle (to fish)
  angler
  angling
Anglican
  Anglicanism
anglice (in English)
anglicise
  anglicize
  anglicism
Anglomania
Anglophile
Anglophobe
  Anglophobia
angostura
anguish
angular
  angularity
anhydrous
aniline
animal
  animalcule
  animal's (of the animal)
  animals'
    (of the animals)
animate
  animatedly
  animating

animation
animosity (dislike)
  animosities (*pl.*)
animus (hostility)
aniseed
ankle
anklet
annal (story of one year)
  annals
  annalist
anneal
  (to toughen metal, etc.)
annex (to join)
  annexation
annexe (of house)
  annex
annihilate
  annihilating
  annihilation
anniversary
  anniversaries (*pl.*)
annotate
  annotating
  annotation
  annotator
announce
  announcement
  announcer
  announcing
annoy
  annoyance
annual (yearly)
  annually
annuity
  annuities (*pl.*)
  annuitant
annul
  annulled
  annulling
  annulment
  annuls
annular (ring-like)
  annularity
annunciate
  annunciating

annunciation
anode
anodyne
anoint
anomalous (irregular)
  anomalously
  anomaly
  anomalies (*pl.*)
anon. (anonymous)
anon (soon)
anonymous (unnamed)
  anonymity
  anonymously
anorak
another
answer
  answerable
  answered
  answering
antacid
antagonise
  antagonize
  antagonising
  antagonizing
  antagonism
  antagonist
antarctic
antecedent
  antecedents (*pl.*)
  antecedence
antechamber
antedate
  antedating
antediluvian
antelope
antenatal
antenna (of insect)
  antennae (*pl.*)
antenna (radio)
  antennas (*pl.*)
anterior
  anteriority
  anteriorly
ante-room
anthem

anther
anthology
  anthologies (*pl.*)
  anthologist
anthracite
anthrax
anthropo- (man)
anthropoid
anthropology
  anthropological
  anthropologist
anthropomorphic
  anthropomorphism
anti-aircraft
antibiotic
antibody
  antibodies (*pl.*)
antic
antichrist
anticipate
  anticipating
  anticipation
  anticipative
  anticipatory
anticlimax
  anticlimaxes (*pl.*)
  anticlimactic
anticyclone
  anticyclonic
antidepressant
antidote
antifreeze
antigen
antihistamine
antilogarithm
antimacassar
antimony
antipathy
  antipathies (*pl.*)
  antipathetic
antipodes
  antipodean
antiquary
  antiquaries (*pl.*)
  antiquarian

antiquarian's
  (of the antiquarian)
antiquarians'
  (of the antiquarians)
antique (very old)
  antiquated
  antiquity
  antiquities (*pl.*)
antirrhinum
  antirrhinums (*pl.*)
anti-Semitism
  anti-Semite
  anti-Semitic
antiseptic
  antisepsis
  antiseptically
antisocial
  antisocially
antithesis
  antitheses (*pl.*)
antitoxin
  antitoxic
antler
  antlered
antonym
anus
  anal
anvil
anxious
  anxiety
  anxiously
any
  anybody
  anybody's (of anybody)
  anyhow
  anyone
  anyone's (of anyone)
  anything
  anyway
  anywhere
aorta
apace (quickly)
apart
  apartheid
apartment

apathy
  apathetic
  apathetically
ape
  ape's (of the ape)
  apes' (of the apes)
  apery (monkey-house)
ape (to imitate)
  aping
  apery (imitation)
aperient (laxative)
aperitif (cocktail)
aperture
apex
  apexes (*pl.*)
  apices
aphis (greenfly)
  aphides (*pl.*)
aphorism
  aphoristic
aphrodisiac
apiary (for bees)
  apiaries (*pl.*)
  apiarist
  apiculture
apiece (each)
aplomb
apocalypse
  apocalyptic
apocrypha
  apocryphal
apogee
apologia (written excuse)
apology
  apologies (*pl.*)
  apologetic
  apologetically
  apologise
  apologize
  apologising
  apologizing
apophthegm (witticism)
apoplexy
  apoplectic
  apoplectically

apostasy
apostate
apostatise
apostatize
a posteriori
apostle
apostolate
apostolic
apostrophe
apostrophise
apostrophize
apostrophising
apostrophizing
apothecary
apothecaries (*pl.*)
apothecary's
(of the apothecary)
apothecaries'
(of the apothecaries)
apotheosis
appal
appall
appalled
appalling
appals (it)
apparatus
apparatuses (*pl.*)
apparatus (pl.)
apparel
apparelled
appareled
apparent
apparently
apparition (*from* appear)
appeal
appealing
appellant
appear
appearance
appeared
appearing
appease
appeasement
appeaser
appellation

append
appendage
appendix
(addition to a book)
appendices (*pl.*)
appendix (in anatomy)
appendixes (*pl.*)
appendicitis
appertain
appertaining
appetite
appetiser
appetizer
appetising
appetizing
applaud
applause
apple
apple-cart
apple-pie
appliqué
apply
appliance
applicable
applicant
application
applied
applying
appoint
appointment
apportion
apportioning
apposite (apt)
appraise
appraisal
appraisement
appraising
appreciate
appreciable
appreciably
appreciating
appreciation
appreciative
apprehend
apprehension

apprehensive
apprentice
apprentice's
(of the apprentice)
apprentices'
(of the apprentices)
apprenticeship
apprise (to inform)
apprising
apprize (to value)
apprizing
appro. (approval)
approach
approaches (*pl.*)
approachable
approbation
appropriate
appropriately
appropriateness
appropriating
appropriation
appropriator
approve
approval
approving
approximate
approximately
approximating
approximation
appurtenance (accessory)
apricot
a priori
apron
apropos
apt
aptitude
aptly
aptness
aqua-, aque- (water)
aqualung
aquarium
aquatic
aquatint
aqueduct
aqueous

aquiline (eagle-like)
arabesque
Arabian
  Arabic
arable
arbiter
  arbitrage
arbitrary
  arbitrarily
  arbitrariness
arbitrate
  arbitrating
  arbitration
  arbitrator
arbour (garden bower)
  arbor
arc
  arced
  arcked
  arcing
  arcking
arcade
arch (cheeky)
  archly
  archness
arch (of building)
  arches (*pl.*)
archaeology
  archaeological
  archaeologically
  archaeologist
archaic
  archaism
  archaistic
archangel
archbishop
  archbishopric
  archbishop's
    (of the archbishop)
  archbishops'
    (of the archbishops)
archdeacon
  archdeaconry
archdiocese
archduke

archducal
archduchess
archduchesses (*pl.*)
archduchy
arch-enemy
archer
archery
archetype
archetypal
archiepiscopal
  archiepiscopate
archipelago
  archipelagos,
    archipelagoes(*pl.*)
architect
  architect's
    (of the architect)
  architects'
    (of the architects)
architectural
architecturally
architecture
architrave
archive
  archivist
arctic
ardent
  ardently
  ardour
  ardor
arduous
  arduously
are
  aren't (are not)
area (space)
arena
argosy
argot (slang)
argue
  arguable
  arguably
  arguing
  argument
  argumentative
aria (song)

arid
  aridity
aright
arise
  arisen
  arising
  arose
aristocracy
  aristocrat
  aristocratically
arithmetic
  arithmetical
  arithmetically
  arithmetician
ark (Noah's)
arm (of body)
  armchair
  armful
  armlet
  arm's (of the arm)
  arms' (of the arms)
armada
Armageddon
armament
armature
armistice
armour
  armor
  armourer
  armorer
  armoury
  armory
  armouries (*pl.*)
  armories (pl.)
arms (coat of)
  armorial
arms (weapons)
army
  armies (*pl.*)
  army's (of the army)
  armies' (of the armies)
aroma
  aromatic
arose (*from* arise)
around

arouse
  arousal
  arousing
arraign (to accuse)
  arraignment
arrange (to put in order)
  arranged
  arrangement
  arranging
arrant (thorough)
array
arrears
arrest
arrive
  arrival
  arriving
arrogant (proud)
  arrogance
  arrogantly
arrogate
      (to claim unduly)
  arrogating
  arrogation
arrow
arrowroot
arsenal
arsenic
  arsenical
  arsenious
arson
  arsonist
art
  artist
  artiste (performer)
  artistic
  artistically
  artistry
  artist's (of the artist)
  artists' (of the artists)
artefact, artifact
artery
  arteries (pl.)
  arterial
artesian
artful

artfully
artfulness
arthritis
  arthritic
artichoke
article
articulate
  articulating
  articulation
  articulately
artifact, artefact
artifice
  artificer
artificial
  artificiality
  artificially
artillery
  artilleryman
  artillerymen (pl.)
  artilleryman's
      (of the artilleryman)
  artillerymen's
      (of the artillerymen)
artisan
artist (see art)
artiste (performer)
artless
  artlessly
  artlessness
arty
Aryan
asbestos
  asbestosis
ascend (to go up)
  ascendancy,
                    ascendency
  ascendant
  ascension
  ascent (going up)
ascertain
  ascertainable
  ascertainment
ascetic (abstinent)
  ascetically
  asceticism

ascribe
  ascribable
  ascribing
  ascription
aseptic (surgically clean)
  asepsis
ash (cinders)
  ashes (pl.)
  ashen
  ashy
ash (tree)
ashamed
ashore
Asia
  Asiatic
aside
asinine
  asininity
ask
askance
askew
asleep
asp (snake)
asparagus
  asparagus (pl.)
aspect
aspen (tree)
asperity (harshness)
  asperities (pl.)
aspersion (slander)
asphalt
asphyxia
  asphyxiant
  asphyxiate
  asphyxiating
  asphyxiation
aspic (jelly)
aspidistra
aspirate (letter H)
aspire (to seek to attain)
  aspirant
  aspiration
  aspired
  aspiring
  aspirin

ass
  asses (*pl.*)
  ass's (of the ass)
  asses' (of the asses)
assail
  assailant
assassin
  assassin's
      (of the assassin)
  assassins'
      (of the assassins)
  assassinate
  assassinating
  assassination
  assassinator
assault
  assaulter
assay (to test)
  assayer
assemble
  assemblage
  assembling
assembly
  assemblies (*pl.*)
assent (agreement)
assert (to insist)
  assertion
  assertive
assess (to fix amount)
  assessable
  assessment
  assessor
asset (possession)
assiduous
  assiduity
  assiduously
assign
  assignable
  assignation
  assignee
  assignment
assimilate
  assimilating
  assimilation
assist

assistance (help)
assistant (helper)
assize
associate
  associate's
      (of the associate)
  associates'
      (of the associates)
  associating
  association
assort
  assortment
assuage
  assuagement
  assuaging
assume
  assuming
  assumption
assure
  assurance
  assuredly
  assurer
  assuring
aster (plant)
asterisk
asteroid (planet)
astern
asthma
  asthmatic
astir (moving about)
astigmatism
  astigmatic
astonish
  astonishment
astound
astral
astrakhan
astray
astride
astringent
  astringency
astrology
  astrologer
astronaut
  astronautics

astronomy
  astronomer
  astronomic
  astronomical
  astronomically
astute
  astutely
  astuteness
asunder
asylum
asymmetry
  asymmetric
  asymmetrical
  asymmetrically
atheist
  atheism
athlete
  athlete's (of the athlete)
  athletes'
      (of the athletes)
  athletics
atlas
  atlases (*pl.*)
atmosphere
  atmospheric
atoll
atom
  atomic
  atomically
  atomisation
  atomization
  atomise
  atomize
  atomiser
  atomizer
  atomising
  atomizing
atone
  atonement
  atoning
atrocious
  atrociously
  atrocity
  atrocities (*pl.*)
atrophy

atrophied
atrophies
atrophying
attach (to fix)
  attachable
  attachment
attaché
  attaché case
attack (to fight against)
  attacker
attain
  attainable
  attainment
attempt
attend
  attendance
      (being present)
  attendant
      (person present)
  attendants (*pl.*)
  attention
  attentive
  attentively
attenuate
  attenuating
  attenuation
  attenuator
attest
  attestation
  attestor
  attestator
attic
attire (clothes, to clothe)
  attiring
attitude
attorney
  attorneys (*pl.*)
  attorney's
    (of the attorney)
  attorneys'
    (of the attorneys)
attract
  attraction
  attractive
  attractiveness

attribute
  attributable
  attributing
  attribution
  attributive
  attributively
attrition
attune
atypical (not typical)
  atypically
aubergine
auburn
auction
  auctioneer
  auctioneer's
    (of the auctioneer)
  auctioneers'
    (of the auctioneers)
  auctioning
audacious
  audaciously
  audacity
audible
  audibility
  audibly
audience
audio- (hearing)
  audiometer
  audiometric
  audiometry
  audio-typist
  audio-visual
audit
  audited
  auditing
  auditor
  auditor's
    (of the auditor)
  auditors'
    (of the auditors)
audition
auditorium
au fond
auger (tool)
aught (anything)

augment
  augmentation
au gratin
augur (to predict)
  augured
  auguring
  augurs
  augury
  auguries (*pl.*)
August (month)
august (noble)
auk (sea-bird)
aunt
  auntie, aunty
  aunt's (of the aunt)
  aunts' (of the aunts)
au pair
aura
  aurae (*pl.*)
  auras (*pl.*)
aural (by ear)
  aurally
au revoir
auspices
auspicious (favourable)
  auspiciously
austere
  austerely
  austerity
  austerities (*pl.*)
autarchy (absolute power)
  autarchies (*pl.*)
autarky (self-sufficiency)
authentic
  authentically
  authenticate
  authenticating
  authentication
  authenticity
author
  author's (of the author)
  authors'
    (of the authors)
  authoress (*fem.*)
  authoresses (*pl.*)

authoress's
  (of the authoress)
authoresses'
  (of the authoresses)
authorship
authorise
authorize
authorisation
authorization
authorising
authorizing
authority
  authorities (*pl.*)
  authoritarian
  authoritative
  authoritatively
autism
  autistic
auto- (self)
autobiography
  autobiographies (*pl.*)
  autobiographic
  autobiographical
  autobiographically
autocrat
  autocracy
  autocracies (*pl.*)
  autocratic
  autocratically
autogenous
autogiro, autogyro
autograph
automation
automatic
  automatically
  automatism
automaton
  automatons, automata
    (*pl.*)
automobile
automotive
autonomous
  autonomy
autopilot
autopsy

autopsies (*pl.*)
autostrada
autostrade (*pl.*)
auto-suggestion
autumn
  autumnal
auxiliary
avail
  availability
  available
avalanche
avant-garde
avarice
  avaricious
avenge
  avenger
  avenging
avenue
aver
  averred
  averring
  avers
average
  averaging
averse (opposed)
  aversion (dislike)
avert (to prevent)
  avertable
  avertible
aviary (for birds)
  aviaries (*pl.*)
aviation
aviator
aviator's
    (of the aviator)
aviators'
    (of the aviators)
avid
  avidity
  avidly
avocado
avocation
avoid
  avoidable
  avoidably

avoidance
avuncular
await
  awaited
  awaiting
awake
awaken
awakening
awaking
awoke
awaked
award
aware
  awareness
away
awe
  awesome
awful
  awfully
  awfulness
aweigh (anchor lifted)
awhile
awkward
  awkwardly
  awkwardness
awl (tool)
awning
awry (crooked)
axe
ax
  axing
axial
  axially
axiom
  axiomatic
  axiomatically
axis
  axes (*pl.*)
axle
ayah
ay, aye (yes)
azalea
azimuth
  azimuthal
azure

babble

B

babble (of voices)
 babbler
 babbling
babe
Babel (tower of)
baboon
baby
 babies (*pl.*)
 baby's (of the baby)
 babies' (of the babies)
 babyish
 baby-sitter
bachelor
 bachelor's
   (of the bachelor)
 bachelors'
   (of the bachelors)
 bachelorhood
bacillus
 bacilli (*pl.*)
 bacillary
back
 backache
 back bench
 back benches (*pl.*)
 back-bencher
 backbone
 back-breaking
 backed
 backer
 backgammon
 background
 backstairs
 backwater
backbite
 backbiter
 backbiting
backdate
 backdating

backfire
 backfiring
backward
 backwardness
bacon
bacterium
 bacteria (*pl.*)
 bacterial
 bacteriological
 bacteriologist
 bacteriology
bad
 badly
 bad-tempered
bade (from bid)
badge
badger (animal)
badger (to pester)
 badgered
 badgering
badminton
baffle
 baffling
bag
 bagged
 baggier
 bagging
 baggy
bagatelle
baggage
bagpipe
bail (cricket)
bail (security)
bail (*see* bale)
bailiff
 bailiff's (of the bailiff)
 bailiffs' (of the bailiffs)
bairn
bait (for fish)
bait (to torment)
baize
bake
 baker
 baker's (of the baker)
 bakers' (of the bakers)

bakery
 bakeries (*pl.*)
 baking
baksheesh (tip)
 bakshish
balalaika
balance
 balancing
balcony
 balconies (*pl.*)
bald
 bald-headed
 baldness
balderdash
bale, bail
   (out of aeroplane)
 baling, bailing
bale, bail
   (to pump out a boat)
bale (of merchandise)
 baling
baleful (evil)
 balefully
balk, baulk
   (billiards, timber)
balk, baulk (to hinder)
ball
 ball-bearing
 ball bearing
 ball-point
ballad
ballast
ballerina
 ballerina's
   (of the ballerina)
 ballerinas'
   (of the ballerinas)
ballet
 ballet dancer
ballistic
balloon
ballot (to vote)
 balloted
 balloting
ballyhoo

balm
  balmy (fragrant)
baloney, boloney
balsam
baluster
  balustrade
bamboo
bamboozle
  bamboozling
ban
  banned
  banning
  bans
banal
  banality
  banalities (*pl.*)
  banally
banana
band
  bandsman
  bandsmen (*pl.*)
  bandsman's
    (of the bandsman)
  bandsmen's
    (of the bandsmen)
bandage
  bandaging
bandit
  banditry
bandoleer, bandolier
bandy (crooked)
  bandy-legged
bandy
  (to exchange remarks)
  bandied
  bandies
  bandying
bane (ruin)
  baneful
  banefully
bang
bangle
banish
  banishment
banister, bannister

banjo
  banjos (*pl.*)
bank
  banker
  bank holiday
  banknote
bankrupt
  bankruptcy
  bankruptcies (*pl.*)
  bankrupt's
    (of the bankrupt)
  bankrupts'
    (of the bankrupts)
banner
banns (for wedding)
banquet
  banqueting
bantam
  bantam-weight
banter (to tease)
  bantered
  bantering
baptise
  baptize
  baptising
  baptizing
  baptism
bar (of pub)
  barmaid
  barmaid's
    (of the barmaid)
  barmaids'
    (of the barmaids)
  barman
  barmen (*pl.*)
  barman's
    (of the barman)
  barmen's
    (of the barmen)
  bartender
bar (to prevent)
  barred
  barring
  bars
bar (of metal, etc.)

bar (except)
bar (law court)
barb
  barbed wire
barbarian
  barbaric
  barbarism
  barbarous
  barbarously
barbecue
barber
  barber's (of the barber)
  barbers' (of the barbers)
barbitone
  barbiturate
  barbituric
bard
bare (uncovered)
  bareback
  barefaced
  barefoot
  bareheaded
  barelegged
  bareness
barely (scarcely)
bargain
barge (boat)
  bargee
  barge-pole
barge (to push)
  barging
baritone
  baritone's
    (of the baritone)
  baritones'
    (of the baritones)
barium
bark (dog's)
bark (of tree)
bark, barque (ship)
barley
  barley sugar
barmy (silly)
  barmier
  barmily

barn

barn
 barnyard
barnacle
barometer
 barometric
baron
 baron's (of the baron)
 barons' (of the barons)
 baroness (*fem.*)
 baronesses (*pl.*)
 baroness's
    (of the baroness)
 baronesses'
   (of the baronesses)
 baronet
 baronial
 barony
baroque
barque, bark (ship)
barrack (for soldiers)
barrack (to jeer)
barrage
barrel
 barrelled
 barreled
barren
 barrenness
barricade
 barricading
barrier
barrister
 barrister's
    (of the barrister)
 barristers'
    (of the barristers)
barrow
barter
 bartered
 barterer
 bartering
basalt
base
 baseless
 basely
 baseness

basing
basement
bashful
 bashfully
 bashfulness
basic
 basically
basin
basis
 bases (*pl.*)
bask
basket
 basketball
bas-relief
bass, bast (fibre)
bass (fish)
bass (music)
 basses (*pl.*)
 bass's (of the bass)
 basses' (of the basses)
 bass clef
basset (hound)
bassoon
bast, bass (fibre)
bastard
 bastardy
baste (cooking or sewing)
 basting
bastion
bat
 batsman
 batsman's
    (of the batsman)
 batsmen's
    (of the batsmen)
 batted
 batting
batch
 batches (*pl.*)
bate (to restrain)
 bated breath
 bating
bath
 bathing
bathe (to go swimming)

bather
 bathing
bathos
batik
batman (soldier servant)
 batmen (*pl.*)
 batman's
       (of the batman)
 batmen's
       (of the batmen)
baton (conductor's)
battalion
batten (to close)
 battened
 battening
batter (to beat)
 battered
 battering
batter (for pastry)
battery
 batteries (*pl.*)
battle
 battleaxe
 battleax
 battledress
 battleship
 battling
battlement
batty (crazy)
 battier
bauble (cheap jewel)
baulk, balk
       (billiards, timber)
baulk, balk (to hinder)
bauxite
bawd (debauched person)
 bawdier
 bawdiest
 bawdy
bawl (to shout)
bay (laurel)
 bay-leaf
bay (gulf)
bay (of a hound)
 baying

20

bay (compartment)
  bay window
bayonet
  bayoneted
  bayoneting
bazaar
bazooka
be
  been
  being
beach (shore)
  beachcomber
  beachhead
beacon
bead
  beady
beadle
beagle
  beagling
beak
beaker (cup)
beam
bean (vegetable)
  beanfeast
  beanstalk
bear (animal)
  bear's (of the bear)
  bears' (of the bears)
bear (to carry)
  bearable
  bearer
  bore
  born (of a baby)
  borne (carried)
beard
bearing (of a machine)
beast
  beastlier
  beastliness
  beastly
beat (to hit)
  beaten
  beater
beat (rhythm)
beatific

beau
  beaux (*pl.*)
beauty
  beauties (*pl.*)
  beauteous
  beautician
  beautified
  beautiful
  beautifully
  beautify
  beautifying
beaver
becalm
because
beckon (to signal)
become
  became
  becoming
bed
  bedclothes
  bedded
  bedding
  bedridden
  bedrock
  bed-sitter
  bed-sitting-room
bedaub
bedevil
  bedevilled
  bedeviled
  bedevilling
  bedeviling
bedlam
  bedlamite
bedouin
bedraggle
bee
  bee's (of the bee)
  bees' (of the bees)
  beehive
  beeswax
beech (tree)
beef
  beefeater
  beefier

  beefsteak
  beefy
beeline
been (*from* be)
beer (drink)
  beeriness
  beery
beet (vegetable)
  beetroot
beetle (insect)
  beetle's (of the beetle)
  beetles' (of the beetles)
befall
  befallen
  befell
befit
  befitted
  befitting
before
  beforehand
befoul
befriend
beg
  beggar
  beggared
  beggaring
  beggarliness
  beggarly
  beggar's (of the beggar)
  beggars'
    (of the beggars)
  beggary
  begged
  begging
  begs
beget
  begetter
  begot
  begotten
begin
  began
  beginner
  beginner's
    (of the beginner)

beginners'
        (of the beginners)
beginning
begins
begun
begone (go away)
begonia
begrudge
  begrudging
beguile
  beguilement
  beguiler
  beguiling
behalf
behave
  behaving
  behaviour
  behavior
behead
  beheaded
behind
  behindhand
behold
  beheld
  beholden
        (under obligation)
  beholder
  beholding
behove (to be necessary)
beige
being
belabour
  belabor
  belaboured
  belabored, belabord
  belabouring
  belaboring
belated
belay (nautical term)
belch
  belched
beleaguer
  beleaguered
  beleaguering
belfry

belfries (*pl.*)
belie
  belying
belief
  believable
  believe
  believer
  believing
belittle
  belittler
  belittling
bell (for ringing)
belladonna
belle (pretty girl)
belles lettres
bellicose
  bellicosity
belligerent
  belligerence
bellow (to shout)
bellows (air pump)
belly
  bellies (*pl.*)
  bellyful
belong
beloved
below (under)
belt
bemoan
bemuse
bench
  benches (*pl.*)
  bencher
bend
  bent
beneath
benediction (blessing)
benefaction (doing good)
  benefactor
  benefactor's
        (of the benefactor)
  benefactors'
        (of the benefactors)
  benefactress (*fem.*)
  benefactresses (*pl.*)

benefice (church living)
beneficence (kindness)
  beneficent
beneficial (advantageous)
  beneficially
  beneficiary
  beneficiaries (*pl.*)
benefit
  benefited
  benefiter
  benefiting
benevolent
  benevolence
  benevolently
benighted
benign
  benignancy
  benignant
benison (blessing)
bent (skill)
benumb
  benumbed
benzene (petroleum fluid)
benzine (cleaning fluid)
bequeath
  bequest
berate
  berating
bereave
  bereavement
  bereft
  bereaved
beret (cap)
berry (fruit)
  berries (*pl.*)
berserk, berserker
berth (nautical)
beryl
beseech
  beseeched
  beseeches
  besought
beset
  besetting
beside

besides
besiege
  besieging
besom (broom)
besotted
besought (*from* beseech)
bespeak
  bespoke
  bespoken
best
bestial
  bestialism
  bestiality
  bestialities (*pl.*)
  bestially
bestir
  bestirred
  bestirring
  bestirs
bestow
  bestowal
bestride
  bestriding
  bestrode
bet
  betted
  better
  betting
bête noire
  bêtes noires (*pl.*)
betel (leaf)
betide
betimes
betoken
betray
  betrayal
  betrayed
betroth
  betrothal
  betrothed
better
  best
better (to improve)
  bettered
  bettering

betterment
between
betwixt
bevel
  bevelled
  beveled
  bevelling
  beveling
beverage
bevy
  bevies (*pl.*)
bewail
beware
bewilder
  bewildered
  bewildering
  bewilderment
  bewilders
bewitch
  bewitched
  bewitches
beyond
biannual (half-yearly)
  biannually
bias
  biased
  biases (*pl.*)
  biasing
bible
  biblical
bibliography
  bibliographies (*pl.*)
  bibliographer
  bibliographic
  bibliographical
  bibliographically
bibliophile, bibliophil
bibulous
bicarbonate
bicentenary
  bicentenaries (*pl.*)
  bicentennial
biceps
bicker
  bickered

bickering
bicycle
  bicycling
  bicyclist
bid
  bidden
  bidder
  bidding
  bade
bide (to wait)
  biding
bidet
biennial (every two years)
  biennially
bier (coffin stand)
bifocal
bifurcate
  bifurcating
  bifurcation
big
  bigger
bigamy
  bigamies (*pl.*)
  bigamist
  bigamist's
        (of the bigamist)
  bigamists'
        (of the bigamists)
  bigamous
  bigamously
bigot
  bigoted
  bigotry
bigwig
bijou
  bijoux (*pl.*)
bike (bicycle)
bikini
bilateral
  bilaterally
bilberry
  bilberries (*pl.*)
bile
  biliary
bilge

23

bilingual
  bilingualism
  bilinguist
bilious
  biliousness
bilk (to cheat)
bill
  bill of fare
bill (beak)
billet
  billeted
  billetee
  billeter
  billeting
billet doux
  billets doux (*pl.*)
billiards
billion (UK million million)
billio
  (US thousand million)
  billionaire
billow
  billowy
bimonthly
  (every two months)
  bimonthly
  (twice a month)
bin
binary
binaural
bind
  binder
  bindery
  bound
binge
bingo
binnacle
binocular
binomial
bio- (*life*)
biochemist
  biochemical
  biochemistry
biography
  biographies (*pl.*)

biographer
biographical
biographically
biology
  biological
  biologically
  biologist
  biologist's
    (of the biologist)
  biologists'
    (of the biologists)
bionics
biopsy
  biopsies (*pl.*)
bipartite
  bipartisan
biped
biplane
bipolar
birch (tree)
birch (whip)
bird
  bird's (of the bird)
  birds' (of the birds)
  bird's-eye
  birdie (golf)
birth
  birthday
  birthplace
  birthrate
  birthright
biscuit
bisect
  bisection
  bisector
bisexual
  bisexually
bishop
  bishopric
  bishop's (of the bishop)
  bishops'
    (of the bishops)
bismuth
bison
bistro

bitch
  bitches (*pl.*)
bite
  bit
  biter
  bites
  biting
  bitten
bitter (beer)
bitter (sour)
  bitterer
  bitterly
  bitterness
bittern (bird)
bitumen
  bituminous
bivalve
bivouac
  bivouacked
  bivouacking
bizarre (unusual)
  bizarrely
  bizarreness
blab
  blabbing
  blabbed
  blabs
black
  blackberry
  blackberries (*pl.*)
  blackbird
  blackbird's
    (of the blackbird)
  blackbirds'
    (of the blackbirds)
  blackboard
  blacken
  blackened
  blackening
  black market
  black marketeer
  blackness
  blackout
  blacked out
blackguard

blackguardly
blackguard's
(of the blackguard)
blackguards'
(of the blackguards)
blackmail
blackmailed
blackmailer
blacksmith
blacksmith's
(of the blacksmith)
blacksmiths'
(of the blacksmiths)
bladder
blade
blame
blameless
blamelessly
blaming
blanch (to whiten)
blancmange
bland (gentle)
blandly
blandish (to flatter)
blandishment
blank
blank cheque
blank check
blanket
blanketed
blanketing
blare
blaring
blarney
blasé
blaspheme
blasphemer
blaspheming
blasphemous
blasphemously
blasphemy
blasphemies (*pl.*)
blast
blast-off
blatant

blatancy
blatantly
blaze
blazing
blazer
blazon (coat of arms)
bleach
bleak
bleaker
bleakly
bleakness
blear
blear-eyed
blearily
bleariness
bleary
bleary-eyed
bleat
bleed
bled
bleeder
blemish
blemishes (*pl.*)
blench
blenched
blenches
blend
blender
bless
blessed (sacred)
blest
blesses
blessing
blew (*from* blow)
blight
blighter
blind
blind alley
blindfold
blindly
blindness
blink
blinkered
bliss
blissful

blissfully
blissfulness
blister
blistered
blistering
blithe
blithely
blitheness
blithering
blizzard
bloat
bloated
bloater
blob
bloc (group)
block
blockage
blockbuster
blockade
blockading
blockhead
bloke
bloke's (of the bloke)
blokes' (of the blokes)
blond (*male*)
blonde (*fem.*)
blood
bloodcurdling
bloodhound
blood pressure
bloodshed
bloodshot
bloodthirsty
blood vessel
bloody
bloom
bloomer
blossom
blot
blots
blotted
blotter
blotting
blotch
blotches (*pl.*)

25

blotchy
blouse
blow
  blew
  blower
  blown
  blows
blowzy (red-faced)
blub (to cry)
  blubbed
  blubbing
  blubs
blubber (of whale)
  blubbery
blubber (to sob)
  blubbered
bludgeon
  bludgeoned
  bludgeoning
blue
  bluebell
  blueberry
  blueberries (*pl.*)
  blue-chip
  blue-collar
  blue-eyed
  blueness
  blue-pencil
  blue-pencilled
  blue-penciled
bluff (to deceive)
bluff (hearty)
  bluffness
blunder
  blundered
  blunderer
  blundering
  blunders
blunderbuss
blunt
  bluntly
  bluntness
blur
  blurred
  blurriness

blurs
blurb
blurt
blush
  blushes (*pl.*)
  blushed
  blushes
bluster
  blustered
  blustering
  blusters
  blustery
boa (fur wrap)
boa (snake)
  boa-constrictor
boar (male pig)
  boar's (of the boar)
  boars' (of the boars)
board
  boarder
board (of wood)
boast
  boaster
  boastful
  boastfully
  boastfulness
boat
  boat's (of the boat)
  boats' (of the boats)
  boatswain (bosun)
bob
  bobbed
  bobbing
  bobs
bobbin
bobby
  bobbies (*pl.*)
  bobby's (of the bobby)
  bobbies'
          (of the bobbies)
bob-sled, bobsleigh
bode
  boding
bodice
bodkin

body
  bodies (*pl.*)
  bodied
  bodies' (of the bodies)
  bodiless
  bodily
  bodyguard
  body's (of the body)
bogey (golf)
boggle
  boggling
bogie (undercarriage)
bogus
bogy, bogey (goblin)
  bogeys, bogies (*pl.*)
boil
  boiler
boisterous
  boisterously
bold
  boldly
bole (clay)
bole (of tree)
bollard
boloney, baloney
Bolshevik
  Bolshevism
  Bolshevist
bolster
  bolstered
  bolstering
bolt
bomb
  bomber
  bombshell
bombard
  bombardier
  bombarding
  bombardment
bombast
  bombastic
  bombastically
bona fide (in good faith)
  bona fides (good faith)
bonanza

bond
bondage
bone
boneless
bony
bonfire
bonhomie
bonnet
bonneted
bonny
bonnier
bonus
bonuses (*pl.*)
bon voyage
boo
booed
booing
booby
boobies (*pl.*)
book
bookable
booklet
book's (of the book)
books' (of the books)
book token
bookie (bookmaker)
bookies (*pl.*)
bookie's (of the bookie)
bookies'
(of the bookies)
bookkeeper
bookkeeping
boom
boomerang
boor (lout)
boorish
boost (to strengthen)
booster
boot
bootee
bootlace
bootless (profitless)
bootleg
bootlegged
bootlegger

bootlegging
booth
booty
booze
boozer
boozing
borax
boracic
border (edge)
bordered
bordering
bore (to weary)
boredom
boring
bore (*from* to bear)
bore (to pierce)
boring
born (of a baby)
borne (carried)
borough (town)
borrow (money, etc.)
borrower
bosh (nonsense)
bosom
boss
bosses (*pl.*)
bosses' (of the bosses)
bossier
bossiness
bossily
boss's (of the boss)
bossy
bosun (boatswain)
botany
botanical
botanist
botch
both
bother
botheration
bothered
bothering
bothersome
bottle
bottling

bottleneck
bottom
bottomless
bottommost
botulism
boudoir
bough (branch)
bought (purchased)
boulder (large stone)
boulevard
bounce
bouncing
bound (to jump)
bound (*from* bind)
boundary
boundaries (*pl.*)
bounder (rascal)
boundless
bounteous
bounty
bounties (*pl.*)
bountiful
bouquet
bourbon
bourgeois
bourgeoisie
bout
boutique
bovine
bow (to bend forward)
bow (for violin, etc)
bow (knot)
bow-tie
bow (forepart of ship)
bow (weapon)
bowdlerise
bowdlerize
bowdlerising
bowdlerizing
bowel (intestine)
bower (summer-house)
bowl (in cricket)
bowler
bowler's (of the bowler)

bowlers'
    (of the bowlers)
bowling
bowl (basin)
bow-legs
  bow-legged
box
  boxer
  boxer's (of the boxer)
  boxers' (of the boxers)
box
  boxes (*pl.*)
box-office
boy
  boys (*pl.*)
  boyhood
  boy-friend
  boyish
  boyishly
  boyishness
  boy's (of the boy)
  boys' (of the boys)
boycott
  boycotted
  boycotting
brace
  bracing
bracelet
braces
bracken
bracket
  bracketed
  bracketing
brackish
brad
  bradawl
brag
  brags
  braggart
  bragged
  bragging
braid
Braille
brain
  brainier

brainless
brain's (of the brain)
brains' (of the brains)
brainwashed
brainwashing
brainwave
brainy
braise (to cook)
  braising
brake (to slow down)
  braking
brake (vehicle)
bramble
bran
branch
  branches (*pl.*)
brand
  brand-new
brandy
  brandies (*pl.*)
brash
brass
  brasses (*pl.*)
brassard
brassière
brat
bravado
brave
  bravely
  bravery
  braving
bravo (cry of approval)
  bravos (*pl.*)
bravo (ruffian)
  bravoes (*pl.*)
bravura
brawl
brawn
  brawny
bray
braze (to weld)
  brazing
brazen (impudent)
  brazenness
brazen (made of brass)

brazen
  (out, to be unashamed)
brazier (brass-worker)
brazier (pan)
breach
bread (food)
breadth
break
  breakable
  breakage
  breakfast
  breakthrough
bream
breast
  breast-feeding
  breast-fed
breath
  breathalyser
  breathalyzer
  breathing
  breathless
  breathtaking
breathe (to take breaths)
  breather
  breathing
breech (of gun)
  breech-loader
  breech-loading
breeches (trousers)
breed
  bred
breeze
  breezily
  breezy
brethren
brevity
  brevities (*pl.*)
brew
  brewer
  brewer's (of the brewer)
  brewers'
    (of the brewers)
  brewery
  breweries (*pl.*)
briar, brier

bribe
bribable
bribery
bribing
bric-à-brac
brick
brickbat
bricklayer
bricklayer's
(of the bricklayer)
bricklayers'
(of the bricklayers)
bricklaying
bride
bridal
bridegroom
bridesmaid
bridge
bridging
bridgehead
bridle
bridle-path
bridling
brief
brief-case
briefly
brier, briar
brigade
brigadier
brigadier's
(of the brigadier)
brigadiers'
(of the brigadiers)
brigand
bright
brighten
(to make bright)
brightened
brightening
brightly
Brighton
brilliant
brilliance
brilliantly
brim

brim-full
brimful
brimstone
brine
briny
bring
brought
brink
brisk
briskly
brisket
bristle
bristling
bristly
Britain
British
Briton (British subject)
Britannia
Britannic
Brittany (in France)
brittle
brittleness
broach (to open, begin)
broached
broaches
broad
broaden
broadened
broadening
broadly
broadcast
broadcaster
broadcaster's
(of the broadcaster)
broadcasters'
(of the broadcasters)
broadminded
broadside
brocade
broccoli
brochure
brogue
broil
broiler
broke (*from* break)

broke (bankrupt)
broken
broken-hearted
broker
brokerage
bromide
bronchial
bronchitic
bronchitis
bronco (horse)
broncos (*pl.*)
bronze
brooch (jewel)
brooches (*pl.*)
brood
broody
brook (stream)
brooklet
brook (to tolerate)
broom (brush)
broom (shrub)
broth
brothel
brother
brothers (*pl.*)
brotherhood
brother-in-law
brothers-in-law (*pl.*)
brother-in-law's
(of the brother-in-law)
brothers-in-law's
(of the brothers-in-law)
brotherliness
brotherly
brother's
(of the brother)
brothers'
(of the brothers)
brougham (carriage)
brought (*from* bring)
brow
browbeaten
brown
Brownie (junior Guide)
browse

29

browsing
bruise
  bruiser
  bruising
brunette
brunt
brush
  brushes (*pl.*)
  brushing
brusque
  brusquely
  brusqueness
Brussels
  Brussels sprouts
brute
  brutal
  brutalisation
  brutalization
  brutalise
  brutalize
  brutalising
  brutalizing
  brutality
  brutalities (*pl.*)
  brutally
  brute's (of the brute)
  brutes' (of the brutes)
bubble
  bubbling
  bubbly
buccaneer
buck (male deer, rabbit)
buck (to jump)
buck (up, to hurry)
buck (in card-game)
  buck-passer
  buckpassing
  pass the buck
buck rarebit (food)
bucket
  bucketful
  bucketfuls (*pl.*)
buckle
  buckling
buckram

bucolic
bud
  buds
  budded
  budding
Buddha
  Buddhism
  Buddhist
buddleia
budge
  budging
budgerigar
budget
  budgetary
  budgeted
  budgeting
buff
buffalo
  buffaloes (*pl.*)
  buffalo's
           (of the buffalo)
  buffaloes'
           (of the buffaloes)
buffer
  buffered
  buffering
buffet (to knock)
  buffeted
  buffeting
  buffets
buffet (for food)
buffoon
  buffoonery
  buffooneries (*pl.*)
bug (to listen in)
  bugged
  bugging
bug (insect)
bugbear
buggy (small cart)
  buggies (*pl.*)
  buggy's (of the buggy)
  buggies' (of the buggies)
bugle
  bugler

bugling
build
  builder
  building
  built
bulb
  bulbous
bulge
  bulging
bulk
  bulkier
  bulky
bulkhead
bull
  bullfighter
  bullish
  bullock
  bull's (of the bull)
  bulls' (of the bulls)
bulldoze
  bulldozer
  bulldozing
bullet
  bullet-proof
bulletin
bullfinch
  bullfinches (*pl.*)
bullion
bullock
bull's-eye
bully
  bullied
  bullies (*pl.*)
  bullies' (of the bullies)
  bullying
  bullyrag
  bully's (of the bully)
bulrush
bulwark
bum
bumble-bee
bump
  bumper
  bumpier
  bumpily

bumpiness
bumpy
bumpkin
bumptious
  bumptiously
  bumptiousness
bun
bunch
  bunches (*pl.*)
bundle
  bundling
bung
  bunged up
bungalow
bungle
  bungler
  bungling
bunion
bunk (bed in ship)
bunk (to run away)
bunker (in golf)
  bunkered
  bunkering
bunkum
bunny
  bunnies (*pl.*)
  bunny's (of the bunny)
  bunnies'
      (of the bunnies)
Bunsen burner
bunting
buoy (float)
  buoyancy
  buoyant
  buoyantly
  buoyed (up)
  buoying
bur, burr (of a plant)
burble
  burbling
burden
  burdened
  burdening
  burdensome
bureau

bureaux (*pl.*)
bureaus (*pl.*)
bureaucracy
bureaucrat
bureaucratic
bureaucratically
burgeon
  burgeoning
burgle
  burglar
  burglary
  burglaries (*pl.*)
  burgling
burgomaster
burgundy
burial
burlesque
burly
  burlier
  burliness
burn
  burned
  burner
  burning
  burnt
burnish
  burnished
  burnisher
  burnishing
burr (sound)
burrow
bursar
  bursary
  bursaries (*pl.*)
burst
bury
  burial
  buried
  buries
  burying
bus
  buses (*pl.*)
  bussed
  bussing
busby

busbies (*pl.*)
bush
  bushes (*pl.*)
  bushy
bushel
business
  businesses (*pl.*)
  business-like
bust
bustle
  bustling
busy
  busier
  busily
  busybody
  busybodies (*pl.*)
  busying
  busyness (being busy)
but
butcher
  butchers (*pl.*)
  butchered
  butcherer
  butchering
  butcher's
      (of the butcher)
  butchers'
      (of the butchers)
  butchery
  butcheries (*pl.*)
butler
  butlers (*pl.*)
  butler's (of the butler)
  butlers' (of the butlers)
butt (to push)
butts (for shooting)
butt (thick end)
butt (barrel)
butter
  buttered
  butter-fingered
  butter fingers
  buttering
  buttery
buttercup

butterfly
  butterflies (*pl.*)
  butterfly's
    (of the butterfly)
  butterflies'
    (of the butterflies)
buttery (food store)
  butteries (*pl.*)
buttock
button
  buttoned
buttress
  buttresses (*pl.*)
buxom
  buxomness
buy
  bought
  buyer
  buyer's (of the buyer)
  buyers' (of the buyers)
  buying
buzz
buzzard
by
  by and by
bye (in cricket)
by-election
bygone
by-law
byline
bypass
  bypasses (*pl.*)
bypath
by-play
by-product
byre (cow-house)
byroad
bystander
byword

C

cab
  cabby
  cabbies (*pl.*)
  cabby's (of the cabby)
  cabbies' (of the cabbies)
cabaret
cabbage
cabin
cabinet
cable
  cablegram
  cabling
cache (hiding place)
cackle
  cackling
cacophony (ugly noise)
  cacophonous
cactus
  cacti, cactuses (*pl.*)
cad
  caddish
  caddishly
  cad's (of the cad)
  cads' (of the cads)
cadaver
  cadaverous
caddie (golf)
  caddying
caddis
  caddis-worm
caddy (tea)
  caddies (*pl.*)
cadence (rhythm)
cadenza (in music)
cadet
  cadet corps
  cadet's (of the cadet)
  cadets' (of the cadets)
cadge

  cádging
cadmium
Caesarean (birth)
café
  cafés (*pl.*)
cafeteria
caffeine
cage
cagey (shrewd)
  cagier
  cagiest
  cagily
  caginess
cairn
caisson
cajole
  cajolery
  cajoling
cake
  cake's (of the cake)
  cakes' (of the cakes)
  caking
calabash
calamine (ointment)
calamity
  calamities (*pl.*)
  calamitous
calcify
  calcification
  calcified
  calcifying
calcium
calculate
  calculable
  calculating
  calculation
  calculator
calculus
calendar (table of dates)
calender (machine)
  calendered
  calendering
calends, kalends
calf
  calves (*pl.*)

calving
calf (of leg)
  calves (*pl.*)
calibre
  caliber
  calibrate
  calibrating
  calibration
calico
caliph
  caliphate
call
  caller
  caller's (of the caller)
  callers' (of the callers)
calligraphy
  calligrapher
  calligraphic
  calligraphist
calliper
  caliper
callisthenic
  calisthenic
callous (unfeeling)
  callously
  callousness
callow (inexperienced)
callus (hardened skin)
  calluses (*pl.*)
  callosity
calm
  calmly
  calmness
calomel
calorie
  calories (*pl.*)
  calorific
  calorimeter
  calorimetric
  calorimetry
calumny
  calumnies (*pl.*)
  calumniate
  calumniating
  calumniator

calumnious
calve
  calving
calypso
calyx
  calyxes, calyces (*pl.*)
cam
camaraderie
camber
  cambered
cambric
came (*from* come)
camel
  camel-hair
camellia
Camembert
cameo
  cameos (*pl.*)
camera
  camera's
    (of the camera)
  cameras'
    (of the cameras)
camisole
camomile (herb)
camouflage
  camouflaging
camp
campaign
camphor
  camphorated
campus
  campuses (*pl.*)
can
  canned
  cannery
  canning
can
  can't (cannot)
canal
  canalisation
  canalization
  canalise
  canalize
canary (bird)

canaries (*pl.*)
canary's (of the canary)
canaries'
    (of the canaries)
can-can
cancel
  cancellation
  cancelled
  canceled
  cancelling
  canceling
  cancels
cancer
  cancerous
candelabra, candelabrum
  candelabra,
      candelabras,
      candelabrums(*pl.*)
candid (outspoken)
  candidly
  candour
  candor
candidate
  candidacy
  candidacies (*pl.*)
  candidature
candle
  candlelight
  candlestick
candour (frankness)
  candor
candy (sweetmeat)
  candies (*pl.*)
  candied (sugared)
  candying
cane
  caning
canine
canister
canker
cannabis
cannery
  canneries (*pl.*)
cannibal
  cannibalisation

cannibalization
cannibalise
cannibalize
cannibalising
cannibalizing
cannibalism
cannibal's
    (of the cannibal)
cannibals'
    (of the cannibals)
cannon (gun)
  cannonade
  cannon's
    (of the cannon)
  cannons'
    (of the cannons)
cannot, can't
canny (shrewd)
  cannier
  cannily
  canniness
canoe
  canoes (*pl.*)
  canoeing
  canoeist
canon
  (Church law, dignitary)
  canonical
  canonisation
  canonization
  canonise
  canonize
  canonising
  canonizing
  canonry
canon (music)
canopy
  canopies (*pl.*)
  canopied
cant (jargon)
cant (hypocrisy)
cantabile
  (with singing tone)
cantaloup, cantaloupe
    (melon)

cantankerous
  cantankerously
cantata
  cantatas (*pl.*)
canteen
canter (easy gallop)
  cantered
  cantering
cantilever
  cantilevered
canto (part of poem)
  cantos (*pl.*)
canton (Swiss county)
  cantonal
cantonment
cantor (singer)
canvas (cloth)
  canvases (*pl.*)
canvass (for votes)
  canvassed
  canvasser
  canvasses
  canvassing
canyon
caoutchouc
cap
  capped
  capping
  caps
capable
  capability
  capabilities (*pl.*)
  capably
capacious
capacity
  capacities (*pl.*)
  capacitance (*electr.*)
  capacitive
  capacitor (*electr.*)
cape
caper (to jump)
  capered
  capering
caper (spice)
  caper-sauce

capillary
  capillaries (*pl.*)
capital
  capitalisation
  capitalization
  capitalise
  capitalize
  capitalising
  capitalizing
  capitalism
  capitalist
  capitalistic
  capitally
capitation
    (counting people)
Capitol (building)
capitulate (to give in)
  capitulating
  capitulation
capon
caprice
  capricious
  capriciously
capsize
  capsizable
  capsizing
capstan
capsule
  capsular
captain
  captaincy
  captaincies (*pl.*)
  captain's
    (of the captain)
  captains'
    (of the captains)
caption
  captioned
captious (peevish)
  captiously
  captiousness
captivate (to delight)
  captivating
  captivation
captive

captivity
capture
  captor
  capturing
car
  car's (of the car)
  cars' (of the cars)
carabiniere
  carabinieri (*pl.*)
carafe
caramel
carat (weight)
caravan
  caravanning
  caravaning
caraway (seed)
carbide (chemical)
carbine (rifle)
carbohydrate
carbolic
carbon
  carbonaceous
  carbonate
  carbon dioxide
  carbonic
  carbonisation
  carbonization
  carbonise
  carbonize
  carbonising
  carbonizing
carborundum
carboy (large jar)
carbuncle
carburettor
  carburetor
carcass, carcase
  carcasses, carcases (*pl.*)
carcinoma
  carcinogenic
card
  cardboard
  card-carrying
cardiac
cardigan

cardinal (of Church)
cardinal (most important)
cardio- (heart)
  cardiogram
  cardiograph
  cardiographer
  cardiographic
  cardiography
care
  carefree
  careful
  carefully
  careless
  carelessly
  carelessness
  careworn
  caring
careen
  (to turn ship on side)
  careened
  careening
career (in life)
  careerist
career (to rush about)
  careering
caress
  caresses (*pl.*)
  caressed
  caresses
  caressing
caretaker
  caretaker's
    (of the caretaker)
  caretakers'
    (of the caretakers)
  caretaking
cargo
  cargoes (*pl.*)
caricature
  caricaturing
  caricaturist
caries (tooth decay)
carillon
carminative (drug)
carmine (colour)

carnage
carnal
  carnally
carnation
carnival
carnivore (flesh-eater)
  carnivorous
carol
  carolled
  caroled
  caroller
  caroler
  carolling
  caroling
carotid (artery)
carouse
  carousal
  carousing
carousel (roundabout)
carp (to grumble)
carp (fish)
carpenter
  carpentering
  carpenter's
    (of the carpenter)
  carpenters'
    (of the carpenters)
  carpentry
carpet
  carpeted
  carpeting
carriage
carrier
carrion
carrot (vegetable)
  carroty
carry
  carried
  carrier
  carries
  carrying
cart
  cartage
  carter
carte blanche

cartel
cartilage
  cartilaginous
cartography
  cartographer
  cartographic
carton (cardboard)
cartoon (drawing)
  cartoonist
cartridge
carve (to cut up)
  carving
  carving knife
caryatid (pillar)
cascade
  cascading
cascara
case
  casing
casein (basis of cheese)
casement
cash
  cashed
  cashes
cash and carry
cashew (nut)
cashier (of a bank, etc.)
  cashier's
      (of the cashier)
  cashiers'
      (of the cashiers)
cashier (to dismiss)
  cashiered
  cashiering
cashmere
casino
  casinos (*pl.*)
cask
casket
casserole
cassette
cassock
cast (to throw)
  cast-off
cast (of actors)

castanet
castaway
caste (social class)
  casteless
castellated
castigate
  castigating
  castigation
castle
castor, caster (of chairleg)
castor, caster (sugar)
castor oil
castrate
  castrating
  castration
  castrato (singer)
  castrati (*pl.*)
casual
  casually
  casualness
casualty
  casualties (*pl.*)
casuist (arguer)
  casuistry
cat
  catcall
  catnap
  cat's (of the cat)
  cats' (of the cats)
  cat's eye
  cattish
  cattily
  catty
catabolism
cataclysm (upheaval)
  cataclysmal
  cataclysmic
  cataclysmically
catacomb
catalepsy
  cataleptic
catalogue
  catalog
  cataloguer
  cataloger

  cataloguing
  cataloging
catalyse
  catalyze
  catalysation
  catalyzation
  catalyser
  catalyzer
  catalysis
  catalyses (*pl.*)
  catalyst
  catalytic
catamaran
catapult
cataract
catarrh
  catarrhal
catastrophe
  catastrophic
  catastrophically
catch
  catches
  catchment
  catchy
  caught
catechise
      (to ask questions)
  catechize
  catechising
  catechizing
  catechism
categoric
  categorical
  categorically
category
  categories (*pl.*)
  categorise
      (to make a list)
  categorize
  categorising
  categorizing
cater
  catered
  caterer
  catering

caterpillar
  caterpillar's
    (of the caterpillar)
  caterpillars'
    (of the caterpillars)
caterwaul
catgut
catharsis
  cathartic
cathedral
catheter
cathode
  cathodic
catholic
  catholicism
  catholicity
catkin
catsup
  ketchup
cattle
caucus
  caucuses (*pl.*)
caught (*from* catch)
caul (of a baby)
cauldron
cauliflower
caulk
  (to make watertight)
cause
  causal
  causation
  causative
  causing
causeway
caustic
  caustically
cauterise
  cauterize
  cauterisation
  cauterization
  cauterising
  cauterizing
  cautery
    (surgical instrument)
  cauteries (*pl.*)

caution
  cautionary
  cautious
  cautiously
cavalcade
cavalier
  cavalier's
    (of the cavalier)
  cavaliers'
    (of the cavaliers)
cavalry
cave
  caving
caveat (warning)
cavern
  cavernous
caviare
  caviar
cavil (to object)
  cavilled
  caviled
  cavilling
  caviling
  cavils
cavity
  cavities (*pl.*)
cavort
caw
cayenne
cease
  ceaseless
  ceaselessly
  ceasing
  cessation
cedar
cede (to yield)
  ceding
  cession
cedilla
ceiling (of a room)
celandine
celebrate
  celebrant
  celebrating
  celebration

  celebrator
celebrity
  celebrities (*pl.*)
celerity (speed)
celery (vegetable)
  celeriac
celestial
  celestially
celibate (unmarried)
  celibacy
cell
cellar
  cellarage
cello
  cellos (*pl.*)
  cellist
  cellist's (of the cellist)
  cellists' (of the cellists)
cellophane
cellular
celluloid
cellulose
Celsius (centigrade)
Celt
  Celtic
cement
cemetery
  cemeteries (*pl.*)
cenotaph
censer (for incense)
censor (official)
  censored
  censoring
  censorious
  censorship
censure (blame)
  censured
  censuring
census (count of people)
  censuses (*pl.*)
cent (money)
centaur (mythical horse)
centenary
  (hundredth anniversary)
  centenaries (*pl.*)

centenarian
(person aged ddd)
centennial
centigrade
centigram
centilitre
centiliter
centime (money)
centimetre
centimeter
centipede
central
centralisation
centralization
centralise
centralize
centralising
centralizing
centrally
centre
center
centred
centered
centre-forward
centre-piece
centerpiece
centring
centering
centrifugal
(away from centre)
centrifugally
centrifuge
centripetal
(towards centre)
centrist
centuple (hundredfold)
centurion
century
centuries (*pl.*)
century's
(of the century)
centuries'
(of the centuries)
cephalic
cephalitis

ceramic
cereal (corn)
cerebellum
cerebral
cerebration
(working of brain)
cerebro-spinal
cerebrum
(part of brain)
ceremony
ceremonies (*pl.*)
ceremonial
ceremonially
ceremonious
ceremoniously
cerise (cherry-coloured)
certain
certainly
certainty
certainties (*pl.*)
certitude
certify
certifiable
certificate
certification
certified
certifies
certifying
certitude
cervix
cervical
cessation (ceasing)
cession (yielding)
cesspit
cesspool
chafe (to rub)
chafing
chaff (to tease)
chaff (husks)
chaffinch
chaffinches (*pl.*)
chagrin
chagrined
chain
chair

chaired
chairing
chairman
chairmen (*pl.*)
chairman's
(of the chairman)
chairmen's
(of the chairmen)
chairwoman
chairwomen (*pl.*)
chairwoman's
(of the chairwoman)
chairwomen's
(of the chairwomen)
chaise longue
chaises longues (*pl.*)
chalcedony
chalet
chalice
chalk
chalky
challenge
challenger
challenging
chamber
chambermaid
chambermaid's
(of the chambermaid)
chambermaids'
(of the chambermaids)
chamberlain
chameleon
chamfer
chamfered
chamfering
chamois
champ (to munch)
champagne
champion
championed
championing
championship
chance
chancing
chancy

chancel (part of church)
chancellor (official)
  chancellery
      (of an embassy)
  chancelleries (*pl.*)
chancery (law court)
  chanceries (*pl.*)
chandelier
chandler
change
  changeable
  changing
changeling
channel
  channelled
  chaneled
  channelling
  chaneling
chant
chantry
  chantries (*pl.*)
chaos
  chaotic
  chaotically
chap (fellow)
chap
  chapped
chapel
chaperon
  chaperonage
  chaperoned
  chaperoning
chaplain
  chaplaincy
chaplet (wreath)
chapter
char (house work)
  charred
  charlady
  charladies (*pl.*)
  charlady's
    (of the charlady)
  charladies'
    (of the charladies)
  charring

charwoman
charwomen (*pl.*)
charwoman's
  (of the charwoman)
charwomen's
  (of the charwomen)
char (to scorch)
  charred
  charring
charabanc
character
  characterisation
  characterization
  characterise
  characterize
  characterising
  characterizing
  characteristic
  characteristically
charade
charcoal
charge
  chargeable
  charging
chargé d'affaires
  chargés d'affaires (*pl.*)
chariot
  charioteer
charisma
  charismatic
charity
  charities (*pl.*)
  charitable
  charitably
charlatan
charlotte
  charlotte russe
charm
  charmer
chart
charter
  chartered
  charterer
  chartering
charwoman

charwomen (*pl.*)
chary (careful)
  charily
  chariness
chase
  chaser
  chasing
chasm
chassis
  chassis (*pl.*)
chaste
  chastely
  chasten
  chastened
  chastening
  chastity
chastise
  chastisement
  chastising
chat
  chats
  chatted
  chatter
  chatterbox
  chattering
  chatting
  chatty
château
  châteaus, châteaux (*pl.*)
chattel
chatelaine
chauffeur
  chauffeurs (*pl.*)
  chauffeur's
    (of the chauffeur)
  chauffeurs'
    (of the chauffeurs)
  chauffeuse (*fem.*)
chauvinism
  chauvinist
  chauvinistic
cheap
  cheaper
  cheaply
  cheapness

cheat
check (to restrain or test)
  checkmate
  checkmating
cheek
  cheekier
  cheekily
  cheekiness
  cheeky
cheep (chick's chirp)
cheer
  cheerily
  cheerless
  cheery
cheerful
  cheerfully
  cheerfulness
cheese
  cheese-paring
cheetah (animal)
chef
  chef's (of the chef)
  chefs' (of the chefs)
chef-d'oeuvre
  chefs-d'oeuvre (pl.)
chemical
  chemically
chemise
chemist
  chemistry
  chemist's
     (of the chemist)
  chemists'
     (of the chemists)
cheque (order on bank)
  check
chequer
  (to mark with squares)
  checker
  chequered
  checkered
chequered (varied)
  checkered
cherish
cheroot

cherry
  cherries (pl.)
cherub
  cherubic
  cherubically
chess
  chessboard
chest
  chestnut
chevalier
chevron
  chevroned
chevy, chivy, chivvy
  chevied, chivied, chivvied
chew
  chewy
Chianti
chic (elegant)
chicanery (trickery)
chichi
chick
  chicken
  chickenpox
  chicken's
     (of the chicken)
  chickens'
     (of the chicken)
  chickweed
chicory
chide (to scold)
  chided
  chid
  chidden
  chiding
chief
  chief's (of the chief)
  chiefs' (of the chiefs)
  chieftain
  chieftaincy
chiffon
chilblain
child
  children (pl.)
  childbirth

childhood
childish
children's
     (of the children)
child's (of the child)
chill
  chilled
  chillier
  chilly
chilli (spice)
  chili
  chillies (pl.)
  chilies (pl.)
chime
  chiming
chimney
  chimneys (pl.)
chimpanzee
chin
China
  Chinese
china (porcelain)
chink
chintz
  chintzes (pl.)
chip
  chipped
  chipping
  chips
chipmunk
chiropodist
  chiropodist's
     (of the chiropodist)
  chiropodists'
     (of the chiropodists)
  chiropody
chiropractic
  chiropractor
  chiropraxy
chirp
chirrup
  chirruped
  chirruping
chisel (tool)
chisel (to cheat)

chiselled
chiseled
chiseller
chiseler
chiselling
chiseling
chisels
chit (short note)
chit (young child)
chit-chat
chivalry
  chivalrous
  chivalrously
chive
chivvy, chivy, chevy
  chivvied, chivied,
          chevied
chlorate
  (chem. compound)
chloride
  (chem. compound)
chlorine (chem. element)
  chlorinate
  chlorinating
  chlorination
chlorodyne
chloroform
chlorophyll
chock
  chock-a-block
  chock-full
chocolate
choice
  choicely
  choiceness
  choicest
choir
choke
  choker (high collar)
  choking
choler (anger)
  choleric
cholera (disease)
cholesterol
choose

choosing
choosy, choosey
chose
chosen
chop
  chopped
  chopper
  chopping
  chopstick
choppy (of sea, rough)
chop-suey
choral
  chorally
chorale (hymn)
  choral
chord (music)
chord (maths)
chore (task)
choreography
  choreographer
  choreographic
chorister
chortle
  chortling
chorus
  choruses (*pl.*)
chosen (*from* choose)
chow (dog)
Christ
  Christendom
  Christian
  Christianity
  Christmas
  Christmassy
christen
  christened
  christening
chromate
chrom- (colour)
  chromatic
  chromatin
  chrome
  chromic
  chromium
  chromosome

chromosphere
chron- (time)
  chronic (continuous)
  chronically
  chronicle
  chronology
  chronologies (*pl.*)
  chronological
  chronologically
  chronometer
chrys- (gold)
  chrysalis
  chrysalises (*pl.*)
  chrysanthemum
  chrysanthemums (*pl.*)
chub (fish)
chubby
  chubbier
chuck
  chucker-out
chuckle
  chuckling
chug
  chugging
chukker, chukka,
        chukkar(polo)
chum
  chummed
  chumming
  chummy
chump
chunk
  chunky
Church
  church-goer
  churchwarden
churlish (sulky)
churn
chute (sloping passage)
chutney
cicada
cicatrice (scar)
cicatrise (to heal)
  cicatrize
  cicatrising

cicatrizing
cider
cigar
  cigarette
  cigaret
cinder
  Cinderella
cinema
  cinematic
  cinematograph
  cinematography
cineraria (plant)
cinerary (for ashes)
  cinerarium
  cinerary urn
cinnamon
cipher, cypher
circa (approximately)
circle
  circling
circuit
  circuitous
  circuitry
  circuitries (*pl.*)
circular
  circularising
  circularizing
circulate
  circulating
  circulation
circum- (around)
  circumcise
  circumcising
  circumcision
  circumference
  circumflex
  circumlocution
  circumnavigate
  circumnavigation
  circumscribe
  circumscribing
  circumscription
  circumspect
  circumspection
  circumstance

circumstantial
circumstantially
circumvent
circumvention
circus
  circuses (*pl.*)
cirrhosis
cirrus (cloud)
cist (tomb)
cistern
citadel
cite (to quote)
  citation
  citing
citizen
  citizen's (of the citizen)
  citizens' (of the citizens)
  citizenship
citron (tree)
  citrate
  citric (acid)
  citrus
    (orange, lemon, etc.)
city
  cities (*pl.*)
  city's (of the city)
  cities' (of the cities)
civet
civic
  civic centre
  civic center
civil
  civilian
  civilian's
    (of the civilian)
  civilians'
    (of the civilians)
  civility
  civilities (*pl.*)
  civilly
civilise
civilize
civilisation
civilization
civilising

civilizing
civvies (civilian clothes)
clad (clothed)
  cladding
claim
  claimable
  claimant
    (one who claims)
clairvoyance
clairvoyant
clam (shellfish)
clamant (noisy)
clamber
  clambered
  clambering
clammy
  clamminess
clamour
  clamor
  clamorous
clamp
clan
  clannish
clandestine
  clandestinely
clang
  clanger (bad mistake)
  clangour (noise)
  clangor
clap
  clapped
  clapping
  claps
  claptrap
claret
clarify
  clarification
  clarified
  clarifies
  clarifying
clarinet
  clarinettist,
        clarinetist
  clarinetist
clarion (loud)

clarity (clearness)
clash
clasp
class (in school)
  classroom
class (social position)
  classless
  classy
classic
  classical
  classically
  classicism
  classicist
  classics
classify
  classifiable
  classification
  classified
  classifies
  classifying
clatter
  clattered
  clattering
clause
claustral
claustrophobia
  claustrophobic
clavichord
clavicle (collar-bone)
  clavicular
claw
clay
clean
  cleanable
  cleaner (more clean)
  cleaner (person)
  cleanliness
  cleanly
cleanse
  cleansing
clear
  clearance
  clearly
clear-cut
cleave (to stick to)

clave
cleaved
cleaving
cleave (to split)
cleavage
cleaved
cleaving
cleft
clove
cloven
clef
clematis
clement
  clemency
clench (to close tightly)
clergy
  clergyman
  clergymen (pl.)
  clergyman's
    (of the clergyman)
  clergymen's
    (of the clergymen)
cleric
  clerical
clerk
  clerk's (of the clerk)
  clerks' (of the clerks)
clever
  cleverer
  cleverly
clew, clue (thread)
cliché
click
client
  clientele
  client's (of the client)
  clients' (of the clients)
cliff
climacteric
climate (weather)
  climatic
  climatically
  climatology
climax
  climaxes (pl.)

climactic
climb
  climbable
  climber
clime (region)
clinch (boxing, settling)
cling
  clung
clinic
  clinical
  clinically
clink
  clinker
clip
  clipped
  clipping
  clips
clipboard
clipper (sailing ship)
clique
  cliquey
  cliquish
clitoris
cloak
  cloakroom
clobber
  clobbered
  clobbering
cloche
clock
  clockwise
  clockwork
clod
  clodhopper
clog
  clogged
  clogging
  clogs
cloister
  cloistered
  cloistral
close (near)
close (to shut)
  closing
  closure

closet
  closeted
clot
  clots
  clotted
  clotting
cloth (material)
clothe (to dress)
  clad
  clothed
  clothes (garments)
  clothier
  clothing
cloud
  cloudier
  cloudy
clout (to hit)
clove (*see* cleave)
  cloven
clove (spice)
clover
  clover-leaf
clown
cloy
club (to hit)
  clubbed
  clubbing
club (association)
cluck
clue (to mystery)
  clueless
clue, clew (thread)
clump
clumsy
  clumsier
  clumsily
  clumsiness
clung (*from* cling)
cluster
  clustered
  clustering
clutch
clutter
  cluttered
  cluttering

coach (carriage)
  coaches (*pl.*)
  coachman
coach (to teach)
coagulate
  coagulating
  coagulation
coal
coalesce
  coalescence
  coalescent
  coalescing
coalition
coarse (rough)
  coarsely
  coarsen
  coarsened
  coarseness
  coarsening
coast
  coastal
  coaster
  coastguard
coat (garment)
coat (to cover)
coax
coaxial
cob
cobalt
cobble
  cobbler
  cobbling
cobra
cobweb
  cobwebbed
cocaine
  cocain
coccyx (base of spine)
  coccygeal
cochineal
cochlea (of the ear)
cock (bird)
  cockcrow
  cockerel
cock-eyed

cockade
cockatoo
  cockatoos (*pl.*)
cockchafer
cockle
cockney
  cockneys (*pl.*)
  cockney's
     (of the cockney)
  cockneys'
     (of the cockneys)
cockpit
cockroach
cocksure
cocktail
cocky (conceited)
  cockier
  cockily
coco (tree)
  coconut
cocoa (drink)
cocoon
cocotte
cod
  codling (small cod)
  cod's roe
coda (music)
coddle
  coddling
code
  coding
codeine (drug)
codger
codicil
codify
  codification
  codified
  codifying
coeducation
  coeducational
coefficient
coerce
  coercing
  coercion
coexist

coexistence
coffee
coffer (box)
coffin
cog
  cog-wheel
cogent
  cogency
  cogently
cogitate
  cogitating
  cogitation
cognac
cognate (related)
cognisance (knowledge)
  cognizance
cognisant
  cognizant
cognition (knowing)
  cognitive
cognomen (nickname)
cohabit
  cohabitation
  cohabited
  cohabiting
cohere
  coherence
  coherent
  coherently
  coherer
  cohering
  cohesion
  cohesive
cohort
coiffeur (hairdresser)
  coiffeurs (*pl.*)
  coiffeuse (*fem.*)
  coiffeuses (*pl.*)
  coiffure (hair style)
coil
coin
  coinage
  coiner
coincide
  coincidence

coincident
coincidental
coincidentally
coinciding
coir (fibre)
coition, coitus
coke
  coking
col (mountain pass)
colander (strainer)
cold
  cold-blooded
  colder
  coldly
  cold-shoulder
  cold-shouldered
cole (cabbage)
  coleslaw
colic
  colicky
Coliseum (in London)
  Colosseum (in Rome)
colitis
collaborate
  collaborating
  collaboration
  collaborator
collage
    (patchwork picture)
collapse
  collapsible
  collapsing
collar
  collared
  collarette
  collaret
  collaring
collate
  collating
  collation
  collator
collateral
collation (meal)
colleague
collect

collection
collector
collector's
    (of the collector)
collectors'
    (of the collectors)
collect (prayer)
collective
  collectively
  collectivism
  collectivist
colleen
college
  collegial
  collegian
  collegiate
collide
  colliding
  collision
collie (dog)
collier
  colliery
  collieries (*pl.*)
collision
collocate (to arrange)
  collocating
  collocation
colloid
  colloidal
colloquial
  colloquialism
  colloquially
  colloquy
  colloquies (*pl.*)
collude
  colluding
  collusion
  collusive
cologne
colon (gut)
  colitis
colon (punctuation mark)
colonel
  colonelcy

colonel's
    (of the colonel)
colonels'
    (of the colonels)
colonnade
colony
  colonies (*pl.*)
  colonial
  colonialism
  colonisation
  colonization
  colonise
  colonize
  coloniser
  colonizer
  colonising
  colonizing
  colonist
coloration (*from* colour)
coloratura (singer)
colossal
  colossally
  colossus (large statue)
colour
  color
  coloration
  coloured
  colored
  colourful
  colorful
  colourfully
  colorfully
  colouring
  coloring
  colourless
  colorless
colt
  coltish
columbine
column
  columnar
  columnist
coma (unconsciousness)
  comatose (unconscious)
comb

combat
combatant
combative
combe, coomb (valley)
combine
  combinable
  combination
  combining
combustion
  combustible
come
  came
  coming
comedy
  comedies (*pl.*)
  comedian
  comedian's
    (of the comedian)
  comedians'
    (of the comedians)
  comedienne (*fem.*)
comely (pretty)
  comelier
  comeliness
comestible
comet
come-uppance
comfit (sweetmeat)
comfort
  comfortable
  comfortably
  comforter
comic
  comical
  comicality
  comicalities (*pl.*)
  comically
comity (friendship)
  comities (*pl.*)
comma
  (punctuation mark)
command
  commandant
  commander
  commandment

commandeer (to seize)
  commandeered
  commandeering
commando
  commandos (*pl.*)
commemorate
  commemorating
  commemoration
  commemorative
commence
  commencement
  commencing
commend (to praise)
  commendable
  commendably
  commendation
commensurate
  commensurable
  commensurably
  commensurately
comment (remark)
  commentary
  commentaries (*pl.*)
  commentator
commerce
  commercial
  commercialisation
  commercialization
  commercialise
  commercialize
  commercialising
  commercializing
  commercialism
  commercially
commiserate (to pity)
  commiserating
  commiseration
commissar (political boss)
commissariat
  (food supply)
commission
  commissionaire
  commissioner
commit
  commitment

commits
committal
committed
committing
committee
commode
commodious
commodity
commodities (*pl.*)
commodore
common
commoner
Common Market
commonplace
commonwealth
commotion
communal
communally
commune (to discuss)
communing
commune (settlement)
communicate
communicable
communicating
communication
communicative
communion
communicant
communiqué
communism
communist
community
communities (*pl.*)
commute
commutable
commutation
commutator (*electr.*)
commuter (traveller)
commuter's
  (of the commuter)
commuters'
  (of the commuters)
commuting
compact
companion

companionable
company
companies (*pl.*)
company's
  (of the company)
companies'
  (of the companies)
compare
comparable
comparably
comparative
comparatively
comparing
comparison
compartment
compartmentalisation
compartmentalization
compartmentalise
compartmentalize
compass
compasses (*pl.*)
compassion
compassionate
compatible
compatibility
compatibly
compatriot
compel
compelled
compelling
compels
compendious
compendium
compensate
compensating
compensation
compensator
compensatory
compère
compèring
compete
competing
competition
competitive
competitively

competitor
competitor's
  (of the competitor)
competitors'
  (of the competitors)
competent (capable)
competence (skill)
competently
compile
compilation
compiler
compiling
complacent (smug)
complacency
complacently
complain
complainant
complainer
complaint
complaisant (willing)
complaisance
    (willingness)
complement (to add to)
complementary
complete
completely
completing
completion
complex
complexity
complexities (*pl.*)
complexion
complicate
complicacy
complicating
complication
complicity
  (sharing in crime)
compliment (praise)
complimentary
compline (church service)
comply
compliance
compliant
complied

47

complies
complying
component
comport (to behave)
comportment
(behaviour)
compose
composer (of music)
composing
composition
composure (calmness)
composite
compositely
compositor (in printing)
compos mentis
compost (garden refuse)
compote (of fruit)
compound
comprehend
comprehensibility
comprehensible
comprehensibly
comprehension
comprehensive
comprehensively
compress
compressibility
compressible
compression
compressor
comprise
comprising
compromise
compromising
comptometer
comptroller
compulsory
compulsion
compulsive
compulsively
compulsorily
compunction
compute
computable
computation

computer
computerisation
computerization
computerise
computerize
computerising
computerizing
computing
comrade
comradely
comradeship
con (to cheat)
conned
conning
cons
con (to inspect)
conned
conning
con (to steer a ship)
conning-tower
concave
concavity
concavities (*pl.*)
conceal (to hide)
concealed
concealing
concealment
concede (to yield)
conceding
concession
conceit (pride)
conceited
conceive (to imagine)
conceivable
conceivably
conceiving
conceive
(to become pregnant)
conceiving
conception
concentrate
concentrating
concentration
concentrator
concentric

concentrically
concentricity
concept
conception
conceptual
conceptualise
conceptualize
conceptualising
conceptualizing
concern
concert
concertina
concerto
concertos (*pl.*)
concert (to plan together)
concession
concessionaire
concessionnaire
concessionary
concierge
concierge's
(of the concierge)
concierges'
(of the concierges)
conciliate
conciliating
conciliation
conciliator
conciliatory
concise
concisely
conciseness
conclave
conclude
concluding
conclusion
conclusive
conclusively
concoct
concoction
concomitant
concomitance
concord
concordance
concordant

48

concourse
concrete
  concretely
  concreteness
concubine
  concubinage
concur
  concurred
  concurrence
  concurrent
  concurrently
  concurring
  concurs
concuss
  concussed
  concussion
condemn
  condemnation
  condemnatory
condense
  condensation
  condenser
  condensing
condescend
  condescension
condign (severe)
  condignly
condiment
condition
  conditional
  conditionally
condole (to sympathise)
  condolatory
  condolence
  condoler
  condoling
condom
condone (to forgive)
  condonation
  condoning
conduce
  conducing
  conducive
conduct (behaviour)
conduct (electr.)

conductance
conductivity
conductor
conductor (of orchestra)
  conductor's
    (of the conductor)
  conductors'
    (of the conductors)
conductor (bus)
  conductress (fem.)
  conductresses (pl.)
conduit
cone
coney, cony (rabbit)
  coneys, conies (pl.)
confabulate
  confabulating
  confabulation
confection
  confectioner
  confectioner's
    (of the confectioner)
  confectioners'
    (of the confectioners)
  confectionery
confederate
  confederacy
  confederacies (pl.)
  confederating
  confederation
confer
  conference
  conferment
  conferred
  conferring
  confers
confess
  confession
  confessional
  confessor
confetti
confidant (person)
  confidante (fem.)
confide
  confidence

confident
confidential
confidentiality
confidentially
confidently
confiding
configuration
confine
  confinement
  confining
confirm
  confirmable
  confirmation
  confirmative
  confirmatory
confiscate
  confiscating
  confiscation
  confiscator
conflagration
conflict
conform
  conformable
  conformance
  conformation (shape)
  conformity
confound
confrère, confrere
confront
  confrontation
confuse
  confusing
  confusion
confute (to prove wrong)
  confutation
  confuting
congeal (to freeze)
  congealed
  congealing
  congelation
congenial (sympathetic)
  congeniality
  congenially
congenital (inborn)
  congenitally

conger
  conger-eel
congest
  congestion
  congestive
conglomerate
  conglomerating
  conglomeration
congratulate
  congratulating
  congratulation
  congratulatory
congregate
  congregating
  congregation
  congregational
congress
  congresses (*pl.*)
  congressional
congruent
  congruence
congruous (suitable)
  congruity
conic (*from* cone)
  conical
  conically
conifer
  coniferous
conjecture
  conjecturable
  conjecturably
  conjectural
  conjecturing
conjoin
  conjoint
  conjointly
conjugal
conjugate (*grammar*)
  conjugating
  conjugation
conjunction
conjunctive (*grammar*)
  conjunctival
conjunctivitis (eye disease)
conjure

conjurer, conjuror
conjuring
conkers (chestnuts)
connect
  connection, connexion
  connective
  connector, connecter
conning-tower
connive
  connivance
  conniving
connoisseur
  connoisseur's
    (of the connoisseur)
  connoisseurs'
    (of the connoisseurs)
connote
  connotation
  connoting
connubial
  connubially
conquer
  conquerable
  conquered
  conqueror
  conquest
consanguinity
  consanguineous
conscience
  conscientious
      (painstaking)
  conscientiously
  conscientiousness
conscious
  consciously
  consciousness
conscript
  conscription
  conscript's
    (of the conscript)
  conscripts'
    (of the conscripts)
consecrate
  consecrating
  consecration

consecutive
  consecutively
consensus
consent
consequence
  consequential
  consequently
conservatoire
conserve
  conservancy
  conservation
  conservatism
  conservative
  conservatory
  conservatories (*pl.*)
  conserving
consider
  considerable
  considerably
  considerate
  considerately
  considerateness
  consideration
  considered
  considering
consign
  consignee (receiver)
  consignment
  consignor (sender)
  consigner
consist
  consistence
  consistency
  consistencies (*pl.*)
  consistent
console
    (to sympathise with)
  consolable
  consolation
  consolatory
  consoler
  consoling
console (cabinet)
consolidate
  consolidating

consolidation
consols (Govt. securities)
consommé
consonant
consort (husband or wife)
consort
    (to come together)
consortium
  consortia (*pl.*)
conspicuous
  conspicuously
  conspicuousness
conspire
  conspiracy
  conspiracies (*pl.*)
  conspirator
  conspiratorial
  conspiring
constable
  constable's
    (of the constable)
  constables'
    (of the constables)
  constabulary
  constabularies (*pl.*)
constant
  constancy
  constantly
constellation
    (cluster of stars)
consternation
constipate
  constipated
  constipating
  constipation
constituency
  constituencies (*pl.*)
  constituent
constitute
  constituting
  constitution
  constitutional
  constitutionally
constrain
  constrained (repressed)

constraint (repression)
constrict
  constriction
  constrictive
  constrictor
construct
  construction
  constructional
  constructive
  constructively
  constructor
construe
  construing
consul
  consular
  consulate
  consul's (of the consul)
  consuls' (of the consuls)
consult
  consultant
  consultation
  consultative
consume
  consumable
  consumer
  consumer's
    (of the consumer)
  consumers'
    (of the consumers)
  consuming
consumption
consumptive
consummate
  consummately
  consummation
contact
  contactor
contagion
  contagious
contain
  container
  containerisation
  containerization
  containerise
  containerize

containment
contaminate
  contaminant
  contaminating
  contamination
contemplate
  contemplating
  contemplation
  contemplative
  contemplatively
contemporaneous
  contemporary
  contemporaries (*pl.*)
contempt
  contemptible
  contemptibly
  contemptuous
  contemptuously
contend
(to compete or struggle)
  contention
  contentious
content
    (amount contained)
content (satisfied)
  contentment
contention (dispute)
  contentious
contest
  contestable
  contestant
context
contiguous
  contiguously
  contiguity
continence (restraint)
  continent
continent (mainland)
  continental
contingent
  contingency
    (chance happening)
  contingencies (*pl.*)
contingent
    (group of soldiers)

continue
  continual
  continually
  continuance
  continuation
  continuing
  continuity
  continuous
  continuously
contort
  contortion
  contortionist
contour
contraband
contraception
  contraceptive
contract
  contraction
  contractor
  contractor's
    (of the contractor)
  contractors'
    (of the contractors)
  contractual
  contractually
contradict
  contradiction
  contradictory
contralto
  contraltos (*pl.*)
  contralto's
    (of the contralto)
  contraltos'
    (of the contraltos)
contraption
contrary
  contrarily
  contrariness
contrast
contravene
  contravening
  contravention
contretemps (mishap)
contribute
  contributing

contribution
contributor
contributory
contrite (penitent)
  contritely
  contrition
contrive
    (to plan or invent)
  contrivance
  contriving
control
  controllable
  controlled
  controller
  controlling
  controls
controversial
  controversially
  controversy
  controversies (*pl.*)
  controvert
  controvertible
contumacy
  contumacious
  contumely
contuse
  contusion
conundrum
conurbation
convalesce
  convalescence
  convalescent
  convalescing
convection
  convector
convene
  convener
  convening
  convention
convenient
  convenience
  conveniently
convent
convention
  conventional

  conventionality
  conventionally
converge
  convergence
  convergent
  converging
conversant
    (acquainted with)
converse (opposite)
  conversely
converse (to talk)
  conversation
  conversational
  conversationalist
  conversationally
  conversazione
  conversaziones (*pl.*)
  conversazioni (pl.)
  conversing
convert
  conversion
  converter
  convertor (alt.)
  convertibility
  convertible
convex
  convexity
convey
  conveyance
  conveyancer (lawyer)
  conveyancing
  conveyor, conveyer
  conveyor belt
  belt conveyer
convict
  conviction
  convict's
    (of the convict)
  convicts'
    (of the convicts)
convince
  convincing
  convincingly
convivial
  conviviality

convivially
convocation
convoke
  convoking
convolute
  convolution
convolvulus
  convolvuluses (*pl.*)
convoy
convulse
  convulsing
  convulsion
  convulsive
  convulsively
cony, coney (rabbit)
  conies, coneys (*pl.*)
coo
  cooed
  cooing
cook
  cooker
  cookery
  cook's (of the cook)
  cooks' (of the cooks)
cool
  coolant
  cooler
  cool-headed
  cooling
  coolly
  coolness
coolie (labourer)
coomb, combe (valley)
coop (to enclose)
  cooped (up)
co-op (society or store)
co-operate
  cooperate
  co-operating
  co-operation
  co-operative
  co-operator
co-opt
  co-option
co-ordinate

co-ordinating
co-ordination
cop (policeman)
  cop's (of the cop)
  cops' (of the cops)
cope (to manage)
  coping
cope (cloak)
copeck (Russian money)
  kopek, kopeck
co-pilot
  copilot
copious (abundant)
  copiously
copper (metal)
  copperplate
copper (policeman)
coppice, copse
      (small wood)
copra
copse (coppice)
copulate
  copulating
  copulation
copy
  copies (*pl.*)
  copied
  copier
  copies
  copying
  copyright
  copyrighted
coquette
  coquetry
  coquetted
  coquetting
  coquettish
coral
cord (string)
  cordage
  cordite
cordial (drink)
cordial (friendly)
  cordiality
  cordially

cordon
  cordon bleu
  cordoned
  cordoning
corduroy
core
co-respondent
      (in divorce case)
  corespondent
cork
  corkage
  corkscrew
corm
cormorant
corn
  cornflour (in cooking)
  cornflower (blue flower)
  cornstarch
cornea (of the eye)
  corneal
cornelian (cherry)
cornelian (precious stone)
corner
  cornered
  cornering
cornet
cornice
corny (old-fashioned)
corollary
  corollaries (*pl.*)
corona
  coronae, coronas (*pl.*)
  coronation
coronary (thrombosis)
coroner
coronet
  coroneted
corporal (soldier)
  corporal's
      (of the corporal)
  corporals'
      (of the corporals)
corporal (of the body)
  corporal punishment
corporate

corporation
corporeal (not spiritual)
corps (group of people)
  corps de ballet
corpse (dead body)
corpulent
  corpulence
corpuscle
  corpuscular
corral (to enclose cattle)
  corralled
  corralling
correct
  correction
  corrective
  correctly
  correctness
  corrector
correlate
  correlating
  correlation
  correlative
  correlativity
correspond
  correspondence
  correspondent
corridor
corrigendum
  corrigenda (*pl.*)
corroborate (to confirm)
  corroborating
  corroboration
  corroborative
corrode
  corrodible
  corroding
  corrosion
  corrosive
corrugate
  corrugated
  corrugation
corrupt
  corrupter
  corruptibility
  corruptible

corruption
corruptive
corruptly
corruptness
corsage
corset
cortège
  cortege
cortex
  cortical
cortisone
corundum (mineral)
corvée (hard task)
corvette (small ship)
cosecant, cosec (*maths.*)
cosh
co-signatory
  cosignatory
  co-signatories (*pl.*)
cosine, cos (*maths.*)
cos lettuce
cosmetic
  cosmetician
cosmic
  cosmically
cosmonaut
cosmopolitan
cosmos
cossack
cosset
  cosseted
  cosseting
cost
  costlier
  costly
co-star
  costar
costard (apple)
coster
  costermonger
  costermonger's
    (of the costermonger)
  costermongers'
    (of the costermongers)
costive (constipated)

costume
  costumier
cosy
  cozy
  cosier
  cozier
  cosily
  cozily
  cosiness
  coziness
cosy (for teapot)
  cozy
  cosies (*pl.*)
  cozies (*pl.*)
cot (baby's)
cotangent, cot (*maths.*)
coterie
cottage
  cottager
cotton
  cottonwool
cotyledon (botany)
couch
  couches (*pl.*)
couch-grass
cough
could (*from* can)
  couldn't (could not)
council (County, etc.)
  councillor
counsel
    (lawyer or advice)
  counselled
  counseled
  counselling
  counseling
  counsellor
  counselor
  counsels
count
  countless
count (nobleman)
  count's (of the count)
  counts' (of the counts).
  countess (*fem.*)

countesses (*pl.*)
countess's
   (of the countess)
countesses'
   (of the countesses)
countdown
countenance
counter (of shop)
counter (to oppose)
  countered
  countering
counteract
  counteracting
  counteraction
counter-attraction
  counterattraction
counterbalance
  counterbalancing
counter-clockwise
counterfeit
counterfoil
counter-irritant
  counterirritant
countermand
countermine
  countermining
counterpane
counterpart
counterpoint
counterpoise
countersign
countersink
  countersunk
counterweight
country
  countries (*pl.*)
  country's
    (of the country)
  countries'
    (of the countries)
countrified
countrify
countryman
countrymen (*pl.*)

countryman's
  (of the countryman)
countrymen's
  (of the countrymen)
county
  counties (*pl.*)
  county council
  county councillor
coup
  coup d'état
  coup de grace
couple
  couplet (poetry)
  coupling
coupon
courage
  courageous
  courageously
courier
course (lectures, etc.)
course (of a meal)
course (golf)
course (direction)
court (tennis, etc.)
court (to woo)
  courtier
  courting
  courtship
court
  courtyard
courtesan
courtesy (politeness)
  courtesies (*pl.*)
  courteous
  courteously
courtly (polite)
court-martial
  court-martials (*pl.*)
  courts-martial (*pl.*)
  court-martialled
  court-martialed
  court-martialling
  court-martialing
cousin
  cousinly

cousin's (of the cousin)
cousins' (of the cousins)
couture
couturier
couturière (*fem.*)
cove (bay)
cove (fellow)
coven (of witches)
covenant
cover
  coverage
  covered
  covering
  coverlet
  cover-up
covert (small wood)
covert (secret)
  covertly
covet (to wish for)
  coveted
  coveting
  covetous
covey (flock of birds)
  coveys (*pl.*)
cow
  cowboy
  cowherd
  cowhide
  cowman
  cowmen (*pl.*)
cow (to subdue)
  cowed
coward
  cowardice
  cowardliness
  cowardly
cower (to crouch)
  cowered
  cowering
cowl (hood)
cowrie, cowry (shell)
cowslip
cox
  coxswain
  coxcomb (fop)

coy
  coyly
  coyness
cozen (to cheat)
  cozenage
crab
  crabbed
  crabby
crack
  cracker
crackle
  crackling
cradle
  cradling
craft (boat)
craft (guile)
  craftier
  craftily
  crafty (sly)
craft (skilled trade)
  craftsman
  craftsmen (pl.)
  craftsmanship
crag
  craggy
crake
cram
  crammed
  crammer
  cramming
  crams
cramp
cranberry
  cranberries (pl.)
crane (hoisting machine)
  cranage
crane (bird)
crane (to stretch neck)
  craning
cranium
  cranial
crank (engine part)
  crankcase
  crankshaft
crank (odd person)

crankier
crankiness
cranky
cranny
  crannies (pl.)
crape (black crêpe)
crapulent
  crapulence
  crapulous
crash
crash-land
crass (stupid)
crate (packing case)
crater (of volcano)
cravat
crave (to long for)
  craving
craven (cowardly)
crawfish, crayfish
crawl
  crawler
crayon
craze
  crazier
  crazily
  craziness
  crazy
creak (noise)
  creaky
cream
  creamery
  creameries (pl.)
  creamier
  creaminess
  creamy
crease
  creasing
create
  creating
  creation
  creative
  creatively
  creativity
  creator
creature

creature's
    (of the creature)
creatures'
    (of the creatures)
crèche
credence
credential
credible
  credibility
  credibly
credit
  creditable
  creditably
  credited
  crediting
  creditor
  creditor's
      (of the creditor)
  creditors'
      (of the creditors)
credo
credulity
  credulous
creed
creek (small stream)
creep
  creeper
  creepier
  creepily
  creepiness
  creepy
  crept
cremate
  cremating
  cremation
  crematorium
  crematory
  crematoria,
      crematoriums(pl.)
  crematories
Creole
creosote
crêpe (fabric)
  crepe
crepitate (to creak)

crepitating
crepitation
crepuscular
crescendo
  crescendos (*pl.*)
crescent
cress
crest
  crestfallen
cretin (idiot)
  cretinism
  cretinous
cretonne (cloth)
crevasse (in glacier)
crevice (crack)
crew (*from* crow)
crew (of a ship)
crib (child's cot)
crib (to cheat)
  cribbed
  cribber
  cribbing
  cribs
cribbage (game)
crick
cricket
  cricketer
  cricketer's
      (of the cricketer)
  cricketers'
      (of the cricketers)
cricket (insect)
cried (*from* cry)
  crier
  cries
crime
  criminal
  criminally
  criminologist
  criminology
crimson
cringe
  cringing
crinkle
  crinkling

crinkly
crinoline
cripple
  crippling
crisis
  crises (*pl.*)
crisp
  crispness
criss-cross
  criss-crossed
  criss-crossing
criterion
  criteria (*pl.*)
critic
  critical
  critically
  criticise
  criticize
  criticising
  criticizing
  criticism
  critic's (of the critic)
  critics' (of the critics)
critique (critical essay)
croak
crochet (knitting)
  crocheted
  crocheting
crock
crockery
crocodile
  crocodile's
      (of the crocodile)
  crocodiles'
      (of the crocodiles)
crocus
  crocuses (*pl.*)
croft
  crofter
croissant
crony
  cronies (*pl.*)
  crony's (of the crony)
  cronies' (of the cronies)
crook (to bend)

crooked
crookeder
crookedly
crook (criminal)
croon
  crooner
crop (of corn, etc.)
crop (to cut)
  cropped
  cropping
  cropper (fall)
croquet (game)
croquette (rissole)
crore (of rupees)
crosier (bishop's staff)
cross (angry)
  crossly
  crossness
cross
  crosses (*pl.*)
  crossing
cross-breed
  cross-bred
cross-examine
  cross-examination
  cross-examiner
  cross-examining
cross-eyed
cross-legged
cross-purpose
cross-question
  cross-questioned
  cross-questioner
  cross-questioning
cross-reference
crossroad
cross-section
crossword (puzzle)
crotch
    (of body or trousers)
crotchet (music)
crotchety (peevish)
crouch
croup
croupier

57

croûton, crouton
crow
  crowing
crow (bird)
crowed (*from* to crow)
crowbar
crowd (of people)
crown
crucial
  crucially
crucible
crucify
  crucified
  crucifix
  crucifixes (*pl.*)
  crucifixion
  crucifying
crude
  crudely
  cruder
  crudity
  crudities (*pl.*)
cruel
  crueller
  cruelly
  cruelty
  cruelties (*pl.*)
cruet
cruise
  cruiser
  cruising
crumb
  crumby
crumble
  crumbling
  crumbly
crumpet
crumple
  crumpling
crunch
  crunchy
crupper
crusade
  crusader
  crusading

crush
  crushed
crust
  crustily
  crusty
crustacea (shellfish)
  crustacean
  crustaceous
crutch
  crutches (*pl.*)
crux
  cruxes, cruces (*pl.*)
cry
  cries (*pl.*)
  cried
  crier
  crying
crypt- (hidden)
  crypt (under church)
  cryptic (obscure)
  cryptically
  cryptogam (plant)
  cryptogram (code)
  cryptograph
  cryptographer
  cryptographic
  cryptography
crystal
  crystalline
  crystallisation
  crystallization
  crystallise
  crystallize
  crystallographer
  crystallography
cub
cubby-hole
cube
  cubic
  cubicle
cuckold
cuckoo
  cuckoo's
        (of the cuckoo)

cuckoos'
    (of the cuckoos)
cucumber
cuddle
  cuddling
  cuddly
cudgel
  cudgelled
  cudgeled
  cudgelling
  cudgeling
  cudgels
cue (actor's)
cue (billiards)
cuff (of coat)
cuff (to hit)
cuisine
cul-de-sac
  culs-de-sac (*pl.*)
culinary
cull (to pick flowers)
cull (to kill animals)
culminate
  culminating
  culmination
culottes
culpable
  culpability
  culpably
culprit
  culprit's (of the culprit)
  culprits' (of the culprits)
cult
cultivate
  cultivatable
  cultivating
  cultivation
  cultivator
culture
  cultural
  culturally
  culturing
culvert
cumbersome
cummerbund

cumulative
  cumulatively
cumulus (cloud)
cunning
  cunningly
cup
  cupful
  cupfuls (*pl.*)
  cupped
  cupping
cupboard
cupidity
cupola
cur
  currish
curaçao
curate
  curate's (of the curate)
  curates' (of the curates)
  curacy
  curacies (*pl.*)
curator
curb, kerb (road edge)
  curbstone, kerbstone
curb (harness)
curb (to restrain)
curd
  curdle
  curdling
cure
  curability
  curable
  curative
  curing
curé (priest)
curette (knife)
curfew
curio
  curios (*pl.*)
curious
    (inquisitive, peculiar)
  curiosity
  curiosities (*pl.*)
  curiously
curl

curler
curly
curlew (bird)
curmudgeon
currant (fruit)
currency (money)
  currencies (*pl.*)
current (*electr.*)
current (at present)
  currently
current (flow)
curriculum
  curricula (*pl.*)
  curriculums (*pl.*)
  curriculum vitae
curry (spice)
  curried
curry (to groom)
  curried
  curries
  curry-comb
  currying
curse
  cursing
cursive (handwriting)
cursor
(of slide rule, computer)
cursory (rapid)
  cursorily
curt
  curtly
  curtness
curtail
  curtailed
  curtailment
curtain
  curtained
  curtaining
curtsy, curtsey
  curtsies, curtseys (*pl.*)
  curtsied, curtseyed
  curtsies, curtseys
  curtsying, curtseying
curve
  curvature

curving
cushion
cuss
  cussed
  cussedness
custard
custody (imprisonment)
  custodial
  custodian
custom
  customarily
  customary
  custom-built
  customisation
  customization
  customise
  customize
  customising
  customizing
  custom-made
customer
  customer's
      (of the customer)
  customers'
      (of the customers)
cut
  cutter
  cutting
cutaneous
cutback
cute
  cutely
  cuteness
cuticle
cutlass
  cutlasses (*pl.*)
cutler
  cutlery
cutlet
cuttlefish
cyanide (chem.)
cyanosis (disease)
cybernetics
cyclamen
cycle

cycling
cyclist
cyclist's (of the cyclist)
cyclists' (of the cyclists)
cyclometer
cyclic
cyclical
cyclically
cyclone
cyclonic
cygnet (young swan)
cylinder
cylindrical
cylindrically
cymbal (gong)
cymbalist
cynic
cynical
cynically
cynicism
cynosure
cypher, cipher
cypress (tree)
cypresses (*pl.*)
cyst (bladder)
cystitis
cytology
Czech
Czechoslovakia

D

dab
dabbed
dabbing
dabs
dab (fish)
dab (clever person)
dabble
dabbler
dabbling

da capo
(from the beginning)
dace (fish)
dachshund
dad
daddy
daddies (*pl.*)
daddies' (of daddies)
dad's (of dad)
dads' (of dads)
daddy's (of daddy)
dado
dados (*pl.*)
dadoes (pl.)
daffodil
daft
dafter
dagger
dago
dagos (*pl.*)
dahlia
dahlias (*pl.*)
daily (every day)
dailies (*pl.*)
dainty
daintier
daintily
daintiness
dairy
dairies (*pl.*)
dairymaid
dairymaid's
(of the dairymaid)
dairymaids'
(of the dairymaids)
dais (platform)
daises (*pl.*)
daisy
daisies (*pl.*)
dale (valley)
dally (to dawdle)
dalliance
dallied
dallies
dallying

Dalmatian
dam (barrier)
dammed
damming
damage
damageable
damaging
damask
dame
damn
(to condemn, curse)
damnable
damnably
damnation
damned
damning
damp
dampen
dampened
damper
dampness
damsel
damson
dance
dancer
dancer's (of the dancer)
dancers'
(of the dancers)
dancing
dandelion
dandle
dandling
dandruff
dandy
dandies (*pl.*)
dandified
danger
dangerous
dangerously
dangle
dangling
dank
dankness
daphne (shrub)
dapper

dapple
dare
  daredevil
  daring
dark
  darken
  darker
  darkly
  darkness
darling
darn
dart
dash
  dashboard
dastardly
data (*from* datum)
date
  dating
date (fruit)
dative (*grammar*)
daub
  dauber
daughter
  daughter-in-law
  daughters-in-law (*pl.*)
  daughter-in-law's
  (of the daughter-in-law)
  daughters-in-law's
 (of the daughters-in-law)
  daughter's
    (of the daughter)
  daughters'
    (of the daughters)
daunt
  dauntless
  dauntlessly
Dauphin
davit
dawdle
  dawdler
  dawdling
dawn
day
  days (*pl.*)
  daily

daybreak
daylight
day's (of the day)
days' (of the days)
day to day
daze
dazzle
  dazzling
deacon
  deaconess (*fem.*)
dead
  deaden
  deadened
  deadening
  dead heat
  deadlier
  deadline
  deadliness
  deadlock
  deadlocked
  deadly
deaf
  deafen
  deafened
  deafening
  deafeningly
  deafer
  deafness
deal
  dealer
  dealing
  dealt
dean
  deanery
  deaneries (*pl.*)
dear (expensive)
  dearer
  dearly
  dearness
dear (darling)
  dearest
dearth (scarcity)
death
  deathless
  deathlike

deathly
death-rate
débâcle
debar
  debarred
  debarring
debark
  debarkation
debase
  debasement
  debasing
debate
  debatable
  debatably
  debating
debauch (to pervert)
  debauchee
  debaucher
  debauchery
  debaucheries (*pl.*)
debenture
debilitate
  debilitating
  debilitation
  debility
debit
  debitable
  debited
  debiting
debonair
debouch (to emerge)
  debouchment
debrief
debris
debt
  debtor
  debtor's (of the debtor)
  debtors' (of the debtors)
debunk
debus
  debussed
  debussing
début
  débutant
  débutante (*fem.*)

decade
decadent
  decadence
decamp
decant
  decanter
decapitate
  decapitating
  decapitation
decarbonise
  decarbonize
  decarbonisation
  decarbonization
  decarbonising
  decarbonizing
decathlon
decay
decease (death)
  deceased
deceit
  deceitful
  deceitfully
deceive
  deceiver
  deceiving
decelerate
  decelerating
  deceleration
decent (respectable)
  decency
  decencies (*pl.*)
  decently
decentralise
  decentralize
  decentralisation
  decentralization
  decentralising
  decentralizing
deception
  deceptive
  deceptively
decibel
decide
  deciding
  decidedly

deciduous
decimal
  decimalisation
  decimalization
  decimalise
  decimalize
decimate (to kill)
  decimating
  decimation
decipher
  deciphered
  deciphering
  decipherment
decision
  decisive
  decisively
deck (to adorn)
  decked
  decking
deck (of ship)
declaim
  declamation
  declamatory
declare
  declaration
  declaring
declassify
  declassification
  declassified
decline (*grammar*)
  declension
  declinable
  declining
decline (slope down)
  declination
  declining
decline (to deteriorate)
  declining
decline (to refuse)
  declining
declivity
  declivities (*pl.*)
decoction
decode
  decoder

decoding
décolleté
  décolletage
decompose
  decomposable
  decomposing
  decomposition
decompress
  decompression
  decompressor
decongestant
decontaminate
  decontaminating
  decontamination
decontrol
  decontrolled
  decontrolling
décor
decorate
  decorating
  decoration
  decorative
  decorator
decorum
  decorous
  decorously
decoy
decrease
  decreasing
decree
  decreeing
decrement
decrepit
  decrepitude
decry
  decried
  decries
  decrying
dedicate
  dedicating
  dedication
  dedicatory
deduce (to infer)
  deducible
  deducing

deduction

deduct (to subtract)

deductible

deduction

deed

deem

deep

  deepen

  deepened

  deepening

  deeper

  deep-laid

  deeply

  deep-seated

deep-freeze

  deep-freezer

  deep-freezing

  deep-frozen

deep-fry

  deep-fried

  deep-frying

deer (animal)

de-escalate

  de-escalation

deface

  defacing

de facto

defame

  defamation

  defamatory

  defaming

default

  defaulter

defeat

  defeatism

  defeatist

defecate, defaecate

  defecating, defaecating

  defecation, defaecation

defect (failure)

  defective

defect (to desert)

  defection

  defector

defence

defense

defenceless

defenseless

defensibilty

defensible

defensibly

defensive

defend

defendant

defendant's

    (of the defendant)

defendants'

    (of the defendants)

defender

defer (to postpone)

deferment

deferred

deferring

defers

defer (to yield)

deference

deferential

deferentially

deferred

deferring

defers

defiant (*from* defy)

defiantly

defiance

deficient

deficiency

deficiencies (*pl.*)

deficit

defile

defilement

defiling

define

definable

defining

definition

definite

definitely

definitive

definitively

deflate

deflating

deflation

deflationary

deflect

deflection

deflector

deflower

deflowered

deflowering

defoliate

defoliant

defoliating

defoliation

defoliator

deform

deformation

deformity

deformities (*pl.*)

defraud

defray

defrayable

defrayal

defreeze

defreezing

defrost

deft (neat)

deftly

deftness

defunct

defuse

defusing

defy

defiance

defiant

defiantly

defied

defier

defies

defying

dégagé

degenerate

degeneracy

degenerating

degeneration

degenerative

degrade
  degradation
  degrading
degree
dehydrate
  dehydrating
  dehydration
de-ice
  deice
  de-icer
  deicer
  de-icing
  deicing
deify
  deifying
  deification
deign
deism
deity
  deities (*pl.*)
deject
  dejected
  dejection
de jure
delay
  delaying
delectable
delegate
  delegacy
  delegacies (*pl.*)
  delegating
  delegation
delete (to cross out)
  deleting
  deletion
deleterious (harmful)
deliberate (intentional)
  deliberately
deliberate (to consider)
  deliberating
  deliberation
delicate
  delicacy
  delicacies (*pl.*)
  delicately

delicatessen
delicious
  deliciously
delight
  delightful
  delightfully
delimit
  delimitation
delineate
  delineating
  delineation
  delineator
delinquent
  delinquency
  delinquencies (*pl.*)
deliquesce
  deliquescence
  deliquescent
delirium
  delirious
deliver
  deliverance
  delivered
  deliverer
  delivering
  delivery
  deliveries (*pl.*)
delouse
  delousing
delta
delude (to deceive)
  deluding
  delusion
  delusive
deluge (rain storm)
de luxe
delve
  delving
demagnetise
  demagnetize
  demagnetisation
  demagnetization
  demagnetising
  demagnetizing
demagogue

demagoguery
demagogic
demagogy
demand
demarcate
  demarcating
  demarcation
démarche
demean (to behave)
  demeanour (behaviour)
  demeanor
demented
dementia
demesne (estate)
demilitarise
  demilitarize
  demilitarising
  demilitarizing
demise (to bequeath)
  demising
demist
  demister
demitasse
demobilise
  demobilize
  demobilisation
  demobilization
  demobilising
  demobilizing
democracy
  democracies (*pl.*)
  democratic
  democratically
  democratisation
  democratization
  democratise
  democratize
  democratising
  democratizing
demolish
  demolition
demon
  demonic
  demon's (of the demon)

demons'
(of the demons)
demonstrate
demonstrable
demonstrating
demonstration
demonstrative
demonstrator
demoralise
demoralize
demoralisation
demoralization
demoralising
demoralizing
demote (to lower)
demoting
demotion
demount
demur (to object)
demurred
demurring
demurs
demurrage
(late delivery penalty)
demure (modest)
demurely
den
denationalise
denationalize
denationalisation
denationalization
denationalising
denationalizing
denaturalise
denaturalize
dengue (fever)
denial (*from* deny)
denier (thread thickness)
denigrate
denigrating
denigration
denigrator
denim (cloth)
denizen (inhabitant)
denominate

denominating
denomination
denominational
denominator
denote
denoting
dénouement
denouement
denounce
denouncement
denouncer
denouncing
de nouveau
de novo
dense
densely
denseness
denser
density
densities (*pl.*)
dent
dental
dentifrice
dentine
dentition
denture
dentist
dentistry
dentist's (of the dentist)
dentists'
(of the dentists)
denude
denudation
denuding
denunciate
denunciating
denunciation
denunciator
deny
denial
denied
denies
denying
deodorise
deodorize

deodorant
deodorisation
deodorization
deodorising
deodorizing
deo volente, D.V.
(God willing)
depart
departure
department
departmental
departmentalise
departmentalize
departmentally
depend
dependable
dependant (person)
dependent
dependence
dependency
dependencies (*pl.*)
dependent (relying)
depersonalise
depersonalize
depict
depiction
depilatory (hair remover)
depilatories (*pl.*)
deplete
depleting
depletion
deplore
deplorable
deplorably
deploring
deploy
deployment
depopulate
depopulating
depopulation
deport
deportation
deportee
deportment (behaviour)
depose

deposing
deposition
deposit
  deposited
  depositing
  depositor
  depository (store)
  depositories (*pl.*)
depot
deprave (to corrupt)
  depraved
  depraving
  depravity
deprecate (to disapprove)
  deprecating
  deprecation
  deprecator
  deprecatory
depreciate
  (to decrease in value)
  depreciating
  depreciation
depredation (plundering)
  depredator
depress
  depressant
  depressed
  depression
  depressive
depressurise
  depressurize
  depressurisation
  depressurization
  depressurising
  depressurizing
deprive (to take away)
  deprival
  deprivation
  depriving
depth
depute
  deputation
  deputing
  deputise
  deputize

deputising
deputizing
deputy
deputies (*pl.*)
deputy's (of the deputy)
deputies'
     (of the deputies)
derail
  derailment
derange
  derangement
  deranging
derelict
  dereliction
deride
  deriding
  derision
  derisive
  derisory
de rigueur
derive
  derivation
  derivative
  deriving
dermatitis
  dermatologist
  dermatology
derogate
  derogating
  derogation
  derogatory
  derogatorily
derrick
dervish
descant (melody)
descend (to go down)
  descendant (person)
  descent
(going down, inheritance)
describe
  describable
  describing
  description
  descriptive
desecrate (to profane)

desecrating
desecration
desecrator
desecrater
desegregate
  desegregating
  desegregation
desensitise
  desensitize
desert (to abandon)
  deserter
  desertion
desert (barren region)
deserts (rewards)
deserve
  deservedly
  deserving
déshabillé, dishabille
desiccate (to dry)
  desiccating
  desiccation
  desiccator
desideratum
  desiderata (*pl.*)
design
  designer
  designer's
     (of the designer)
  designers'
     (of the designers)
designate
  designating
  designation
desire
  desirability
  desirable
  desirably
  desiring
  desirous
desist
desk
desolate
  desolation
despair
despatch, dispatch

dispatch
desperado
  desperadoes (*pl.*)
desperate (in despair)
  desperately
  desperation
despicable (*from* despise)
  despicably
despise
  despising
despite (notwithstanding)
despoil
  despoiler
  despoliation
despond
  despondency
  despondent
  despondently
despot
  despotic
  despotically
  despotism
dessert (fruit or sweet)
destination
destine
  destiny
  destinies (*pl.*)
destitute
  destitution
destroy
  destroyer
  destruction
  destructive
  destructively
  destructiveness
  destructor
desultory
  desultorily
  desultoriness
detach
  detachable
  detachment
detail
detain
detect

detectable
detection
detective
detective's
     (of the detective)
detectives'
     (of the detectives)
detector
détente
detention (*from* detain)
deter
  deterred
  deterrent
  deterring
  deters
detergent
deteriorate
  deteriorating
  deterioration
determine
  determinable
  determinant
  determination
  determining
  determinism
detest
  detestable
  detestation
dethrone
  dethroning
  dethronement
detonate
  detonating
  detonation
  detonator
detour
detract
  detraction
  detractor
detriment
  detrimental
  detrimentally
deuce (devil)
deuce (in tennis)
devalue

devaluation
devaluing
devastate
  devastating
  devastation
  devastator
develop
  developer
  development
  developmental
deviate
  deviant
  deviating
  deviation
device (contrivance)
devil
  devilment
  devilish
  devilishly
  devilled
  deviled
  devilry
devious
  deviously
  deviousness
devise (to plan)
  devising
devise (to bequeath)
  devising
devoid
devolve
  devolution
  devolving
devote
  devotee
  devoting
  devotion
devour
  devoured
devout
  devoutly
  devoutness
dew
  dewy
dexterity

dextrous
dexterous
dextrously
dexterously
dextrose (kind of glucose)
diabetes
diabetic
diabolic
diabolical
diabolically
diadem
diaeresis
diagnose
diagnosing
diagnosis
diagnoses (*pl.*)
diagnostic
diagnostician
diagonal
diagonally
diagram
diagrammatic
diagrammatically
dial
dialled
dialed
dialler
dialer
dialling
dialing
dials
dialect
dialectic
dialogue
diameter
diametric
diametrical
diametrically
diamond
diapason
diaper
diaphanous
diaphragm
diarchy
diarchies (*pl.*)

diarrhoea
diarrhea
diary
diaries (*pl.*)
diarist
diastole (heart function)
diastolic
diathermy
diatom (alga)
diatomic
    (having two atoms)
diatribe (fierce criticism)
dibble
dibber
dice
dicing
dicey (risky)
dichotomy
    (division in two)
dicker (to haggle)
dickered
dicky (shaky)
dickey
dicotyledon (botany)
dictaphone
dictate
dictating
dictation
dictator
dictatorial
dictatorially
dictator's
    (of the dictator)
dictators'
    (of the dictators)
diction
dictionary
dictionaries (*pl.*)
didactic
didactically
didacticism
diddle
diddling
didn't (did not)
die (to end life)

died
die-hard
dying
die (game)
dice (*pl.*)
die (tool)
dies (*pl.*)
dielectric
diesel
diet
dietary
dieted
dietetics
dietician, dietitian
dieting
diets
differ
differed
difference
different
differential
differentially
differentiate
differentiating
differentiation
differing
difficult
difficulty
difficulties (*pl.*)
diffident
diffidently
diffidence
diffract
diffraction
diffuse
diffuser
diffusing
diffusion
diffusive
dig
digger
digging
digs
dug
digest

disable

digestibility
digestible
digestion
digestive
digit
 digital
digitalin (poison)
 digitalis (drug)
dignify
 dignified (stately)
dignity
 dignitary (official)
 dignitaries (pl.)
digress
 digressed
 digresses
 digression
 digressive
dike, dyke
dilapidate
 dilapidating
 dilapidation
dilate
 dilatability
 dilatable
 dilatation
 dilating
 dilation
 dilator
dilatory (delaying)
 dilatorily
 dilatoriness
dilemma
dilettante
 dilettanti,
   dilettantes(pl.)
diligent
 diligently
 diligence
dill (herb)
dilly-dally
 dilly-dallied
 dilly-dallies
 dilly-dallying
dilute

diluent
diluting
dilution
diluvial
dim
 dimly
 dimmed
 dimmer
 dimming
dime (coin)
dimension
 dimensional
diminish
 diminution
 diminutive
diminuendo
dimity (fabric)
dimple
 dimpling
din
dinar (Yugoslav money)
dine
 dined
 diner (person)
 dining
 dinner (meal)
dinghy (boat)
 dinghies (pl.)
dingy (dark)
 dingier
 dingily
 dinginess
dinner
dinosaur
dint
diocese
 dioceses (pl.)
 diocesan
diode
diorama
dioxide
dip
 dipped
 dipper
 dipping

dips
diphtheria
diphthong
diploma
 diplomas (pl.)
diplomacy
 diplomacies (pl.)
 diplomat
 diplomatic
 diplomatically
 diplomatist
 diplomat's
   (of the diplomat)
 diplomats'
   (of the diplomats)
dipsomania
 dipsomaniac
dire
 direr
 direful
direct
 directing
 direction
 directional
 directive
 director
 directorate
 directory
 directories (pl.)
dirge (sad song)
dirigible (airship)
dirndl
dirt
 dirtied
 dirtier
 dirtily
 dirtiness
 dirty
 dirtying
disable
 disabled
 disability
 disabilities (pl.)
 disablement
 disabling

69

disabuse
  disabusing
disadvantage
  disadvantageous
disaffected
  disaffection
disagree
  disagreeable
  disagreeably
  disagreeing
  disagreement
disallow
disappear
  disappearance
  disappeared
  disappearing
disappoint
  disappointment
disapprove
  disapproval
  disapproving
disarm
  disarmament
disarrange
  disarrangement
  disarranging
disarray
disassociate
  disassociating
  disassociation
disaster
  disastrous
  disastrously
disband
  disbandment
disbar
  disbarred
  disbarring
disbelieve
  disbelief
  disbeliever
  disbelieving
disburden
  disburdened
disburse

disbursement
disbursing
disc
  disk (computer)
  disk
  disc-brake
  disc-jockey
discard
discern
  discernible
  discernment
discharge
  discharging
disciple
  disciple's
      (of the disciple)
  disciples'
      (of the disciples)
discipline
  disciplinarian
  disciplinary
  disciplining
disclaim
  disclaimer
disclose
  disclosing
  disclosure
discolour
  discolor
  discoloration
  discoloured
  discolored
discomfit (to disconcert)
  discomfited
  discomfiting
  discomfiture
discomfort
      (lack of comfort)
discompose
  discomposing
  discomposure
disconcert (to fluster)
disconnect
  disconnection
disconsolate

disconsolately
discontent
discontinue
  discontinuance
  discontinuing
  discontinuity
  discontinuities (*pl.*)
  discontinuous
discord
  discordance
  discordant
discothèque, discotheque
discount
discourage
  discouragement
  discouraging
discourse
  discoursing
discourteous
  discourteously
  discourtesy
  discourtesies (*pl.*)
discover
  discovered
  discoverer
  discovering
  discovery
  discoveries (*pl.*)
discredit
  discredited
  discrediting
discreet (prudent)
  discreetly
  discretion
discrepance, discrepancy
  discrepancies (*pl.*)
  discrepant
discrete (separate)
  discretely
discriminate
  discriminating
  discrimination
  discriminatory
discursive
discus (heavy disc)

discuses, disci (*pl.*)
discuss (to talk over)
discussion
disdain
disdainful
disdainfully
disease
disembark
disembarkation
disembody
disembodied
disembodiment
disembowel
disenchant
disenchantment
disengage
disengagement
disengaging
disentangle
disentanglement
disentangling
disestablish
disestablishment
disfavour
disfavor
disfavoured
disfavored
disfigure
disfigured
disfigurement
disfiguring
disgorge
disgorging
disgrace
disgraceful
disgracefully
disgracing
disgruntled
disguise
disguising
disgust
dish
dishes (*pl.*)
dishabille, déshabillé
dishearten

disheartened
dishevelled
disheveled
dishonest
dishonestly
dishonesty
dishonour
dishonor
dishonourable
dishonorable
dishonourably
dishonorably
dishonoured
dishonored
disillusion
disincentive
disinclination
disinclined
disinfect
disinfectant
disinfection
disinherit
disinheritance
disinherited
disinheriting
disintegrate
disintegrating
disintegration
disintegrator
disinter
disinterment
disinterred
disinterring
disinterested
disjointed
dislike
dislikable
dislocate
dislocating
dislocation
dislodge
dislodgement
dislodgment
dislodging
disloyal

disloyally
disloyalty
dismal
dismally
dismantle
dismantling
dismay
dismayed
dismember
dismembered
dismembering
dismemberment
dismiss
dismissal
dismount
disobedient
disobedience
disobediently
disobey
disobeyed
disoblige
disobliging
disorder
disordered
disordering
disorderliness
disorderly
disorganise
disorganize
disorganisation
disorganization
disorganising
disorganizing
disorientate
disorientation
disown
disparage
disparaging
disparagement
disparate (different)
disparity
disparities (*pl.*)
dispassionate
dispassionately
dispatch, despatch

71

dispatcher
dispel
  dispels
  dispelled
  dispelling
dispense
  dispensary
  dispensaries (*pl.*)
  dispensation
  dispenser
  dispenser's
     (of the dispenser)
  dispensers'
     (of the dispensers)
  dispensing
disperse
  dispersal
  dispersing
  dispersion
dispirit
  dispirited
displace
  displacement
  displacing
display
displease
  displeasing
  displeasure
disport
dispose
  disposable
  disposal
  disposing
disposition
dispossess
  dispossession
     (taking away)
disproportion
  disproportionate
  disproportionately
disprove
  disproving
dispute
  disputable
  disputably

disputant
disputing
disqualify
  disqualification
  disqualified
  disqualifying
disquiet
  disquieten
  disquietened
  disquieted
  disquietening
  disquieting
  disquietude
disquisition
disregard
disrepair
disreputable
  disreputably
  disrepute
disrespect
  disrespectful
  disrespectfully
disrobe
  disrobing
disrupt
  disruption
  disruptive
dissatisfy
  dissatisfaction
  dissatisfied
  dissatisfies
dissect
  dissection
  dissector
dissemble
  dissembler
  dissembling
disseminate
  disseminating
  dissemination
  disseminator
dissent
  dissenter
  dissension
  dissertation

disservice
dissidence (disagreement)
  dissident
  dissident's
     (of the dissident)
  dissidents'
     (of the dissidents)
dissimilar
  dissimilarity
  dissimilarities (*pl.*)
dissimulate (to deceive)
  dissimulating
  dissimulation
  dissimulator
dissipate
  dissipating
  dissipation
dissociate
  dissociating
  dissociation
dissolute
  dissolutely
  dissoluteness
dissolve
  dissoluble
  dissolution
  dissolvent
  dissolving
dissonance
  dissonant
dissuade
  dissuading
  dissuasion
  dissuasive
distaff
  distaffs (*pl.*)
distance
  distant
  distantly
distaste
  distasteful
  distastefully
distemper
  distempered
  distempering

distend
  distensible
  distension
distil
  distill
  distillation
  distilled
  distiller
  distillery
  distilleries (*pl.*)
  distilling
  distils
distinct
  distinction
  distinctive
  distinctly
distingué
distinguish
  distinguishable
distort
  distortion
  distortionless
distract
  distraction
distrain (to seize goods)
  distraint
    (seizure of goods)
distrait
distraught
distress
distribute
  distributing
  distribution
  distributive
  distributor
district
  district nurse
distrust
  distrustful
disturb
  disturbance
  disturber
disunite
  disunion
  disuniting

disunity
disuse
  disusing
ditch
  ditches (*pl.*)
  ditcher
dither
  dithered
  dithering
  dithery
ditto
ditty
  ditties (*pl.*)
diuresis
  diuretic
diurnal (in a day)
  diurnally
diva (prima donna)
divagate
  divagating
  divagation
divan
dive
  diver
  diver's (of the diver)
  divers' (of the divers)
  diving
diverge
  divergence
  divergent
  diverging
divers (various)
diverse (different)
  diversely
  diversity
diversify
  diversification
  diversified
  diversifies
  diversifying
diversion (amusement)
divert (to turn aside)
  diversion
    (alternative route)
divertissement

divest
divide
  dividend
  divider
  dividing
divine (God-like)
  divinely
  divinity
  divinities (*pl.*)
divine (to discover)
  divination
  diviner
  divining
division
  divisible
  divisional
  divisive
  (causing disagreement)
  divisively
  divisor
divorce
  divorcee
  divorcing
divot
divulge
  divulging
dizzy
  dizzier
  dizzily
  dizziness
do
  doer
  does
  doesn't (does not)
  doing
  done
  don't (do not)
docile
  docilely
  docility
dock
  docker
  docker's (of the docker)
  dockers'
    (of the dockers)

dockyard
docket
  docketed
  docketing
doctor
  doctors (*pl.*)
  doctor's (of the doctor)
  doctors' (of the doctors)
  doctorate
  doctored
  doctoring
doctrine
  doctrinaire
  doctrinal
document
  documentary
  documentaries (*pl.*)
  documentation
dodder
  dodderer
  doddery
dodge
  dodging
  dodgy
doe (deer)
doff
dog
  doggie (diminutive)
  doggy (dog-like)
  dog's (of the dog)
  dogs' (of the dogs)
dog (to follow)
  dogs
  dogged
  dogging
dog-ear
  dog-eared
dogged (stubborn)
  doggedly
doggerel
dogma
  dogmas (*pl.*)
  dogmatic
  dogmatically
  dogmatise

dogmatize
dogmatising
dogmatizing
dogmatism
do-gooder
doing (*from* do)
doily
  doilies (*pl.*)
do-it-yourself, DIY
dolce far niente
doldrums
dole (to give out)
  doling
dole (payment)
doleful
  dolefully
doll
  dolled
  dolly
  dollies (*pl.*)
  doll's (of the doll)
  dolls' (of the dolls)
dollar (money)
dollop
dolour (sorrow)
  dolor
  dolorous
dolphin
dolt
domain
dome
Domesday-Book
domestic
  domestically
  domesticate
  domesticity
domicile
  domiciliary
dominate
  dominance
  dominant
  dominantly
  dominating
  domination
domineer

domineered
domineering
dominical
dominion
domino
  dominoes (*pl.*)
don
  donnish
don (to put on)
  donned
  donning
  dons
donate
  donating
  donation
done (*from* do)
donkey
  donkey's
    (of the donkey)
  donkeys'
    (of the donkeys)
donor (giver)
  donor's (of the donor)
  donors' (of the donors)
don't (do not)
doodle
    (to draw aimlessly)
  doodler
  doodling
doodle (*to cheat*)
doom
  doomed
door
dope
  dopey
  doping
dormant
  dormancy
dormer (window)
dormitory
  dormitories (*pl.*)
  dormitory's
    (of the dormitory)
  dormitories'
    (of the dormitories)

dormouse
  dormice (*pl.*)
dorsal
  dorsally
dory (fish)
  dories (*pl.*)
dose
  dosage
  dosing
  dosimeter
doss
  doss-house
dossier
dot
  dotted
  dottier
  dottiest
  dottily
  dotting
  dotty (crazy)
dot (dowry)
dote
  dotage
  dotard
  doting
double
  double-barrelled
  double-breasted
  doubling
  doubly
double entendre
doubt
  doubter
  doubtful
  doubtfully
  doubtfulness
  doubtless
douche
  douching
dough
  doughnut
doughty
  doughtier
  doughtily
  doughtiness

dour (grim)
  dourly
  dourness
douse
  (to drench, extinguish)
  dousing
dove
  dovecot
  dovecote
  dovetail
  dovetailed
dowager
  dowager's
      (of the dowager)
  dowagers'
      (of the dowagers)
dowdy
  dowdier
  dowdily
  dowdiness
dowel
dower
  dower-house
down
  downcast
  downfall
  downfallen
  downhearted
  downpour
  downright
  downstairs
  downtrodden
  downward
down (feathers or fluff)
  downy
Downs
dowry
  dowries (*pl.*)
dowse (for water)
  dowser
  dowsing
doyen
doze
  dozing
dozen

drab
drachma (Greek money)
Draconian (very severe)
draft
  (detachment of men)
draft (of money)
draft (rough copy)
drag
  dragged
  dragging
  drags
dragoman
  dragomans, dragomen
      (*pl.*)
dragon
  dragonfly
  dragonflies (*pl.*)
  dragon's
      (of the dragon)
  dragons'
      (of the dragons)
dragoon
  dragooned
drain
  drainage
drama
  dramatic
  dramatically
  dramatisation
  dramatization
  dramatise
  dramatize
  dramatising
  dramatizing
  dramatis personae
  dramatist
drank (*from* drink)
drape
  draper
  draper's (of the draper)
  drapers' (of the drapers)
  drapery
  draperies (*pl.*)
  draping
drastic

drastically
draught (of air)
  draft
  draughtier
  draftier
  draughty
  drafty
draught (drink)
  draft
draughts (game)
  checkers
draughtsman
  draftsman
  draughtsmen (*pl.*)
  draftsmen (pl.)
draw
  drawn
  drew
drawback
drawer
drawing-room
drawl
dread
  dreadful
  dreadfully
  dreadfulness
  dreadnought
dream
  dreamed
  dreamer
  dreamier
  dreamily
  dreamless
  dreamt
  dreamy
dreary
  drearier
  drearily
  dreariness
dredge
  dredger
  dredging
dregs
drench
  drenching

dress
  dresses (*pl.*)
  dressed
  dresser
  dresses
  dressmaker
  dressy
dressage
dribble
  dribbler
  dribbling
driblet
dried (*from* dry)
  drier (more dry)
drier, dryer
        (drying machine)
drift
  drifter
drill (military)
drill (dentist's)
drily (*from* dry)
  dryly
drink
  drank
  drinkable
  drinker
  drunk
  drunkard
drip
  drip-dried
  drip-dry
  drip-drying
  dripped
  dripping
  drips
drive
  driven
  driver
  driver's (of the driver)
  drivers' (of the drivers)
  driving
  drove
drivel
  drivelled
  driveled

  driveller
  driveler
  drivelling
  driveling
  drivels
drizzle
  drizzling
  drizzly
drogue (buoy)
droll
  drollery
  drolleries (*pl.*)
  drollness
  drolly
dromedary
  dromedaries (*pl.*)
drone
  droning
droop
drop
  droplet
  drop-out
  drop-outs (*pl.*)
  dropped
  dropper
  dropping
  drops
dropsy
  dropsical
dross
drought
drove (*from* drive)
drove (herd)
  drover
drown
  drowned
drowse
  drowsier
  drowsily
  drowsiness
  drowsing
  drowsy
drudge
  drudgery
  drudging

drug
  drugged
  drugging
  druggist
  drugstore
drugget (fabric)
druid
drum
  drum-major
  drummed
  drummer
  drumming
  drums
drunk (*from* drink)
  drunkard
  drunken
  drunkenly
  drunkenness
dry
  dried
  drier, dryer
          (drying machine)
  drier (more dry)
  dries
  drily
  dryly
  dry-clean
  dry-cleaned
  dry-cleaning
  drying
  dryness
dual (double)
  dualism
  dual-purpose
dub
  dubbed
  dubbing
  dubs
dubbin, dubbing (grease)
dubious
  dubiously
ducal (*from* duke)
ducat (money)
duchess
  duchesses (*pl.*)

duchess's
          (of the duchess)
duchesses'
          (of the duchesses)
drugstore
duchy
  duchies (*pl.*)
duck
  duckling
  duck's (of the duck)
  ducks' (of the ducks)
duck
          (to dive or immerse)
duct
  ductless
  ductile
  ductility
dud
dudgeon
due
  duly
duel (fight)
  duelled
  dueled
  duelling
  dueling
  duellist
duenna
  duennas (*pl.*)
  duenna's
          (of the duenna)
  duennas'
          (of the duennas)
duet
duffel, duffle (cloth, coat)
duffer
dug (*from* dig)
  dug-out
  dug-outs (*pl.*)
duke
  dukery
  dukeries (*pl.*)
dulcet
dull
  dullard

duller
dullness
dully
duly (*from* due)
dumb
  dumb-bell
  dumbly
  dumbness
  dumbfound
  dumfound
dummy
  dummies (*pl.*)
  dummy's
          (of the dummy)
  dummies'
          (of the dummies)
dump
dumpling
dumpy
  dumpiness
dun
  duns
  dunned
  dunning
dun (dull brown)
dunce
  dunce's (of the dunce)
  dunces' (of the dunces)
dune
dung
  dunghill
dungaree
  dungarees (*pl.*)
dungeon
duodecimal
duodecimo
          (size of book)
duodenum
  duodenal
duologue
dupe
  duping
  dupery
duplex
duplicate

77

duplicating
duplication
duplicator
duplicity
durable
  durability
  durably
durance
duration
duress
during
dusk
dust
  duster
  dustiness
  dusty
duty
  duties (*pl.*)
  dutiable
  dutiful
  dutifully
  duty-free
dwarf
  dwarfs (*pl.*)
  dwarf's (of the dwarf)
  dwarfs' (of the dwarfs)
dwell
  dweller
  dwelling
  dwelt
dwindle
  dwindling
dye (to colour)
  dyed
  dyeing
  dyer
dying (*from* die)
dyke, dike
dynamic
  dynamically
dynamite
  dynamiting
dynamo
  dynamos (*pl.*)
dynamometer

dynasty
  dynasties (*pl.*)
dyne (unit)
dys- (bad)
dysentery
dyslexia
  dyslexic
dyspepsia
  dyspeptic

E

each
eager
  eagerly
  eagerness
eagle
  eagle-eyed
  eaglet
ear
  earache
  earful
  earphone
  ear-ring
earl
  earldom
  earl's (of the earl)
  earls' (of the earls)
early
  earlier
  earliness
earmark
earn
  earner
  earnest
  earnestly
  earnestness
earth
  earthed
  earthenware
  earthly
  earthquake

earwig
  earwig's (of the earwig)
  earwigs'
      (of the earwigs)
ease
  easier
  easily
  easiness
  easing
  easy
  easygoing
easel
east
  easterly
  eastern
  eastward
  eastwards
Easter
easy (*see* ease)
eat
  ate
  eatable
  eaten
  eater
  eating
  eats
eaves
eavesdrop
  eavesdropped
  eavesdropper
  eavesdropping
  eavesdrops
ebb
  ebb-tide
ebony
  ebonite
ebullient
  ebullience
  ebulliently
eccentric
  eccentrically
  eccentricity
  eccentricities (*pl.*)
ecclesiastic
  ecclesiastical

ecclesiastically
echelon
echo
  echoes (*pl.*)
  echoed
  echoes
  echoing
éclair
éclat
eclectic
  eclecticism
eclipse
  eclipsing
  ecliptic
eclogue
ecology
  ecological
  ecologically
  ecologist
economy
  economies (*pl.*)
  economic
  economical
  economically
  economise
  economize
  economising
  economizing
  economist
ecstasy
  ecstasies (*pl.*)
  ecstatic
  ecstatically
ecumenical
eczema
eddy
  eddies (*pl.*)
  eddied
  eddying
edelweiss
edge
  edgeways
  edgily
  edginess
  edging

edgy
edible
  edibility
edict
edifice (building)
edify (to instruct)
  edification
  edified
edit
  edited
  edition
  editor
  editorial
  editorially
  editor's (of the editor)
  editors' (of the editors)
educate
  educable
  educatability
  educability
  educatable
  educating
  education
  educational
  educationalist
  educationally
  educationist
  educative
  educator
educe (to develop, infer)
  educible
  educing
  eduction
eel
  eel's (of the eel)
  eels' (of the eels)
  elver (young eel)
eerie (creepy)
  eerier
  eerily
  eeriness
efface
  effaceable
  effacement
  effacing

effect (to accomplish)
  effective (useful)
  effectively
  effectiveness
  effectual (actual)
effeminate
  effeminacy
  effeminately
effervesce
  effervescence
  effervescent
  effervescing
effete
efficacious
  efficaciously
  efficacy
efficient
  efficiency
  efficiently
effigy
  effigies (*pl.*)
efflorescence
  efflorescent
effluent (liquid discharge)
effluvium (bad smell)
efflux
effort
  effortless
  effortlessly
effrontery
  effronteries (*pl.*)
effusive (emotional)
  effusively
  effusiveness
  effusion
egalitarian
egg (to urge)
  egged
egg (bird's)
  eggy
ego
  egocentric
  egocentricity
  egoism (selfishness)
  egoist

egoistic
egoistically
egotism (conceit)
egotist
egotistic
egotistical
egotistically
egregious
    (absurd, shocking)
egregiously
egregiousness
egress (exit)
eiderdown
Eiffel (tower)
eight
eighteen
eighteenth
eighth
eighthly
eightieth
eighty
eighties (*pl.*)
Eire
Eisteddfod
either (.... or)
ejaculate
ejaculating
ejaculation
ejaculatory
eject
ejection
ejector
eke (out)
eking
elaborate (complicated)
elaborately
elaborateness
elaborate (to work out)
elaborating
elaboration
elapse
elapsing
elastic
elastically
elasticity

elate
elating
elation
elbow
elbowed
elder (older)
elderly
eldest
elder (tree)
elect
election
electioneering
elective
elector
electoral
electorate
electric
electrical
electrically
electrician
electricity
electrification
electrified
electrify
electrifying
electrocardiogram (E.C.G.)
electrocardiograph
electrocardiography
electrocute
electrocuting
electrocution
electrode
electrodynamic
electrodynamically
electrolysis
electrolyte
electrolytic
electromagnet
electromagnetic
electrometer
electrometric
electromotive
electromotive force
                    (E.M.F.)
electron

electronic
electronically
electroplate
electroplating
electrostatic
electrotechnical
eleemosynary (charitable)
elegant
elegance
elegantly
elegy
elegies (*pl.*)
elegiac
element
elemental
elementarily
elementary
elephant
elephantine
elephant's
        (of the elephant)
elephants'
        (of the elephants)
elevate
elevating
elevation
elevator
eleven
eleventh
elf
elves (*pl.*)
elfin
elfish
elicit (to get information)
elicited
eliciting
elide (to leave out)
eliding
elision
eligible (suitable)
eligibility
eliminate
eliminating
elimination
eliminator

élite
 élitism
 élitist
elixir
Elizabethan
ellipse
 elliptic
 elliptical
 elliptically
elm
elocution
 elocutionist
elongate
 elongating
 elongation
elope
 elopement
 eloping
eloquence
 eloquent
 eloquently
else
 elsewhere
elucidate
 elucidating
 elucidation
elude (to escape)
 eluding
 elusion
 elusive
 elusiveness
elver (young eel)
elves (*from* elf)
Elysian
emaciate
 emaciating
 emaciation
emanate
 emanating
 emanation
emancipate
 emancipating
 emancipation
 emancipator
emasculate

 emasculating
 emasculation
embalm
 embalmer
 embalmment
embankment
embargo
 embargoes (*pl.*)
 embargoed
 embargoes
 embargoing
embark
 embarkation
embarras de richesse
embarrass
 embarrassed
 embarrasses
 embarrassment
embassy
 embassies (*pl.*)
 embassy's
     (of the embassy)
 embassies'
     (of the embassies)
embattle
 embattling
embed
 embedded
 embedding
embellish
 embellishment
ember
embezzle
 embezzlement
 embezzler
 embezzling
embitter
 embittered
 embittering
 embitterment
emblazon
emblem
 emblematic
 emblematically
embody

embodied
embodies
embodiment
embodying
embolism
embonpoint (plumpness)
emboss
 embossment
embrace
 embracing
embrasure
embrocation
embroider
 embroidered
 embroidery
 embroideries (*pl.*)
embroil
 embroilment
embryo
 embryos (*pl.*)
 embryologist
 embryology
 embryonic
emend (to remove error)
 emendation
emerald
emerge (to appear)
 emergence
 emergent
 emerging
 emersion (reappearance)
emergency
 emergencies (*pl.*)
 emergently
emeritus
emery
emetic
emigrate
     (to leave country)
 emigrant
 emigrating
 emigration
 émigré
eminent (distinguished)
 eminently

eminence
emissary
emissaries (*pl.*)
emit
emission
emits
emitted
emitter
emitting
emollient (softening)
emolument (pay)
emotion
emotional
emotionally
emotive
empathy
emperor
emperor's
(of the emperor)
emperors'
(of the emperors)
emphasise
emphasize
emphasis
emphases (*pl.*)
emphasising
emphasizing
emphatic
emphatically
emphysema (lung disease)
empire
empirical (experimental)
empirically
emplacement
employ
employability
employable
employe
employee (worker)
employee's
(of the employee)
employees'
(of the employees)
employer (boss)

employer's
(of the employer)
employers'
(of the employers)
employment
emporium
empower
empowered
empowering
empress
empresses (*pl.*)
empress's
(of the empress)
empresses'
(of the empresses)
empty
empties (*pl.*)
emptied
emptier
empties
emptily
emptiness
emptying
emu
emulate (to imitate)
emulating
emulation
emulative
emulator
emulsion
emulsification
emulsified
emulsifier
emulsify
enable
enablement
enabling
enact
enactment
enamel
enamelled
enameled
enameller
enameler
enamelling

enameling
enamour
enamor
enamoured
enamored
en bloc
encampment
encase
encasing
enceinte (pregnant)
encephalitis
enchant
enchanter
enchantment
enchantress (*fem.*)
encircle
encirclement
encircling
enclave
enclose
enclosing
enclosure
encode
encoding
encomium (praise)
encompass
encore
encored
encoring
encounter
encountered
encountering
encounters
encourage
encouragement
encouraging
encroach
encroachment
encumber
encumbered
encumbering
encumbrance
encyclical
encyclopedia,
encyclopaedia

encyclopedic,
  encyclopaedic
end
 endless
 endlessly
endanger
 endangered
 endangering
endear
 endeared
 endearing
 endearment
endeavour
 endeavor
 endeavoured
 endeavored
 endeavouring
 endeavoring
endemic
 endemically
endive
endocrine (gland)
endorse, indorse
 endorsement,
   indorsement
 endorser, indorser
 endorsing, indorsing
endow
 endowment
endure
 endurable
 endurance
 enduring
enema
 enemas (*pl.*)
enemy
 enemies (*pl.*)
energise
 energize
 energiser
 energizer
 energising
 energizing
energy
 energies (*pl.*)

energetic
energetically
enervate (to weaken)
 enervating
 enervation
en famille
enfeeble
 enfeeblement
 enfeebling
enforce
 enforceability
 enforceable
 enforcement
 enforcing
enfranchise
 enfranchisement
 enfranchising
engage
 engagement
 engaging
engender
 engendered
 engendering
engine
 engineer
 engineered
 engineering
 engineer's
  (of the engineer)
 engineers'
  (of the engineers)
engorge
 engorged
engrained
engrave
 engraver
 engraving
engross
 engrossment
engulf
enhance
 enhancement
 enhancing
enigma
 enigmatic

enigmatically
enjoin (to command)
enjoy
 enjoyable
 enjoyably
 enjoyment
enlarge
 enlargeable
 enlargement
 enlarger
 enlarging
enlighten
 enlightened
 enlightenment
enlist
 enlistment
enliven
 enlivened
 enlivenment
en masse
enmity
 enmities (*pl.*)
ennoble
 ennoblement
 ennobling
ennui (boredom)
 ennuyé (bored)
 ennuyée (*fem.*)
en passant
enormous
 enormity
 enormities (*pl.*)
 enormously
enough
enquire, inquire
 inquire
 enquiring, inquiring
 inquiring
 enquiry, inquiry
 inquiry
 enquiries, inquiries (*pl.*)
 inquiries
enrage
 enraging
enrapture

enraptured
enrich
enrichment
enrol
enroll
enrolled
enrolling
enrolment
enrollment
enrols
en route
ensconce
ensconcing
ensemble
enshrine
enshrining
ensign
ensign's (of the ensign)
ensigns' (of the ensigns)
enslave
enslavement
enslaving
ensue (to follow)
ensuing
ensure (to make sure)
ensuring
entail
entailment
entangle
entanglement
entangling
entente
enter
entered
entering
enteric
enteritis
enterprise
enterprising
entertain
entertainer
entertainment
enthrall, enthral
enthralled
enthralling

enthralment
enthrallment
enthrone
enthronement
enthroning
enthuse
enthusiasm
enthusiast
enthusiastic
enthusiastically
enthusing
entice
enticement
enticing
entire
entirely
entirety
entitle
entitlement
entitling
entity
entities (*pl.*)
entomb
entombment
entomology
entomological
entomologist
entourage
entr'acte
entrails
entrance (to delight)
entranced
entrancement
entrancing
entrance (way in)
entrant
entrap
entrapped
entrapping
entraps
entreat
entreaty
entreaties (*pl.*)
entrée
entrench

entrenchment
entrepôt
entrepreneur
entrepreneurial
entropy
entrust
entry
entries (*pl.*)
entwine
entwining
enumerate
enumerating
enumeration
enumerator
enunciate
enunciating
enunciation
enunciator
envelop (to cover)
enveloped
enveloping
envelopment
envelope (covering)
envenom
environ
environment
environmental
environmentally
envisage
envisaging
envoy
envoys (*pl.*)
envoy's (of the envoy)
envoys' (of the envoys)
envy
enviable
envied
envies
envious
enviously
envying
enwrap
enwrapped
enwrapping
enwraps

enzyme
eolith (ancient flint)
epaulette
 epaulet
ephemera, ephemeron (fly)
 ephemeras, ephemerae,
  ephemerons(*pl.*)
ephemeral (short-lived)
 ephemerally
epic
 epical
 epically
epicene (both sexes)
epicentre
 epicenter
epicure
 epicurean
 epicureanism
epicycle
 epicyclic
epidemic
epidermis
 epidermal
epidiascope
epigastrium
 epigastric
epiglottis
epigram (clever saying)
 epigrammatic
epigraph (inscription)
epilepsy
 epileptic
epilogue
Epiphany
episcopal
 episcopacy
 episcopalian
 episcopate
episode
 episodic
epistle
 epistolary
epitaph
 (inscription on tomb)
epithet (adjective)

epitome
epitomise
 epitomize
epitomising
 epitomizing
epoch
 epochal
eponym
 eponymous
epsilon
equable
 equability
 equably
equal
 equality
 equalities (*pl.*)
 equalled
 equaled
 equally
 equals
equalise
 equalize
 equaliser
 equalizer
 equalising
 equalizing
equanimity
equate
 equating
 equation
equator
 equatorial
equerry
 equerries (*pl.*)
equestrian
 equestrianism
equidistant
equilateral
equilibrate
 equilibrating
 equilibration
equilibrium
equine
equinox
 equinoctial

equip
 equipage
 equipment
 equipped
 equipping
equipoise
equitable
 equitably
 equity
 equities (*pl.*)
equivalent
 equivalence
equivocal
 equivocally
 equivocate
 equivocating
 equivocation
 equivocator
era
 eras (*pl.*)
eradicate
 eradicable
 eradicating
 eradication
erase
 erasable
 eraser
 erasing
 erasure
ere (before)
erect
 erection
 erector
erg (unit)
ergo (therefore)
ergonomics
ergotism (disease)
ermine
erode
 eroding
 erosion
 erosive
erogenous
erotic
 erotica

erotically
eroticism
erotism
err
  erred
  erring
  errs
errand (short journey)
errant (wandering)
  errancy
  errantry
errata (mistakes)
erratic
  erratically
error
  erroneous
  erroneously
ersatz
erstwhile
eructate (to belch)
  eructating
  eructation
erudite (learned)
  eruditely
  erudition
erupt (of a volcano)
  eruption
  eruptive
  eruptively
erysipelas
escalade (to climb over)
  escalading
escalate (to increase)
  escalating
  escalation
  escalator (moving stairs)
escallop, scallop (shellfish)
escalope (slice of veal)
escapade
escape
  escaper
  escaping
  escapism
  escapologist
escapement (of a clock)

escargot (snail)
escarpment (of a hill)
eschatology
  eschatological
eschew
escort
Eskimo
  Eskimos, Eskimo (pl.)
  Eskimo's
          (of the Eskimo)
  Eskimos'
          (of the Eskimos)
esoteric
  esoterical
  esoterically
  esotericism
espalier
especial
  especially
Esperanto
espionage
esplanade
espouse
  espousal
  espousing
espresso
esprit de corps
espy
  espied
  espies
  espying
Esquire
Esq.
essay
  essays (pl.)
  essayist
essence
  essential
  essentially
establish
  establishable
  establishment
estate
esteem
  estimable

estimate
  estimating
  estimation
  estimator
estrange
  estrangement
estuary
  estuaries (pl.)
et cetera, etc.
etch
  etcher
  etching
eternal
  eternally
  eternity
  eternities (pl.)
ether (drug)
ether (of space)
  ethereal
  ethereally
ethic
  ethical
  ethically
  ethics (morals)
ethnic (about nations)
  ethnically
  ethnological
  ethnology
ethos (custom, belief)
ethyl
  ethylene
etiolate (to make pale)
  etiolation
etiquette
étude (music)
etymology
  etymological
  etymologically
  etymologist
eucalyptus
  eucalyptuses (pl.)
  eucalypti (pl.)
Eucharist
Euclid
  Euclidean

eugenic
  eugenically
  eugenics
eulogy
  eulogies (*pl.*)
  eulogise
  eulogize
  eulogising
  eulogizing
  eulogistic
  eulogistically
eunuch
euphemism
  euphemistic
  euphemistically
euphony (pleasant sound)
  euphonious
euphoria (feeling happy)
  euphoric
euphuism
(affected style of speech)
  euphuistic
Eurasian
eureka
eurhythmics
Eurocrat
Eurodollar
Europe
  European
eustachian (tube in ear)
euthanasia
evacuate
  evacuating
  evacuation
  evacuee
evade
  evading
  evasion
evaluate
  evaluating
  evaluation
evanesce (to disappear)
  evanescent
evangelical
  evangelism

evangelist
evaporate
  evaporating
  evaporation
  evaporator
evasion
  evasive
  evasively
  evasiveness
eve
  evening
  eventide
even
  evenly
  evenness
event
  eventful
  eventfully
  eventual
  eventuality
  eventualities (*pl.*)
  eventually
  eventuate
  eventuating
ever
  everlasting
  evermore
every
  everybody
  everybody's
        (of everybody)
  everyone
  everywhere
evict
  eviction
evidence
  evident
  evidently
evil
  evilly
evince
  evincing
eviscerate (to degut)
  eviscerating
  evisceration

evoke
  evocation
  evocative
  evoking
evolve
  evolution
  evolutionary
  evolutionism
  evolutionist
  evolving
ewe (sheep)
ewer (jug)
exacerbate
  exacerbating
  exacerbation
exact
  exactitude
  exactly
  exactness
exaggerate
  exaggerating
  exaggeration
  exaggerator
exalt
  exaltation
examine
  examination
  examiner
  examiner's
      (of the examiner)
  examiners'
      (of the examiners)
  examining
example
exasperate
  exasperating
  exasperation
excavate
  excavating
  excavation
  excavator
exceed
  exceedingly
excel
  excelled

excellence
excellent
excellently
excelling
excels
Excellency
  Excellencies (*pl.*)
  Excellency's
    (of His Excellency)
  Excellencies'
    (of Their Excellencies)
except
  exception
  exceptional
  exceptionally
excerpt (extract)
excess
  excesses (*pl.*)
  excessive
  excessively
exchange
  exchangeable
  exchanger
  exchanging
exchequer
excise (to cut away)
  excisable
  excising
  excision
excise (tax)
excite
  excitability
  excitable
  excitation
  excitement
  exciter
  exciting
exclaim
  exclamation
  exclamatory
exclude
  excluding
  exclusion
  exclusive
  exclusively

exclusiveness
exclusivity
excommunicate
  excommunicating
  excommunication
excrescence
excrete
  excrement
  excreta
  excreting
  excretion
excruciate
  excruciating
  excruciatingly
exculpate (to pardon)
  exculpating
  exculpation
excursion
excuse
  excusable
  excusably
  excusing
execrate
  execrable
  execrably
  execration
executant (performer)
execute
  executing
  execution
  executioner
  executioner's
    (of the executioner)
  executioners'
    (of the executioners)
executive (manager)
  executive's
    (of the executive)
  executives'
    (of the executives)
executor (of a Will)
  executrix (*fem.*)
  executrices (*pl.*)
exemplary
  exemplarily

exemplify
  exemplification
  exemplified
  exemplifies
exempt
  exemption
exercise
  exercising
exert
  exertion
exhale
  exhaling
  exhalation
exhaust
  exhausted
  exhaustible
  exhaustion
  exhaustive
  exhaustively
exhibit
  exhibited
  exhibition
  exhibitionism
  exhibitionist
  exhibitor
exhibition (scholarship)
  exhibitioner
exhilarate
  exhilarant
  exhilarating
  exhilaration
exhort
  exhortation
exhume
  exhumation
  exhuming
exigency
  exigencies (*pl.*)
  exigent
  exigently
exiguous (scanty)
  exiguity
exile
  exiling
exist

existence
existent
existential
existentialism
exit (way out)
exit (he, she goes out)
exeunt (they go out)
exodus
ex officio
exonerate
exonerating
exoneration
exorbitant
exorbitance
exorbitantly
exorcise
        (to free from evil)
exorcize
exorcising
exorcizing
exorcism
exorcist
exotic
exotica
exotically
expand
expandable
expanse
expansible
expansion
expansive
expansively
expatiate
        (to talk at length)
expatiating
expatriate
expatriating
expatriation
expect
expectancy
expectant
expectation
expectorate (to spit)
expectorant
expectorating

expectoration
expedient
expediency
expediencies (*pl.*)
expedite (to hasten)
expediting
expedition
expeditionary
expeditious
expeditiously
expel
expelled
expelling
expels
expulsion
expend
expendability
expendable
expenditure
expense
expensive
experience
experiencing
experiment
experimental
experimentally
experimentation
experimenter
expert
expertise (skill)
expertly
expertness
expert's (of the expert)
experts' (of the experts)
expiate
expiating
expiation
expire (to breathe out)
expiration
expiratory
expiring
expire (to die, finish)
expiring
expiry
explain

explainable
explanation
explanatory
expletive
explicable
explicate (to explain)
explicating
explicit (definite)
explicitly
explicitness
explode
exploding
explosion
explosive
explosively
exploit
exploitation
exploiter
explore
exploration
exploratory
explorer
explorer's
        (of the explorer)
explorers'
        (of the explorers)
exploring
exponent
exponential
export
exportable
exportation
exporter
exporter's
        (of the exporter)
exporters'
        (of the exporters)
exposé
expose
        (detailed description)
exposing
exposition
exposure
expostulate
expostulating

89

expostulation
expound (to explain)
express
  expressible
  expression
  expressionless
  expressive
  expressively
  expressly
expropriate
  expropriating
  expropriation
  expropriator
expulsion (*from* expel)
expunge
  expunction
  expunging
expurgate
  expurgating
  expurgation
  expurgatory
exquisite
  exquisitely
ex-Service
extant (existing)
extempore
  extemporaneous
  extemporaneously
  extemporisation
  extemporization
  extemporise
  extemporize
  extemporising
  extemporizing
extend
  extendible
  extensible
  extension
  extensive
  extensively
extent (scope)
extenuate (to weaken)
  extenuating
  extenuation
exterior

exterminate (to destroy)
  exterminating
  extermination
  exterminator
external
  externally
extinct
  extinction
extinguish
  extinguisher
extirpate (to root out)
  extirpating
  extirpation
  extirpator
extol
  extolled
  extolling
  extols
extort
  extortion
  extortionate
  extortioner
extra
extract
  extractable
  extraction
  extractive
  extractor
extra-curricular
extradite
  extraditable
  extraditing
  extradition
extra-marital
extramural
extraneous
  extraneously
extraordinary
  extraordinarily
extrapolate
  extrapolating
  extrapolation
extra-sensory
extra-systole (heart-beat)
  extra-systolic

extra-territorial
  extra-territoriality
extravagant
  extravagance
  extravagantly
  extravaganza
extreme
  extremely
  extremist
  extremity
  extremities (*pl.*)
extricate
  extricable
  extricating
  extrication
extrinsic
  extrinsically
extrovert
  extroversion
extrude (to squeeze out)
  extruder
  extruding
  extrusion
exuberant
  exuberance
  exuberantly
exude
  exudation
  exuding
exult
  exultant
  exultation
eye
  eyeball
  eyebrow
  eyed
  eyeful
  eyeing
  eying
  eyelash
  eyelashes (*pl.*)
  eyelid
  eye-opener
  eyepiece
  eyesight

eyesore
eyewash
eyewitness
eyrie (eagle's nest)

F

fable
fabric
fabricate
  fabricating
  fabrication
  fabricator
fabulous
  fabulously
façade
face
  faceless
  facial
  facially
  facing
facet (side or aspect)
  faceted
facetious (humorous)
  facetiously
  facetiousness
facia, fascia (panel)
facial (*from* face)
facile (easy)
  facility
  facilities (*pl.*)
facilitate
  facilitating
  facilitation
facsimile
fact
  factual
  factually
faction
factitious (artificial)
factious (seditious)
factor

factorial
  factorially
  factorisation
  factorization
  factorise
  factorize
  factorising
  factorizing
factory
  factories (*pl.*)
  factory's
        (of the factory)
  factories'
        (of the factories)
factotum
  factotums (*pl.*)
facultative (optional)
faculty
  faculties (*pl.*)
fad
  faddish
  faddy
fade
  fadeless
  fading
faeces
  feces
  faecal
  fecal
fag
  fag-end
  fagged
  fagging
faggot
  fagot
Fahrenheit
faience (porcelain)
fail
  failure
fain (willing)
faint
  fainter
  faint-hearted
  faintly
  faintness

fair (light-coloured)
  fairer
  fair-haired
fair
  (outdoor entertainment)
fair (satisfactory)
  fairer
  fairly
  fairness
fair (clear)
  fairway
fairy
  fairies (*pl.*)
  fairy's (of the fairy)
  fairies' (of the fairies)
  fairy tale
fait accompli
faith
  faithful
  faithfully
  faithfulness
  faithless
  faithlessly
  faithlessness
fake
  faker
  faking
fakir (Indian holy man)
falcon
  falconer
  falconry
fall
  fallen
  fell
fallacy
  fallacies (*pl.*)
  fallacious
fallible
  fallibility
fallow
false
  falsehood
  falsely
  falseness
  falsity

falsetto
  falsettos (*pl.*)
falsify
  falsification
  falsified
  falsifies
falter
  faltered
  faltering
fame
  famous
  famously
familiar
  familiarisation
  familiarization
  familiarise
  familiarize
  familiarising
  familiarizing
  familiarity
  familiarly
family
  families (*pl.*)
  family's (of the family)
  families'
       (of the families)
famine
famish
famous
fan
  fanned
  fanning
  fans
fanatic
  fanatically
  fanaticism
fancy
  fancies (*pl.*)
  fancies
  fancied
  fancier
  fanciful
  fancifully
  fancy-free
fanfare

fantasise
  fantasize
  fantasising
  fantasizing
fantasy
  fantasies (*pl.*)
  fantastic
  fantastically
far
  far-fetched
  far-reached
  far-reaching
  far-seeing
  far-sighted
  farther (more distant)
farad (electrical unit)
farce
  farceur
  farcical
  farcically
fare (to travel)
  farewell
  faring
fare (journey money)
farinaceous
       (made of cereal)
farm
  farmer
  farmer's (of the farmer)
  farmers'
       (of the farmers)
  farmhouse
  farmyard
farrier
  farriery
farther, further
  farthest, furthest
farthing
fascia, facia (panel)
fascicle (part of book)
fascinate
  fascinating
  fascination
  fascinator
Fascism

Fascist
fashion
  fashionable
  fashionably
fast (to go without food)
fast (quick)
  faster
fasten
  fastened
  fastener
  fastening
fastidious
  fastidiously
  fastidiousness
fat
  fat-head
  fatness
  fatter
  fattest
fatal
  fatalism
  fatalist
  fatalistic
  fatalistically
  fatality
  fatalities (*pl.*)
  fatally
fate
  fateful
  fatefully
father
  fathered
  fathering
  father-in-law
  fathers-in-law (*pl.*)
  father-in-law's
    (of the father-in-law)
  fathers-in-law's
    (of the fathers-in-law)
  fatherland
  fatherless
  fatherly
  father's (of the father)
  fathers' (of the fathers)
fathom

fatigue
  fatiguing
fatten
  fattened
  fattening
fatuous
  fatuity
  fatuously
faucet (tap)
fault
  faultfinding
  faultier
  faultily
  faultless
  faulty
faun (deity)
fauna (animals)
fauteuil
faux pas
favour
  favor
  favourable
  favorable
  favourably
  favorably
  favoured
  favored
  favouring
  favoring
  favourite
  favorite
  favouritism
  favoritism
fawn (colour)
fawn (deer)
fawn (to flatter or caress)
fay (fairy)
fealty (allegiance)
fear
  fearful
  fearfully
  fearing
  fearless
  fearlessness
  fearsome

feasible
  feasibility
  feasibly
feast
feat (achievement)
feather
  featherbed
  featherbedding
  feathered
  feathering
  featherweight
  feathery
feature
  featureless
  featuring
febrile (feverish)
February
feckless
fecund (fertile)
  fecundity
fed
  fed-up
federal
  federalisation
  federalization
  federalise
  federalize
  federalising
  federalizing
  federalism
  federalist
  federally
federate
  federating
  federation
fee
feeble
  feebler
  feebly
feed
  fed
  fed-up
  feedback
feel
  feeler

feeling
  feelingly
felt
feet (*pl.* of foot)
feign (to pretend)
feint (pretence)
felicitate (to congratulate)
  felicitating
  felicitation
felicity (happiness)
  felicitous
  felicitously
feline (catlike)
  felinity
fellow
  fellow's (of the fellow)
  fellows' (of the fellows)
  fellowship
felon (criminal)
  felonious
  felony
  felonies (*pl.*)
felt (cloth)
felt (*from* feel)
female
  female's (of the female)
  females' (of the females
feminine
  femininity
  feminism
  feminist
femme de chambre
  femmes de chambre
              (*pl.*)
femme fatale
  femmes fatales (*pl.*)
femur (thigh-bone)
  femoral
fence (sword-play)
  fencer
  fencing
fence (hedge)
fend
  fender
fennel

ferment
  fermentation
fern
  fernery
ferocious
  ferociously
  ferociousness
  ferocity
ferret
  ferreted
  ferreting
ferric
  ferrite
  ferrous
ferrule
ferry
  ferries (pl.)
  ferried
  ferrying
fertile
  fertilisation
  fertilization
  fertilise
  fertilize
  fertiliser
  fertilizer
  fertilising
  fertilizing
  fertility
fervent
  fervency
  fervently
  fervid
  fervour
  fervor
festal
fester
  festered
  festering
festive
  festival
  festively
  festivity
  festivities (pl.)
festoon

fetch
fête
fetid, foetid (smelly)
fetish
  fetishism
fetlock
fetter
  fettered
fettle
feud
feudal
  feudalism
fever
  fevered
  feverish
  feverishly
few
  fewer
fey
fez
  fezzes (pl.)
fiancé (male)
  fiancée (female)
  fiancé's (of the fiancé)
  fiancés' (of the fiancés)
  fiancée's (of the fiancée)
  fiancées'
             (of the fiancées)
fiasco
  fiascos (pl.)
fiat (order or decree)
fib
  fibbed
  fibber
  fibbing
fibre
  fiber
  fibroid
  fibrositis
  fibrous
fickle
  fickleness
  fickly
fiction
  fictional

fictitious (imaginary)
  fictitiously
fiddle (to cheat)
  fiddler
  fiddling
fiddle (violin)
  fiddler
fidelity
fidget
  fidgeted
  fidgets
  fidgety
fiduciary (trustee)
field
  field marshal
fiend
  fiendish
  fiendishly
fierce
  fiercely
  fierceness
  fiercer
fiery
  fierier
  fierily
  fieriness
fife (flute)
fifteen
  fifteenth
fifth
  fifthly
fifty
  fifties
  fiftieth
fig
  fig-leaf
fight
  fighter
  fought
figment
figurative
  figuratively
figure
  figurehead
  figurine

figuring
filament
filbert
filch (to steal)
  filched
  filches
file
  filing
filial
  filially
filibuster
  filibustered
  filibustering
filigree
fill
  filled
  filler
fillet
  filleted
  filleting
  fillets
fillip (stimulus)
filly (young horse)
  fillies (*pl.*)
film
filter
  filtered
  filtering
  filtrate
  filtration
filth
  filthier
  filthiest
  filthily
  filthiness
  filthy
fin
  finned
  finny
final
  finale (end in music)
  finalise
  finalize
  finalising
  finalizing

finalist
finality
finally
finance
  financial
  financially
  financier
  financier's
      (of the financier)
  financiers'
      (of the financiers)
  financing
finch
  finches (*pl.*)
find
  finder
  found
fine
  finely
  fineness
  finer
  finery
fine (to penalise)
  fined
  fining
finesse (subtlety)
  finessing
finger
  finger-board
  fingered
  fingering
  fingerprint
  fingers
finical
  finically
  finicky
finis (end)
finish
finite
  finitely
fiord, fjord
fir (tree)
fire
  fierily
  fieriness

fiery
fire brigade
fire engine
fire extinguisher
firefly
  fireflies (*pl.*)
fireplace
firework
firing
firm (business company)
firm
  firmer
  firmly
  firmness
firmament
first
  first aid
  firstly
  first-rate
firth (estuary)
fiscal
  fiscally
fish
  fish (*pl.*)
  fishes (*pl.*)
  fished
  fisher
  fishery
  fisheries (*pl.*)
  fishes' (of the fishes)
  fishily
  fishmonger
  fish's (of the fish)
  fishy
fission
  fissionable
  fissile
  fissure
fist
  fisticuff
fit
  fits
  fitted
  fitter
  fitting

fit (healthy)
  fitter
  fitness
fit (sudden illness)
fitful
  fitfully
five
  fivefold
  fivepence
  fiver
  fives (game)
fix
  fixation
  fixative
  fixes
  fixed
  fixedly
  fixture
fizz
  fizzle
  fizziness
  fizzling
  fizzy
fjord, fiord
flabbergast
  flabbergasted
flabby
  flabbier
  flabbily
  flabbiness
flaccid
  flaccidity
  flaccidly
flag (to become tired)
  flagged
  flagging
flag (national)
flagellate (to flog)
  flagellating
  flagellation
flageolet (bean)
flageolet (flute)
flagon
flagrant (outrageous)
  flagrancy

  flagrantly
flail (to beat)
flail (stick for threshing)
flair (aptitude)
flake
  flaking
  flaky
flambé
flamboyant
  flamboyance
  flamboyantly
flame
  flaming
flamenco
  flamencos (pl.)
flamingo
  flamingos (pl.)
flammable (inflammable)
flâneur (idler)
flange
flank
flannel
  flannelette
  flannelled
  flanneled
  flannelling
  flanneling
flap
  flapped
  flapper (girl)
  flapping
  flaps
flare (blaze)
  flaring
flash
  flashes (pl.)
  flashy
flask
flat
  flatly
  flatter
flatten
  flattened
  flattening
flatter

  flattered
  flatterer
  flattery
flatulent
  flatulence
flaunt
flautist (flute-player)
flavour
  flavor
  flavoured
  flavored
  flavouring
  flavoring
  flavourless
  flavorless
flaw (blemish)
  flawless
  flawlessly
flax
  flaxen
flay
flea (insect)
  flea's (of the flea)
  fleas' (of the fleas)
fledgling (young bird)
flee (to run away)
  fled
  fleeing
fleece (sheep's wool)
  fleecy
fleece (to plunder)
  fleecing
fleet (fast)
  fleeting (passing quickly)
fleet (of ships, cars, etc.)
flesh
  fleshiness
  fleshy
flew (*from* fly)
flex (electric wire)
flex (to bend)
  flexed
  flexibility
  flexible
flick

flicker
  flickered
  flickering
  flickers
flier, flyer
flight
flighty (fickle)
  flightiness
flimsy
  flimsier
  flimsily
  flimsiness
flinch
  flinched
  flinches
fling
  flung
flint
flippant
  flippantly
  flippancy
flipper
flirt
  flirtation
  flirtatious
  flirt's (of the flirt)
  flirts' (of the flirts)
flit
  flitted
  flitting
float
  floated
  floating
  flotation, floatation·
flock
floe (floating ice)
flog
  flogged
  flogging
  flogs
flood
  floodgate
  floodlight
  floodlighting
  floodlit

  floodlighted
floor (to baffle)
  floored
floor (of a room)
  flooring
flop
  flopped
  floppy
flora (flowers)
  floral
  florist
  florist's (of the florist)
  florists' (of the florists)
florid
floss
  flossy
flotation, floatation
flotilla
  flotillas (*pl.*)
flotsam
flounce
  flouncing
flounder
  floundered
  floundering
flounder (fish)
flour (for bread)
  floury
flourish
flout (to scoff at)
flow
flower (of a plant)
  flowered
  flowering
  flowers
  flowery
flown (*from* fly)
flu (influenza)
fluctuate
  fluctuating
  fluctuation
flue (chimney)
fluent
  fluency
  fluently

fluff
  fluffiness
  fluffy
fluid
  fluidity
fluke (fish)
fluke (lucky chance)
flummox
  flummoxed
flung (*from* fling)
flunkey
  flunky
  flunkeys (*pl.*)
  flunkies (pl.)
  flunkey's
      (of the flunkey)
  flunkeys'
      (of the flunkeys)
fluoresce
  fluorescence
  fluorescent
fluoride
  fluoridation
fluorine
flurry
  flurries (*pl.*)
flush
fluster
  flustered
flute
  flautist
  flutist
flutter
  fluttered
  fluttering
fluvial (of a river)
flux
fly
  flew
  flier
  flown
  fly-by-night
  flyer
  flying
  flyleaf

flyleaves (*pl.*)
flywheel
fly (insect)
  flies (*pl.*)
  flies' (of the flies)
  fly's (of the fly)
  flyweight
foal
foam
fob
  fobbed
  fobbing
focal
fo'c's'le, forecastle
focus
  foci, focuses (*pl.*)
  focuses (*pl.*)
  focused
  focuses
  focusing
fodder
foe
  foes (*pl.*)
foetid, fetid (smelly)
foetus, fetus
  foetuses, fetuses (*pl.*)
  foetal, fetal
fog
  fogbound
  fogged
  foggier
  foggily
  fogginess
  fogging
  foggy
  foghorn
fogey, fogy
  (old-fashioned person)
  fogeys, fogies (*pl.*)
foible
foil (to prevent)
  foiled
foil (thin metal)
foist
fold

foldaway
folder
foliage
folio
  folios (*pl.*)
folk
  folklore
follicle
  follicular
follow
  follower
  followthrough
folly
  follies (*pl.*)
foment
  fomentation
fond
  fonder
  fondly
  fondness
fondant (sweetmeat)
fondle
  fondling
fondue
font
food
  foodstuff
fool
  fooled
  foolery
  foolhardiness
  foolhardy
  foolish
  foolishly
  foolproof
  fool's (of the fool)
  fools' (of the fools)
  foolscap
foot
  feet (*pl.*)
  footage
  football
  footsore
  footlight
  footnote

  footstool
  footwear
footling (silly)
fop
  foppish
forage
  forager
  foraging
foray
  forays (*pl.*)
forbear (to abstain)
  forbearance
  forbearing
  forbears
  forbore
  forborne
forebear, forbear
          (ancestor)
forbid
  forbade, forbad
  forbidden
  forbidding
force
  forceful
  forcefully
  forcefulness
  forcible
  forcibly
  forcing
force majeure
forceps
  forceps (*pl.*)
ford
fore (before, in front of)
forearm
forebode
  foreboding
forecast
  forecaster
forecastle, fo'c's'le
foreclose
  foreclosing
  foreclosure
forecourt
forefather

forefinger
forefront
forego (to go before)
  foregoing
  foregone
  forwent
foreground
forehead
foreign
  foreigner
  foreigner's
    (of the foreigner)
  foreigners'
    (of the foreigners)
  foreignness
foreknowledge
forelock
foreman
  foremen (pl.)
  foreman's
    (of the foreman)
  foremen's
    (of the foremen)
foremost
forenoon
forensic
forerunner
foresee
  foresaw
  foreseeable
  foreseeing
  foreseen
foreshadow
foreshore
foreshorten
  foreshortened
  foreshortening
foresight
foreskin
forest
  forester
  forestry
forestall
  forestalled
  forestalling

foretaste
foretell
  foretold
forethought
forever
forewarn
forewoman
  forewomen (pl.)
  forewoman's
    (of the forewoman)
  forewomen's
    (of the forewomen)
foreword
forfeit
  forfeited
  forfeiture
forgather
  forgathered
  forgathering
forge
  forger
  forgery
  forgeries (pl.)
  forging
forget
  forgetful
  forgetfulness
  forgettable
  forgetting
  forgot
  forgotten
  forgot
forget-me-not
forgive
  forgave
  forgivable
  forgiven
  forgiveness
  forgiving
forgo (to do without)
  forgoes
  forgoing
  forgone
  forwent
fork

fork-lift
forlorn
  forlornly
form
  formation
  formative
  formed
formal
  formalisation
  formalization
  formalise
  formalize
  formalising
  formalizing
  formality
  formalities (pl.)
  formally (properly)
format (shape)
  formatted
  formatting
former
  formerly (before)
Formica
formidable
  formidably
formula
  formulae, formulas (pl.)
  formulas (pl.)
formulate
  formulating
  formulation
fornicate
  fornicating
  fornication
  fornicator
forsake
  forsaken
  forsaking
  forsook
forsooth
forsythia
fort
  fortress
  fortresses (pl.)
forte (loud)

fortissimo (very loud)
forte (special skill)
forth (forward)
forthcoming
forthright
forthwith
fortify
fortification
fortified
fortifies
fortifying
fortitude
fortress
fortresses (*pl.*)
fortress's
(of the fortress)
fortresses'
(of the fortresses)
fortuitous (by chance)
fortuitously
fortuity
fortune
fortunate
fortunately
fortune-teller
fortune-telling
forty
forties (*pl.*)
fortieth
forum
forums, fora (*pl.*)
forward
forwards
fossil
fossilisation
fossilization
fossilise
fossilize
foster
fostered
fostering
fought (*from* fight)
foul (filthy)
foully
fouler

foul-mouthed
foulness
foul (unfair)
foul (unfairness)
found (to establish)
foundation
founder
found (*from* find)
foundling
foundry
foundries (*pl.*)
fount
fountain
four
fourfold
four score
foursome
fourth
fourthly
fourteen
fourteenth
fowl (bird)
fox
foxhound
foyer
fracas (disturbance)
fraction
fractional
fractionally
fractious (quarrelsome)
fracture
fracturing
fragile
fragilely
fragility
fragment
fragmentary
fragmentation
fragrant (sweet-smelling)
fragrantly
fragrance
frail
frailer
frailty
frailties (*pl.*)

frame
frame-up
framework
framing
franc (money)
Frances (*fem.* name)
franchise
Francis (*male* name)
frank (open-hearted)
frankly
frankness
frankfurter
frankincense
frantic
frantically
frater- (brother)
fraternal
fraternally
fraternisation
fraternization
fraternise
fraternize
fraternising
fraternizing
fraternity
fraternities (*pl.*)
Frau
Fräulein
fraud
fraudulence
fraudulent
fraudulently
fraught
fray
frayed (torn)
fray (brawl)
freak
freakish
freckle
free
freed
freedom
freeing
freely
freer

freest
free-for-all
freehold
  freeholder
freelance
  freelancing
freemason
  freemasonry
free trade
  free trader
free-wheel
  free-wheeled
  free-wheeling
freeze
  freezer
  freezing
  froze
  frozen
freight (cargo)
  freightage
  freighter
French fries
frenetic, phrenetic
frenzy
  frenzies (*pl.*)
  frenzied
frequency
  frequencies (*pl.*)
frequent (often)
  frequently
frequent (to visit often)
fresco
  frescoes, frescos (*pl.*)
  frescos (*pl.*)
fresh
  fresher
  freshly
  freshman
  freshness
freshen
  freshened
  freshening
fret
  fretful
  fretted

frets
fretting
fretsaw
fretwork
Freudian
friable (crumbly)
  friability
friar (monk)
  friary
  friaries (*pl.*)
  friar's (of the friar)
  friars' (of the friars)
fricassee
friction
  frictional
Friday
fried (*from* fry)
friend
  friendlier
  friendliness
  friendly
  friend's (of the friend)
  friends' (of the friends)
  friendship
frieze (decoration)
frigate
fright
  frightful
  frightfully
  frightfulness
frighten
  frightened
  frightening
frigid
  frigidity
  frigidly
frill
fringe
  fringe benefit
  fringing
frippery
  fripperies (*pl.*)
Frisbee
frisk (to search)
frisky (lively)

friskiness
fritter
  frittered
  frittering
fritter (fried food)
frivol
  frivolity
  frivolities (*pl.*)
  frivolled
  frivoled
  frivolling
  frivoling
  frivolous
  frivolously
frizzle
frock
frog
  frogman
  frogmen (*pl.*)
  frog's (of the frog)
  frogs' (of the frogs)
frolic
  frolicked
  frolicking
  frolics
  frolicsome
front
  frontage
  frontal
  frontally
  frontier
  frontispiece
frost
  frostbite
  frostbitten
  frostily
  frosty
froth
  frothy
frown
froward (unreasonable)
  frowardness
frowzy
  frowziness
frozen

frugal
  frugality
  frugally
fruit
  fruitarian
  fruiterer
  fruitful
  fruitfully
  fruitfulness
  fruitiness
  fruitless
  fruitlessly
  fruity
fruition
frump
  frumpish
frustrate
  frustation
  frustrating
fry
  fried
  frier
  fries
  fryer
  frying
fry (young fish)
fuchsia (flower)
  fuchsias (*pl.*)
fuddle
  fuddled
fudge
  fudging
fuel
  fuelled
  fueled
  fuelling
  fueling
  fuels
fugal (*from* fugue)
fugitive
fugue (music)
  fugal
fulcrum
fulfil
  fulfill

fulfilled
fulfilling
fulfils
fulfilment
  fulfillment
full
  full-blooded
  fully
fulminate
  fulminating
  fulmination
fulsome
  fulsomely
  fulsomeness
fumble
  fumbling
fume
  fuming
fumigate
  fumigating
  fumigation
  fumigator
fun
  funnier
  funnily
  funny
function
  functional
  functionally
  functionary
  functionaries (*pl.*)
fund
fundamental
  fundamentally
funeral
  funereal (gloomy)
  funerary
fungus
  fungi, funguses (*pl.*)
  fungicidal
  fungicide (fungus killer)
  fungoid (like a fungus)
funicular
funk
  funky

funnel
  funnelled
  funneled
  funnelling
  funneling
fur
  furred (roughened)
  furrier
  furry
furbelow (trimmings)
furbish
  furbished
  furbishes
furious
  furiously
furl
  furled
furlong (eighth of a mile)
furlough (military leave)
furnace
furnish
  furnisher
  furniture
furore
  furor
furrier
furrow
further, farther
  furtherance
  furthered
  furthering
  furthermore
  furthermost
  furthest, farthest
furtive
  furtively
  furtiveness
fury
  furies (*pl.*)
  furious
  furiously
furze
fuse
  fusibility
  fusible

fusing
fusion
fuselage
fusilier
fusillade
fuss
  fussed
  fusses
  fussier
  fussily
  fussiness
  fussy
fusty
futile
  futilely
  futility
future
  futurism
  futurist
  futuristic
  futurologist
  futurology
fuzz
  fuzzily
  fuzziness
  fuzzy

gabardine (cloth)
gabble (to chatter)
  gabbler
  gabbling
gable
gad
  gadabout
  gadded
  gadding
  gads
gadfly
  gadflies (*pl.*)
gadget

gadgetry
Gaelic
gaffe (mistake)
gag
  gagged
  gagging
  gags
gage (pledge)
gaggle (of geese)
gaiety (*from* gay)
  gaily
gain
  gainer
  gainful
  gainfully
gainsay
  gainsaid
  gainsays
  gainsaying
gait (style of walking)
gaiter
  gaitered
gala
galactic
galantine
galanty show
galaxy
  galaxies (*pl.*)
gale
gall (bile)
  gall-bladder
  galling
  gallstone
gallant
  gallantry
galleon (ancient ship)
gallery
  galleries (*pl.*)
galley
  galley-slave
gallivant
gallon
gallop
  galloped
  galloper

galloping
gallows
  gallows (*pl.*)
  gallowses (pl.)
galore
galosh, golosh
  galoshes, goloshes (*pl.*)
galumph
  galumphing ·
galvanic
  galvanisation
  galvanization
  galvanised
  galvanized
  galvanising
  galvanizing
  galvanism
galvanometer
gambit
gamble (to speculate)
  gambler
  gambling
gamboge (yellow resin)
gambol (to jump about)
  gambolled
  gamboled
  gambolling
  gamboling
  gambols
game
  gamekeeper
game (ready, willing)
  gamely
game, gammy (lame)
game (football, etc.)
game (to gamble)
  gaming room
gamin (urchin)
  gamine (*fem.*)
gamma
  gamma radiation
  gamma rays
gammon
gammy (lame)
gamp (umbrella)

gamut
gamy
gander
gang
  gangster
  gangsterism
gangling (loose-limbed)
ganglion
    (swelling on nerve)
  ganglia, ganglions (*pl.*)
gangrene
  gangrenous
gangway
gannet
  gannetry
gantry
  gantries (*pl.*)
gaol, jail (prison)
  jail
  gaoled, jailed
  jailed
  gaoler, jailer, jailor
  jailer
gap
gape
  gaping
garage
  garaging
garb (costume)
garbage (rubbish)
garble
  garbled
garçon (waiter)
garden
  gardened
  gardener
  gardener's
      (of the gardener)
  gardeners'
      (of the gardeners)
  gardening
  gardens
gardenia
· gargantuan (enormous)
gargle

gargling
gargoyle
garish
garland
garlic
  garlicky
garment
garner (to collect)
  garnered
  garnering
garnet (gem)
garnish
  garnished
garret (attic room)
garrison
  garrisoned
garrotte (to strangle)
  garrote
garrulous
  garrulity
  garrulously
garter
  gartered
  gartering
gas
  gases (*pl.*)
  gaseous
  gaslight
  gassed
  gasses
  gassiness
  gassing
  gassy
gash
  gashed
gasify
  gasified
  gasification
  gasifying
gasket
gasoline
  gasolene
gasometer (gas holder)
gasp
gastric

gastritis
gastronome
  gastronomic
  gastronomical
  gastronomy
gastropod (snail, etc.)
  gastropoda (*pl.*)
gate (entrance)
  gateway
gâteau
  gâteaus, gâteaux (*pl.*)
gather
  gathered
  gathering
gauche (awkward)
  gaucherie
  gaucheness
gaudy
  gaudily
  gaudiness
gauge (measure)
  gauging
gaunt
gauntlet
gauss (unit of magnetism)
gauze
  gauzy
gave (*from* give)
gavel (hammer)
gavotte
gawky (clumsy)
  gawkiness
gay
  gaiety
  gaily
gaze
  gazing
gazebo
  gazebos, gazeboes (*pl.*)
gazelle
gazette (newspaper)
  gazetteer
  gazetting (map index)
gazette
      (official publication)

gazetted
gazetting
gazette (newspaper)
gazetteer
(geographical index)
gear
gearbox
gearing
gearless
geese (pl. of goose)
geezer (old man)
Geiger counter
geisha
gel (to become jelly)
gelled
gelling
gels
gelatine
gelatin
gelatinous
geld
(to castrate an animal)
gelding
gelid (very cold)
gelignite
gem
gendarme
(French policeman)
gendarmerie,
gendarmery
gender
gene
genealogy
genealogical
genealogically
genealogist
genera (pl. of genus)
general (soldier)
generalissimo
generalissimos (pl.)
general's
(of the general)
generals'
(of the generals)
general (usual)

generality
generalities (pl.)
generally
generalise
generalize
generalisation
generalization
generalising
generalizing
generate
generating
generation
generative
generator
generic
generically
generous
generously
generosity
Genesis
genetic
genetically
genial
geniality
genially
genie, jinnee (goblin)
genies, genii, jinn (pl.)
genies (pl.)
genital
genitive (grammar)
genitival
genius
geniuses (pl.)
genocide
genre (style)
genteel (well-bred)
genteelism
genteelly
gentility
gentian (plant)
gentile (non-Jew)
gentle (mild or kind)
gentleness
gently
gentleman

gentlemen (pl.)
gentlemanly
gentleman's
(of the gentleman)
gentlemen's
(of the gentlemen)
gentlewoman
gentlewomen (pl.)
gentlewoman's
(of the gentlewoman)
gentlewomen's
(of the gentlewomen)
gentry
genuflect
(to bend the knee)
genuflexion
genuflection
genuine
genuinely
genuineness
genus (biological family)
genera (pl.)
Geoffrey
geo- (earth)
geography
geographer
geographic
geographical
geographically
geology
geological
geologically
geologist
geometry
geometric
geometrical
geometrically
geometrician
geophysics
geophysical
geophysicist
geranium
geraniums (pl.)
gerbil, jerbil
geriatrics

geriatrician

germ

  germicidal

  germicide

germane (relevant)

germinate

  germinating

  germination

geron- (old man)

  gerontocracy

      (rule by old men)

  gerontocracies (pl.)

  gerontology

      (study of old age)

gerrymander

gerund

  gerundive

gestate

  gestating

  gestation

gesticulate

  gesticulating

  gesticulation

gesture

  gesturing

get

  getting

  gets

  got

gewgaw

geyser (hot spring)

geyser (water-heater)

ghastly

  ghastlier

  ghastliness

gherkin

ghetto

  ghettos (pl.)

ghost

  ghostly

ghoul

  ghoulish

giant

  giant's (of the giant)

  giants' (of the giants)

giantess (fem.)

giantesses (pl.)

giantess's

      (of the giantess)

giantesses'

      (of the giantesses)

gibber

gibbered

gibbering

gibberish

gibbers

gibbet (gallows)

gibbon (ape)

gibbous (convex)

gibe (to mock)

  gibing

giblets

giddy

  giddier

  giddily

  giddiness

gift

  gift-wrap

  gift-wrapping

gig (small boat)

gig (small carriage)

gigantic

  gigantically

giggle

  giggler

  giggling

gigolo

  gigolos (pl.)

gild (to paint with gold)

  gilded

  gilt

gill (of a fish)

  gilled (having gills)

gill (quarter pint)

gillie, ghillie

  (sportsman's attendant)

gillyflower

gilt-edged

gimcrack

gimlet

gimmick

  gimmickry

  gimmicky

gin (trap)

gin (drink)

ginger

  gingerbeer

  gingerbread

  gingerly

gingham

gingival

  gingivitis

      (disease of gums)

gipsy, gypsy

  gipsies, gypsies (pl.)

giraffe

gird

  girded

  girt

  girder

  girdle

girl

  girlish

  girlishly

  girlishness

  girl's (of the girl)

  girls' (of the girls)

giro

girth

gist

give

  gave

  given

  giver

  giving

gizzard

glacial

  glaciation

glacé

glacier

glad

  gladden

  gladdened

  gladdening

  gladder

gladly
gladsome
glade
gladiator
gladiolus
  gladioli, gladioluses (*pl.*)
glamour
  glamorisation
  glamorization
  glamorise
  glamorize
  glamorising
  glamorizing
  glamorous
  glamorously
glance
  glancing
gland
  glandular
glare
  glaring
glass
  glasses (*pl.*)
  glassily
  glassware
  glassy
glaucoma (eye-disease)
  glaucous (greyish)
glaze
  glazier
  glazing
gleam
glean (to collect)
  gleaner
glebe
glee
  gleeful
  gleefully
glen
glengarry
glib
  glibber
  glibly
  glibness
glide

glider
gliding
glimmer
  glimmered
  glimmering
glimpse
  glimpsing
glint
glisten
  glistened
  glistening
glitter
  glittered
  glittering
gloaming
gloat
globe
  global
  globally
  globe-trotter
  globe-trotting
globule
  globular
gloom
  gloomier
  gloomily
  gloominess
  gloomy
glorify
  glorification
  glorified
  glorifies
  glorifying
glory
  glories (*pl.*)
  gloried
  glories
  glorious
  gloriously
gloss
  glossier
  glossiness
  glossy
glossary
  glossaries (*pl.*)

glottis
  glottal
glove
  glover
glow
  glow-worm
glower (to frown)
  glowered
  glowering
glucose
glue
  gluey
  gluing
glum
  glumly
  glummer
  glumness
glut
  glutted
gluten (of flour)
  glutinous (gluey)
  glutenous
      (having gluten)
glutton (greedy person)
  gluttonous
  glutton's
      (of the glutton)
  gluttons'
      (of the gluttons)
  gluttony
glycerine
  glycerin
gnarled
gnash
gnat
  gnat's (of the gnat)
  gnats' (of the gnats)
gnaw
  gnawed
gnocchi
gnome
gnu (antelope)
go
  go-between
  goer

goes
going
gone
went
goad
goal
goalkeeper
goalless
goat
goatee (beard)
gobble
gobbling
gobbledegook
gobbledygook
goblet
goblin
god
goddess (*fem.*)
goddesses (*pl.*)
goddess's
(of the goddess)
goddesses'
(of the goddesses)
God-fearing
God-forsaken
godliness
godly
goggle
goggling
goitre
goiter
goitrous
gold
golden
goldfinch
goldilocks
goldsmith
golf
golf-course
golfer
golf-links
Goliath
golliwog
golosh, galosh
goloshes, galoshes (*pl.*)

gondola
gondolas (*pl.*)
gondolier
gone (*from* go)
goner
gong
gonorrhoea
gonorrhea
goo
gooey (sticky)
good
goodbye
good-humoured
good-humored
good-looking
goodly
goodness
goodness' sake
goodnight
goodwill
goody
goodies (*pl.*)
goon
goose
geese (*pl.*)
gooseflesh
gosling
gooseberry
gooseberries (*pl.*)
gore (blood)
gory
gore (to pierce)
goring
gorge (to eat greedily)
gorging
gorge (deep valley)
gorgeous
gorgeously
Gorgonzola
gorilla
gorillas (*pl.*)
gorilla's (of the gorilla)
gorillas' (of the gorillas)
gorse
gosling (*from* goose)

gospel
gospeller
gospeler
gossamer
gossip
gossiper
gossiping
got (*from* get)
gotten
gouache
gouge
gouging
goulash
gourd
gourmand (greedy person)
gourmandism
gourmet
(connoisseur of food)
gout
gouty
govern
governable
governance
governess
governesses (*pl.*)
governess's
(of the governess)
governesses'
(of the governesses)
governor
governor's
(of the governor)
governors'
(of the governors)
government
governmental
gown
grab
grabbed
grabbing
grabs
grace
graceful
gracefully
gracing

gracious
graciously
graciousness
gradation
grade
gradient
grading
gradual
gradualism
gradually
graduate
graduating
graduation
graduator
graffiti
graft
grail
grain
gram, gramme
grammar
grammarian
grammatical
grammatically
gramophone
granary
granaries (*pl.*)
grand
grandchild
grandchildren (*pl.*)
grandchild's
(of the grandchild)
grandchildren's
(of the grandchildren)
granddaughter
grandee
grandeur
grandfather
grandma
grandmama
grandmother
grandpa
grandpapa
grandson
grandson's
(of the grandson)

grandsons'
(of the grandsons)
grandiloquence
grandiloquent
grandiloquently
Grand Prix
grandiose
grandiosely
grandiosity
grange
granite
granny, grannie
grannies (*pl.*)
granny's (of granny)
grannies' (of grannies)
grant
granulate
granulating
granulation
granule
granular
granularity
grape
grapefruit
graph
graphic
graphical
graphically
graphite
graphology
graphologist
grapnel
grapple
grappling
grasp
grass
grassy
grasshopper
grate (to scrape)
grater (scraper)
grating
grate (of fireplace)
grateful
gratefully
graticule

gratify
gratification
gratified
gratifies
gratifying
gratin
gratis
gratitude
gratuitous (free)
gratuitously
gratuity (grant of money)
gratuities (*pl.*)
grave (serious)
gravely
grave (tomb)
graveyard
gravel
gravelled
graveled
gravelly
gravitate
gravitating
gravitation
gravitational
gravity
gravy
gray
grey, gray
grayling (fish)
graze
grazing
grease
greaser
greasier
greasily
greasiness
greasing
greasy
great
greater
greatly
greatness
greed
greedier
greedily

greediness
greedy
green
  greenback
  greener
  greenery
  greengage
  greengrocer
  greengrocer's
    (of the greengrocer)
  greengrocers'
    (of the greengrocers)
  greenness
greet
  greeting
gregarious
  gregariousness
gremlin
grenade
  grenadier
grew (*from* grow)
grey
  gray
  greyer
  grayer
  greying
  graying
  greyhound
  grayhound
  greyish
  grayish
  greyness
  grayness
grid
  gridded
  gridiron
griddle
grief
grieve
  grievance
  grieving
  grievous
  grievously
griffin, griffon, gryphon
    (fabulous beast)

griffon (dog)
griffon (vulture)
grill (to cook)
  grilled
  grill-room
grille (grating)
grim
  grimly
  grimmer
  grimness
grimace
  grimacing
grime
  grimier
  griminess
  grimy
grin
  grinned
  grinning
  grins
grind
  grinder
  ground
grip
  gripped
  gripping
  grips
gripe
  gripes (colic)
  griping (pain)
  grippe (influenza)
grisly (terrifying)
grist
gristle
  gristly (tough)
grit
  gritted
  grits
  gritting
  gritty
grizzle
  grizzled (grey)
grizzle (to whimper)
  grizzling
grizzly (grey)

grizzly bear
groan
groats (oats)
grocer
  grocery
  groceries (*pl.*)
  grocer's (of the grocer)
  grocers' (of the grocers)
grog (alcoholic drink)
groggy (unwell)
  groggier
  grogginess
groin
grommet, grummet
    (washer)
groom
  groom's (of the groom)
  grooms' (of the grooms)
groove
  groovy
grope
  groping
gross (coarse)
  grosser (coarser)
  grossly
  grossness
gross (to make a profit)
gross (twelve dozen)
grotesque
  grotesquely
  grotesqueness
grotto
  grottoes, grottos (*pl.*)
grouchy
ground
  groundless
  groundlessly
ground (*from* grind)
group
  group's (of the group)
  groups' (of the groups)
grouse (to grumble)
  grouser
  grousing
grouse (bird)

grout
grove
grovel
  grovelled
  groveled
  groveller
  groveler
  grovelling
  groveling
  grovels
grow
  grew
  grower
  growing
  grown
  grown-up
  growth
growl
  growler
groyne (breakwater)
grub
  grubbed
  grubbier
  grubbiness
  grubbily
  grubby
grudge
  grudging
  grudgingly
gruelling
  grueling
gruel (porridge)
gruesome
  gruesomely
  gruesomeness
gruff
  gruffer
  gruffly
  gruffness
grumble
  grumbler
  grumbling
grummet, grommet
              (washer)
grumpy

grumpily
grumpiness
grunt
gruyère (cheese)
gryphon, griffin, griffon
              (fabulous beast)
guano
guarantee
  guarantees (*pl.*)
  guaranteed
  guaranteeing
  guarantees
  guarantor
  guaranty
guard
  guard-room
  guard's (of the guard)
  guards' (of the guards)
  guardsman
  guardsmen (*pl.*)
guardian
  guardianship
guava
gubernatorial
Guernsey
guerrilla, guerilla
guess
  guessed
  guesswork
guest (visitor)
guffaw
  guffawing
guide
  guidance
  guide's (of the guide)
  guides' (of the guides)
  guiding
guild (society)
  Guildhall
guilder (Dutch money)
guile (cunning)
  guileless
guillotine
  guillotining
guilt

guiltier
guiltily
guiltiness
guilty
guinea
  guinea-pig
guise
guitar
  guitarist
gulf
  Gulf Stream
gull
  gulled
  gullibility
  gullible
gull (bird)
  gullet
gully (water channel)
  gullies (*pl.*)
gulp
gum (sticky substance)
  gummed
  gumminess
  gumming
  gummy
gum (in mouth)
  gumboil
gumption
gun
  gunned
  gunner
  gunnery
  gunning
  gunpowder
gunnel, gunwale
gurgle
  gurgling
Gurkha
guru (Hindu teacher)
gush
gusset
gust
  gusty
gusto
gut (bowel)

gut (to remove gut)
  gutted
  gutting
gut (to destroy by fire)
  gutted
guts (determination)
gutta-percha
gutter
  guttering
guttersnipe
guttural
  gutturally
guy
  Guy Fawkes
guzzle
  guzzler
  guzzling
gybe (in sailing)
  jibe
  gybing
  jibing
gymkhana
gymnasium, gym
  gymnasiums, gymnasia
     (*pl.*)
  gymnast
  gymnastic
gyne- (woman)
gynaecology
  gynecology
  gynaecological
  gynecological
  gynaecologist
  gynecologist
gypsum
gypsy, gipsy
  gypsies, gipsies (*pl.*)
gyrate
  gyrating
  gyration
  gyratory
gyroscope
  gyroscopic

H

habeas corpus
haberdasher
  haberdashery
habit
  habit-forming
habit (clothes)
  habited (clothed)
habitable
habitat
habitation
habitual (usual)
  habitually
  habituate
  habituated (accustomed)
  habituating
  habituation
  habitude
habitué (frequent visitor)
hack
  hacksaw
  hackle
  hackney
  hackneyed
had
  hadn't (had not)
haddock
hades
haema-, haemo- (blood)
  hema-, hemo-
haematologist
  hematologist
haematology
  hematology
haematoma
  hematoma
haemoglobin
  hemoglobin
haemophilia
  hemophilia

haemophiliac
  hemophiliac
haemorrhage
  hemorrhage
haemorrhoids
  hemorrhoids
hag
haggard
haggis
haggle
  haggler
  haggling
haiku (Japanese poem)
  haiku (*pl.*)
hail (frozen rain)
hail (to greet)
  hailer
hair
  hairbreadth
  hair's breadth
  hairier
  hairiness
  hairless
  hairy
hake (fish)
halcyon
hale (robust)
half
  halves (*pl.*)
  half-caste
  half-hearted
  half holiday
  halfway
  halved
  halving
halibut
halitosis (bad breath)
hall
hallelujah, halleluiah,
      alleluia
hallmark
  hallmarked
hallo, hello, hullo
hallow (make sacred)
  hallowed

Hallowe'en
Halloween
hallucinate
hallucinating
hallucination
hallucinatory
hallucinogen
halo (circle of light)
haloes (*pl.*)
halos (pl.)
halt
haltingly
halter
halve (*from* half)
halving
halyard, halliard
ham
hamburger
hamlet
hammer
hammered
hammering
hammers
hammock
hamper (food basket)
hamper (to hinder)
hampered
hampering
hamster
hamstring
hamstrung
hand
handful
handfuls (*pl.*)
hand-made
(made by hand)
handmaid (girl)
hand-me-down
handcuff
handcuffed
handcuffing
handcuffs
handicap
handicapped
handicapping

handicraft
handiwork
handkerchief
handkerchiefs (*pl.*)
handle
handlebar
handler
handling
handsome (good-looking)
handsomely
handsomeness
handwriting
handwritten
handy
handyman
handymen (*pl.*)
handyman's
(of the handyman)
handymen's
(of the handymen)
handier
handily
handiness
hang
hanged
hanger
hangman
hung (picture, etc.)
hangar (for aircraft)
hanger-on
hangover
hang-up
hank (of cotton, etc.)
hanker (to long for)
hankered
hankering
hanky-panky
hansom (cab)
haphazard
hapless (unlucky)
happen
happened
happening
happy
happier

happily
happiness
happy-go-lucky
harangue
haranguing
harass
harassed
harasses
harassment
harbinger
harbour
harbor
harbourage
harborage
harboured
harbored
harbouring
harboring
harbours
harbors
hard
harder
hard-hearted
hard-headed
hardly
hardness
hardship
harden
hardened
hardener
hardening
hardware
hardy
hardier
hardily (boldly)
hare (animal)
harebell
hare-brained
harelip
hare's (of the hare)
hares' (of the hares)
harem
haricot
hark
harlequin

harlequinade
harlot
harlotry
harm
harmful
harmfully
harmless
harmlessly
harmlessness
harmonic
harmonically
harmonica (mouth-organ)
harmonious
harmoniously
harmonise
harmonize
harmonisation
harmonization
harmonising
harmonizing
harmonium
harmony
harmonies (*pl.*)
harness
harp
harpist
harpoon
harpooned
harpooner
harpsichord
harpy (monster)
harpies (*pl.*)
harrier
harrow (to distress)
harrow (mobile rake)
harry (to harass)
harried
harries
harrying
harsh
harshly
harshness
hart (deer)
hartebeest (antelope)
harum-scarum

harvest
harvester
has
has-been
hasn't (has not)
hash
hashish, hasheesh
hasp
hassle
hassock
haste
hastily
hasty
hasten
hastened
hastening
hat
hatter
hatch (egg)
hatchery
hatcheries (*pl.*)
hatch (opening)
hatchway
hatchet
hate
hateful
hating
hatred
haughty
haughtier
haughtily
haughtiness
haul
haulage
hauled
haulier
haunch
haunt
haunted
hausfrau
hauteur
Havana
have
haven't (have not)
having

haven (refuge)
haver (to hesitate)
havered
havering
haversack
havoc
hawk
hawkish
hawser (rope)
hawthorn
hay
hay fever
haymaker
hayrick
haystack
hazard
hazardous
hazardously
haze
hazier
hazily
haziness
hazy
hazel
head
headache
headachy
header
headless
headline
headlong
headmaster
headmaster's
(of the headmaster)
headmasters'
(of the headmasters)
headmistress
headmistresses (*pl.*)
headmistress's
(of the headmistress)
headmistresses'
(of the headmistresses)
headquarters
headstrong
headway

heal (to cure)
  healer
  healing
health
  healthier
  healthily
  healthy
heap
  heaped
hear
  heard
  hearer
  hearing
  hearsay
hearken
  harken
  hearkened
hearse
heart
  heartbreaking
  heartbroken
  heartbrokenly
  heart disease
  heart failure
  heartfelt
  heartless
  heartlessly
  heart-rending
hearten
  heartened
  heartening
hearth
hearty
  heartier
  heartily
  heartiness
heat
  heater
heath
heathen
  heathenism
heather
heave
  heaved
  heaving

  hove (nautical use)
heaven
  heavenly
heavy
  heavier
  heavily
  heaviness
  heavyweight
hebdomadal (weekly)
Hebrew
  Hebraic
hecatomb
heckle
  heckler
  heckling
hectare (measure of area)
hectic
  hectically
hecto- (hundred)
  hectogram
  hectolitre
  hectoliter
hector (to bully)
  hectored
  hectoring
hedge
  hedgehog
  hedgehop
  hedgehopped
  hedgehopping
  hedgehops
  hedger
  hedgerow
  hedging
hedonism
  (theory of pleasure)
  hedonist
heed
  heedful
  heedless
heel (to lean over)
heel (of foot)
hefty
  heftier
  heftily

heftiness
hegemony (leadership)
heifer
height (*from* high)
heighten
  heightened
  heightening
heinous (atrocious)
heir (inheritor)
  heir apparent
  heiress (*fem.*)
  heiresses (*pl.*)
  heiress's (of the heiress)
  heiresses'
      (of the heiresses)
  heirloom
  heir's (of the heir)
  heirs' (of the heirs)
held (*from* hold)
hele, heal, heel
  (to put plant in earth)
helicopter
helio- (sun)
  heliotrope
  heliograph
heliport
helium
helix
  helices (*pl.*)
  helical
hell
  hellish
  hellishly
  hell's (of hell)
hello, hallo, hullo
helm
  helmsman
helmet
helot (serf)
  helotry
help
  helper
  helpful
  helpfully
  helpfulness

helpmate

helpless
helplessly
helplessness
helpmate
helter-skelter
hem
  hemmed
  hemming
  hemstitch
hemi- (half)
  hemiplegia
  hemiplegic
  hemisphere
  hemispherical
hemlock
hemp
  hempen
hen
  hen-coop
  henpecked
hence
  henceforth
henchman
henna
  hennaed
hepatitis (liver disease)
hepta- (seven)
  heptagon
  heptarchy
her
  hers
  herself
herald
  heraldic
  heraldry
  herald's (of the herald)
  heralds' (of the heralds)
herb
  herbaceous
  herbage
  herbal
  herbalist
  herbicide (plant killer)
  herbivore
    (plant-, grass-eater)

herbivorous
herd
  herdsman
here
  hereabout
  hereafter
  hereby
  herein
  hereof
  hereto
  heretofore
  hereunder
  herewith
heredity
  hereditary
  hereditarily
  hereditament
heresy
  heresies (*pl.*)
  heretic
heritance
  heritable
  heritage
  heritor
hermaphrodite
  hermaphroditic
hermetic
  hermetically
hermit
  hermitage
hernia
hero
  heroes (*pl.*)
  heroes' (of the heroes)
  heroic
  heroically
  heroine (brave woman)
  heroism
  hero's (of the hero)
heroin (drug)
heron (bird)
  heronry
herpes
herring
  herring-bone

herring roe
hesitate
  hesitancy
  hesitant
  hesitantly
  hesitating
  hesitation
hessian
hetero- (other)
  heterodox
  heterodoxy
  heterodyne
  heterogeneous
  heterogenous
  heterogeneity
  heterosexual
heuristic
  (by trial and error)
hew (to cut down)
  hewed
  hewer
  hewn
hexa- (six)
  hexagon
  hexagonal
heyday
hiatus
  hiatuses (*pl.*)
hibernate
  hibernating
  hibernation
  hibernator
hiccup, hiccough
  hiccuped
  hiccuping
  hiccups
hide
  hid
  hidden
  hideaway
  hide-out
  hiding
hidebound
hideous
  hideosity

hideously
hier- (sacred)
  hierarch
  hierarchy
  hierarchies (*pl.*)
  hieroglyph
  hieroglyphic
hi-fi
higgledy-piggledy
high
  height
  higher
  highlight
  Highness
  highly
highfalutin,
              highfaluting
highland
  highlander
highway
  highwayman
  highwaymen (*pl.*)
hijack
  hijacked
  hijacker
hike
  hiker
  hiking
hilarious
  hilarity
hill
  hillier
  hillock
  hilly
hilt
him
  himself
hind
  hindmost, hindermost
  hindsight
hinder
  hindered
  hindering
  hindrance
hinge

hinging
hint
hinterland
hip
  hipped
  hip (of rose bush)
hippo- (horse)
  hippodrome
  hippopotamus
  hippopotamuses (*pl.*)
  hippy, hippie
    hippies (*pl.*)
hire
  hireling
  hire purchase
  hiring
hirsute (hairy)
his
hiss
  hisses (*pl.*)
  hissed
  hisses
  hissing
histology
          (science of tissues)
history
  histories (*pl.*)
  historian
  historic
  historical
  historically
histrionic (theatrical)
  histrionically
hit
  hits
  hitter
  hitting
hitch
  hitch-hike
  hitch-hiker
  hitch-hiking
hitch (fault)
hither
  hitherto
hive

hiving
hoar (grey)
  hoariness
  hoary
hoard (to store)
  hoarder
  hoarding (wooden boards)
hoarse (husky)
  hoarsely
  hoarseness
  hoarser
hoax
  hoaxes (*pl.*)
  hoaxer
hobble
  hobbling
hobbledehoy
hobby
  hobby-horse
  hobbies (*pl.*)
hobgoblin
hobnob
  hobnobbed
  hobnobbing
  hobnobs (he, she)
hobo
  hobos, hoboes (*pl.*)
hock (of horse)
hock (wine)
hockey
hocus (to hoax)
  hocussed
  hocused
  hocussing
  hocusing
hocus-pocus
hod
hodgepodge (mixture)
hoe
  hoed
  hoeing
hog
  hogged
  hoggish
  hog's (of the hog)

hogs' (of the hogs)
hogshead
hog-wash
hogmanay
hoi polloi
    (ordinary people)
hoist
hold
  held
  holdall
  holder
  holdup
hole
  holey (full of holes)
holiday
  holidayer
hollandaise
hollow
holly (tree)
hollyhock
holo- (whole)
  holocaust
  hologram
  holograph
holster
holy (sacred)
  Holy Ghost
  holier
  holiness
homage
home
  home-coming
  homeless
  home-made
  homesick
  homesickness
  homespun
  homestead
  homeward
  homewards
  homework
  homing
homely
  homelier
  homeliness

homicide
homicidal
homily (sermon)
  homilies (*pl.*)
homo- (same)
  homoeopath
  homoeopathy
  homoeopathic
  homogeneous
  homogeneity
  homogenise
  homogenize
  homogenous
        (same kind)
  homologous
    (same relative value)
  homonym
  homonymic
  homophone
  homosexual
  homosexuality
homo sapiens
hone
  honing
honest
  honestly
  honesty
honey
  honeycomb
  honeydew
  honeyed
  honeymoon
  honeymooner
  honeysuckle
honorarium
  honorariums,
        honoraria(*pl.*)
honorary
honorific
honour
  honor
  honourable
  honorable
  honourably
  honorably

honoured
honored
honouring
honoring
hood
hoodlum
hoodwink
  hoodwinked
hoof
  hooves, hoofs (*pl.*)
hook
hookah, hooka (pipe)
hookey, hooky (truancy)
  hooky
hooligan
  hooliganism
  hooligan's
    (of the hooligan)
  hooligans'
    (of the hooligans)
hoop
hoop-la
hoot
  hooter
hop
  hopped
  hopper
  hopping
  hops
hope
  hopeful
  hopefully
  hopeless
  hopelessly
  hopelessness
  hoping
hopscotch
horde (crowd)
horizon
  horizontal
  horizontally
hormone
horn
  horned
  hornless

hornpipe
hornet
  hornet's (of the hornet)
  hornets' (of the hornets)
horoscope
horrendous
horrible
  horribly
horrid
horrific
  horrifically
horrify
  horrified
  horrifies
  horrifying
horror
hors d'oeuvre
horse (animal)
  horseback
  horsehair
  horsepower
  horse-radish
  horseshoe
  horsewhip
  horsewhipped
  horsewhipping
  horsewhips
  horsy
horticulture
  horticultural
  horticulturist
hosanna
hose (pipe)
  hosing
hose (stocking)
  hosier
  hosiery
hospice
hospitable (welcoming)
  hospitably
  hospitality
hospital
  hospitalisation
  hospitalization
  hospitalise

hospitalize
host
  hostess (*fem.*)
  hostesses (*pl.*)
  hostess's
      (of the hostess)
  hostesses'
      (of the hostesses)
  host's (of the host)
  hosts' (of the hosts)
hostage
hostel
hostelry
  hostelries (*pl.*)
hostile
  hostilely
  hostility
  hostilities (*pl.*)
hot
  hotheaded
  hotly
  hotter
  hotchpot (legal)
    hotchpot, hotchpotch
        (cookery)
hotel
  hotelier
hound (dog)
hound (to chase)
hour
  hourly
houri
  houris (*pl.*)
house
  housebreaker
  houseful
  household
  householder
  housekeeper
  housekeeping
  housemaster
  housemaster's
      (of the housemaster)
  housemasters'
      (of the housemasters)

housewife
housewives (*pl.*)
housewife's
      (of the housewife)
housewives'
      (of the housewives)
housework
housing
hovel
hover
  hovercraft
  hovered
  hovering
how
  however
  howsoever
howitzer
howl
  howler (bad mistake)
hoyden
hub
hubbub
huddle
  huddling
hue (colour)
hue (outcry)
huff
  huffily
  huffy
hug
  hugged
  hugging
  hugs
huge
  hugely
  huger
Huguenot
hulk
  hulking
hull
hullabaloo
hullo, hallo, hello
hum
  hummed
  humming

humming-bird
hums
human
humanly
humane (kind)
humanely
humaneness
humanist
humanism
humanistic
humanitarian
humanitarianism
humanity
humanities (*pl.*)
humble
humbleness
humbly
humbug
humbugged
humbugging
humdrum
humerus (arm-bone)
humeral
humid
humidified
humidifier
humidifies
humidify
humidifying
humidity
humiliate
humiliated
humiliating
humiliation
humility
hummock (mound)
humoresque
humour
humor
humorist
humorous
humorously
humoured
humored
humouring

humoring
hump
humpback
humus (of soil)
hunch (lump)
hunchback
hunch (sudden idea)
hundred
hundredfold
hundredth
hundredweight
hung (*from* hang)
hunger
hungrier
hungrily
hungry
hunk
hunt
hunter
hunter's (of the hunter)
hunters' (of the hunters)
huntress (*fem.*)
huntsman
huntsmen (*pl.*)
hurdle
hurdling
hurdy-gurdy
hurl (to throw)
hurly-burly
hurrah, hurray
hurricane
hurry
hurried
hurriedly
hurries
hurrying
hurt
hurtle
hurtling
husband
husbandry
husband's
       (of the husband)
husbands'
       (of the husbands)

hush
husk (shell)
husky (dog)
huskies (*pl.*)
husky (hoarse)
huskily
huskiness
hussar
hussy
hussies (*pl.*)
hustings
hustle
hustler
hustling
hut
hutment
hutted
hutting
hutch
hutches (*pl.*)
hyacinth
hybrid
hydr- (water)
hydra (water-snake)
hydrangea
hydrant
hydrate
hydrating
hydration
hydraulic
hydraulically
hydrocarbon
hydrocephalus
hydrocephalic
hydrocephalous
hydrochloric
hydrodynamic
hydro-electric
hydrofoil
hydrogen
hydrology
hydrolysis
hydrolytic
hydrometer
hydrometric

hydrometry
hydropath
  hydropathic
hydrophobia
hydroplane
hydrostatic
hydrotherapy
  hydrotherapeutic
hydroxide
hyena, hyaena
hygiene
  hygienic
  hygienically
hygro- (wet)
  hygrometer
  hygrometric
  hygroscope
  hygroscopic
hymen (membrane)
  hymeneal
hymn
  hymnal
hyper- (over, beyond)
  hyperbola (curve)
  hyperbole (exaggeration)
  hyperbolic
  hyperbolical
  hypermarket
  hypersensitive
  hypertension
  hypertensive
  hyperthyroidism
hyphen
  hyphenated
hypno- (sleep)
  hypnosis
  hypnotic
  hypnotise
  hypnotize
  hypnotising
  hypnotizing
  hypnotism
  hypnotist
hypo- (under)
hypochondria

hypochondriac
hypocrisy
  hypocrite
  hypocritical
  hypocritically
hypodermis
  hypodermic
  hypodermically
hypotenuse
hypothermia
hypothesis
  hypotheses (*pl.*)
  hypothetical
  hypothetically
hysteria
  hysterical
  hysterically
  hysterics
hysteresis (in magnetism)
hysterectomy

I

I'd (I had, would)
I'll (I shall, will)
I'm (I am)
I've (I have)
ice
  iceberg
  icebreaker
  icecap
  icecream
  ice-hockey
  icicle
  icily
  icing
  icy
ichthyo- (fish)
  ichthyology
  ichthyologist
icon

iconoclasm
iconoclast
idea
ideal
  ideally
idealise
idealize
idealisation
idealization
idealising
idealizing
idealism
idealist
idée fixe
identical
  identically
identify
  identifiable
  identification
  identified
  identifies
  identifying
identity
  identities (*pl.*)
  identikit
ideology
  ideologies (*pl.*)
  ideological
  ideologically
idiom
  idiomatic
  idiomatically
idiosyncrasy
  idiosyncrasies (*pl.*)
  idiosyncratic
  idiosyncratically
idiot
  idiocy
  idiotic
  idiotically
  idiot's (of the idiot)
  idiots' (of the idiots)
idle (lazy)
  idleness
  idler (lazy person)

idler (more idle)
idling
idly
idol (image)
idolater
idolatrous
idolatry
idolise
idolize
idolisation
idolization
idolising
idolizing
idyll
  (rural poem or prose)
idyllic
igloo
igneous
ignite
ignitable
igniter
igniting
ignition
ignoble
ignobly
ignominy
ignominies (*pl.*)
ignominious
ignominiously
ignoramus
ignoramuses (*pl.*)
ignorance
ignorant
ignorantly
ignore
ignoring
ilk
ill
illness
illnesses (*pl.*)
I'll (I will)
illegal
illegality
illegalities (*pl.*)
illegally

illegible (unreadable)
illegibility
illegibly
illegitimate
illegitimacy
illegitimately
illicit (unlawful)
illicitly
illimitable (without limit)
illiterate (can't read)
illiteracy
illogical
illogicality
illogicalities (*pl.*)
illogically
illuminate
illuminating
illumination
illusion (misleading idea)
illusionist
illusive (deceptive)
illusory
illustrate
illustrating
illustration
illustrative
illustrator
illustrious
illustriously
illustriousness
I'm (I am)
image
imagery
imagine
imaginable
imaginary
imagination
imaginative
imaginatively
imagining
imbalance
imbecile
imbecility
imbibe
imbibing

imbroglio
imbroglios (*pl.*)
imbue
imbued
imbuing
imitate
imitating
imitation
imitative
imitator
immaculate
immaculacy
immaculately
immanent (inherent)
immanence
immanency
immaterial
immaterially
immature
immaturely
immaturity
immeasurable
immeasurably
immediacy
immediate
immediately
immemorial (very ancient)
immense
immensely
immensity
immerse
immersing
immersion
immigrate
  (to come as settler)
immigrant
immigrant's
  (of the immigrant)
immigrants'
  (of the immigrants)
immigrating
immigration
imminent
  (happening soon)
imminently

imminence
immiscible (not mixable)
immobile
immobilisation
immobilization
immobilise
immobilize
immobilising
immobilizing
immobility
immoderate
immoderately
immodest
immodestly
immodesty
immoral
immorality
immorally
immortal
immortality
immortally
immortalise
immortalize
immortalisation
immortalization
immortalising
immortalizing
immovable
immovably
immune
immunity
immunise
immunize
immunisation
immunization
immunising
immunizing
immunology
immure
immuring
immutable
immutability
immutably
imp
impish

impishly
impishness
imp's (of the imp)
imps' (of the imps)
impact
impaction
impair
impaired
impairing
impairment
impale
impalement
impaling
impalpable
impalpably
impart
impartial
impartiality
impartially
impassable
impasse
impassioned
impassive
impassively
impassiveness
impassivity
impatience
impatient
impatiently
impeach
impeachable
impeachment
impeccable
impeccability
impeccably
impecunious
impecuniosity
impede
impedance (*electr.*)
impeding
impediment
impedimenta
(army luggage)
impel
impelled

impeller
impelling
impels
impend
impending
impenetrable
impenetrability
impenitence
impenitent
impenitently
imperative
imperatively
imperceptible
imperceptibly
imperfect
imperfection
imperfectly
imperial
imperialism
imperialist
imperialistic
imperially
imperil
imperilled
imperiled
imperilling
imperiling
imperilment
imperils
imperious
imperiously
imperiousness
imperishable
imperishably
impermissible
impermeable
impermeability
impersonal
impersonally
impersonate
impersonating
impersonation
impersonator
impertinence
impertinent

impertinently
imperturbable
  imperturbability
  imperturbably
impervious
  imperviousness
impetigo
impetuous
  impetuosity
  impetuously
impetus
  impetuses (*pl.*)
impinge
  impingement
  impinging
impious
  impiety
implacable
  implacability
  implacably
implant
  implantation
implausible
  implausibility
  implausibly
implement
  implementation
implicate
  implicating
  implication
implicit
  implicitly
implied (*from* imply)
implode
    (to burst inwards)
  imploding
  implosion
  implosive
implore
  imploring
imply
  implication
  implied
  implies
  implying

impolite
  impolitely
  impoliteness
impolitic (not prudent)
  impoliticly
imponderable
  imponderability
import
  importation
  importer
importance
  important
  importantly
importunate
      (very persistent)
  importunately
  importunity
importune
    (to ask persistently)
  importuning
impose
  imposing
  imposition
impossible
  impossibility
  impossibly
impost (tax)
impostor (deceiver)
imposture (fraud)
impotence (helplessness)
  impotent
  impotently
impound
impoverish
  impoverishment
impracticable
  impracticability
  impracticably
impractical
imprecate (to curse)
  imprecation
imprecise
  imprecisely
  imprecision
impregnable

impregnability
impregnably
impregnate
  impregnating
  impregnation
impresario
  impresarios (*pl.*)
  impresario's
      (of the impresario)
  impresarios'
      (of the impresarios)
impress
  impressed
  impressible
impression
  impressionable
  impressionism
impressive
  impressively
  impressiveness
imprest (money advanced)
  imprest account
imprimatur
    (permission to print)
imprint (publisher's name)
imprint
    (to impress or stamp)
imprison
  imprisonment
improbable
  improbability
  improbably
impromptu
improper
  improperly
  impropriety
  improprieties (*pl.*)
improve
  improvable
  improvement
  improver
  improving
improvidence
      (carelessness)
  improvident

improvidently
improvise
　improvisation
　improviser
　improvising
imprudence (indiscretion)
　imprudent
　imprudently
impudence (rudeness)
　impudent
　impudently
impugn (to discredit)
　impugned
　impugning
impulse
　impulsive
　impulsively
impunity
　(without punishment)
impure
　impurity
　impurities (pl.)
impute (to blame)
　imputable
　imputation
　imputing
inability
inaccessible
　inaccessibility
inaccuracy
　inaccuracies (pl.)
　inaccurate
　inaccurately
inaction
inactive
　inactively
　inactivity
inadequacy
　inadequacies (pl.)
　inadequate
　inadequately
inadmissible
　inadmissibility
　inadmissibly
inadvertence

inadvertent
inadvertently
inadvisable
　inadvisability
　inadvisably
inalienable
　(not transferable)
　inalienability
inamorato (lover)
　inamorata (fem.)
inane
　inanely
　inanity
　inanities (pl.)
inanimate
inapplicable
　inapplicably
inappreciable (very small)
　inappreciably
inappropriate
　inappropiateness
　inappropriately
inapt (unsuitable)
　inaptly
　inaptness
　inaptitude
inarticulate
　inarticulately
　inarticulateness
inartistic
　inartistically
inasmuch
inattention
　inattentive
　inattentively
inaudible
　inaudibility
　inaudibly
inaugurate
　inaugural
　inaugurating
　inauguration
　inaugurator
　inauguratory
inauspicious (unlucky)

inauspiciously
inborn
inbreed
　inbred
　inbreeding
incalculable
　incalculability
　incalculably
incandescence
　incandescent
incantation
incapable
　incapability
　incapably
incapacitate
　incapacitating
　incapacitation
　incapacity
incarcerate (to imprison)
　incarcerating
　incarceration
incarnate
　incarnation
incautious
　incautiously
incendiary
　incendiaries (pl.)
　incendiarism
incense (to make angry)
　incensing
incense (perfumed smoke)
incentive
inception
incertitude
incessant
　incessantly
incest
　incestuous
　incestuously
inch
　inches (pl.)
incidence
incident
　incidents (pl.)
　incidental

125

incinerate

incidentally
incinerate
  incinerating
  incineration
  incinerator
incipient
incise
  incision
  incisive
  incisively
  incisor (tooth)
incite (to urge)
  incitation
  incitement
  inciter
  inciting
incivility
  incivilities (*pl.*)
inclement
  inclemency
  inclemently
incline
  inclination
  inclining
include
  including
  inclusion
  inclusive
  inclusively
incognito
incoherence
  incoherent
  incoherently
incombustible
  incombustibility
income
  income tax
incomer
  incoming
incommensurable
        (not comparable)
incommensurate
        (not adequate)
incommode
  incommoded

incommoding
incommodious
incommunicado
incomparable
  incomparably
incompatible
  incompatibility
incompetence
  incompetent
  incompetently
incomplete
  incompletely
  incompleteness
incomprehensible
  incomprehensibility
  incomprehensibly
incompressible
  incompressibility
inconceivable
  inconceivably
inconclusive
  inconclusively
incongruous
  incongruously
  incongruity
  incongruities (*pl.*)
inconsequent
  inconsequential
  inconsequently
inconsiderable
        (very small)
  inconsiderably
inconsiderate
  inconsiderately
inconsistency
  inconsistencies (*pl.*)
  inconsistent
  inconsistently
inconsolable
inconspicuous
  inconspicuously
  inconspicuousness
inconstant
  inconstancy
incontestable

incontestably
incontinence
  incontinent
incontrovertible
  incontrovertibly
inconvenience
  inconvenient
  inconveniently
inconvertible
  inconvertibility
incorporate
  incorporating
  incorporation
incorrect
  incorrectly
  incorrectness
incorrigible
  incorrigibility
  incorrigibly
incorruptible
  incorruptibility
increase
  increasing
  increasingly
incredible (unbelievable)
  incredibility
  incredibly
incredulous (unbelieving)
  incredulity
increment
incriminate
  incriminating
  incrimination
  incriminatory
incrustation
incubate
  incubating
  incubation
  incubator
incubus
  incubuses (*pl.*)
  incubi (*pl.*)
inculcate
        (to suggest strongly)
  inculcating

126

inculcation
inculpate (to accuse)
  inculpating
  inculpation
incumbency
  incumbencies (*pl.*)
  incumbent
incur
  incurred
  incurring
  incurs
incurable
  incurability
  incurably
incurious
incursion
  incursive
indebted
  indebtedness
indecency
  indecencies (*pl.*)
  indecent
  indecently
indecipherable
indecision
  indecisive
  indecisively
indeclinable (*grammar*)
indecorous
  indecorously
  indecorousness
  indecorum
indeed
indefatigable
  indefatigability
  indefatigably
indefensible
  indefensibly
indefinable
indefinite
  indefinitely
indelible
  indelibly
indelicate
  indelicacy

indelicacies (*pl.*)
indelicately
indemnify
  indemnification
  indemnified
  indemnifies
  indemnifying
indemnity
  indemnities (*pl.*)
indent
  indentation
  indented
indenture
independent
  independence
  independently
indescribable
  indescribably
indestructible
  indestructibility
  indestructibly
indeterminable
    (can't be settled)
indeterminate (doubtful)
  indeterminately
index
  indexes (*pl.*)
  indices (*pl.*)
  indexation
indicate
  indicating
  indication
  indicative
  indicatively
  indicator
indict (to accuse)
  indictable
  indictment
indifference
  indifferent
  indifferently
indigenous (native)
indigent (poor)
  indigence (poverty)
indigestion

indigestibility
indigestible
indignant (angry)
  indignantly
  indignation
indignity
  indignities (*pl.*)
indigo
indirect
  indirectly
indiscernible
indiscipline
indiscreet
  indiscretion
  indiscreetly
indiscriminate
  indiscriminately
indispensable
  indispensability
  indispensably
indisposed
  indisposition
indisputable
  indisputably
indistinct
indistinguishable
indite (to write)
  inditing
individual
  individualism
  individualist
  individualistic
  individuality
  individually
individualise
  individualize
individualisation
  individualization
individualising
  individualizing
indivisible
  indivisibility
  indivisibly
indoctrinate
  indoctrination

indoctrinating
indolence
indolent
indolently
indomitable
indomitably
indoor
indoors
indubitable
indubitably
induce
inducement
inducing
induct (to introduce)
induction
inductance (*electr.*)
induction
inductive
inductively
indulge
indulgence
indulgent
indulgently
indulging
industrial
industrialisation
industrialization
industrialise
industrialize
industrialising
industrializing
industrialism
industrialist
industrialist's
    (of the industrialist)
industrialists'
    (of the industrialists)
industrially
industry
industries (*pl.*)
industrious
industriously
inebriate
inebriating
inebriation

inebriety
inedible (uneatable)
inedibility
ineducable
ineffable (indescribable)
ineffably
ineffaceable
ineffaceably
ineffective (not efficient)
ineffectively
ineffectiveness
ineffectual (useless)
ineffectually
inefficient
inefficiency
inefficiencies (*pl.*)
inefficiently
inelastic
inelastically
inelasticity
inelegant
inelegancy
inelegantly
ineligible (unsuitable)
ineligibilty
ineluctable (unavoidable)
inept (silly)
ineptitude (silliness)
ineptly
inequality
inequalities (*pl.*)
inequitable
inequitably
ineradicable
ineradicably
inert
inertia
inertly
inertness
inescapable
inescapably
inessential
inestimable
inestimably
inevitable

inevitableness
inevitability
inevitably
inexact
inexactitude
inexcusable
inexcusably
inexhaustible
inexhaustibly
inexorable
inexorably
inexpedient
inexpediency
inexpediently
inexpensive
inexpensively
inexperience
inexplicable
inexplicably
inexpressible
inexpressibly
inextinguishable
inextricable
inextricably
infallible
infallibility
infallibly
infamous
infamously
infamy
infant
infancy
infanticide
infantile
infant's (of the infant)
infants' (of the infants)
infantry
infantryman
infatuate
infatuation
infect
infection
infectious
infectiousness
infelicity

infelicities (*pl.*)
infelicitous
infelicitously
infer
  inference
  inferential
  inferred
  inferring
  infers
inferior
  inferiority
infernal
  infernally
inferno
  infernos (*pl.*)
infertile
  infertility
infest
  infestation
infidel
  infidelity
  infidelities (*pl.*)
infiltrate
  infiltrating
  infiltration
  infiltrator
infinite (very large)
  infinitely
  infinitude
  infinity
infinitesimal (very small)
  infinitesimally
infinitive (*grammar*)
  infinitival
infirm
  infirmary
  infirmaries (*pl.*)
  infirmity
  infirmities (*pl.*)
inflame
  inflaming
  inflammable
  inflammation
  inflammatory
inflate

inflatable
inflating
inflation
inflationary
inflect
  inflection
  inflective
  inflexion
inflexible
  inflexibility
  inflexibly
inflict
  infliction
influence
  influencing
  influential
  influentially
influenza
influx
inform
  informant
  information
  informative
  informer
informal
  informality
  informally
infraction
infra dig.
infra-red
infrastructure
infrequent
  infrequency
  infrequently
infringe
  infringement
  infringing
infuriate
  infuriating
infuse
  infuser
  infusing
  infusion
ingenious (clever)
  ingeniously

ingenuity
ingénue
ingenuous (naïve)
  ingenuously
  ingenuousness
ingest
  ingestion
inglorious
  ingloriously
ingoing
ingot
ingrain
  ingrained
ingratiate
  ingratiating
ingratitude
ingredient
ingress
ingrowing
inhabit (to dwell in)
  inhabitable
  inhabitant
inhale
  inhalant
  inhalation
  inhaling
inherent
  inherence
  inherently
inherit
  inheritable
  inheritance
  inherited
  inheritor
inhibit (to restrain)
  inhibited
  inhibition
  inhibitory
inhospitable
  inhospitably
inhuman (barbarous)
  inhumanity
  inhumanities (*pl.*)
  inhumanly
inhumane (cruel)

inimical

inhumanely
inimical
inimitable
  inimitably
iniquitous
  iniquitously
  iniquity
  iniquities (*pl.*)
initial (at the beginning)
  initially
initial (to sign)
  initialled
  initialed
  initialling
  initialing
  initials
initiate
  initiating
  initiation
  initiative
  initiator
inject
  injection
injudicious
  injudiciously
injunction
injure
  injuring
  injurious
  injuriously
  injury
  injuries (*pl.*)
injustice
ink
  inky
inkling (hint)
inland
in-law
inlay
  inlaid
inlet
inmate
in memoriam
inmost
inn

innkeeper
innkeeper's
  (of the innkeeper)
innkeepers'
  (of the innkeepers)
innards
innate
  innately
inner
  innermost
innings
  innings (*pl.*)
innocence
  innocent
  innocently
innocuous (harmless)
  innocuously
innovate
  innovating
  innovation
  innovator
innuendo
  innuendoes, innuendos (*pl.*)
  innuendos (pl.)
innumerable
  innumerably
inoculate
  inoculating
  inoculation
inoffensive
  inoffensively
  inoffensiveness
inoperable
  (unfit for operation)
inoperative
  (not functioning)
inoperativeness.
inopportune
  inopportunely
inordinate
  inordinately
inorganic
input
  inputting

inquest
inquire (to investigate)
enquire (to ask)
  inquiring
  inquiry
  inquiries (*pl.*)
inquisition
  inquisitor
  inquisitorial
inquisitive
  inquisitively
  inquisitiveness
inroad
inrush
insalubrious
  insalubrity
insane (mad)
  insanely
  insanity (madness)
insanitary (unhealthy)
  insanitariness
insatiable
  insatiably
inscribe
  inscribing
  inscription
inscrutable
  inscrutability
  inscrutably
insect
  insecticide
  insect's (of the insect)
  insects' (of the insects)
insecure
  insecurely
  insecurity
inseminate
  inseminating
  insemination
insensate (stupid)
insensible (unconscious)
  insensibility
  insensibly
insensitive (unfeeling)
  insensitively

130

insensitiveness
insensitivity
inseparable
inseparably
insert
insertion
inset
insetting
inshore
inside
insider
insidious
insidiously
insidiousness
insight
insignia
insignia (*pl.*)
insignificant
insignificance
insignificantly
insincere
insincerely
insincerity
insinuate
insinuating
insinuation
insinuator
insipid
insipidly
insipidness
insist
insistence
insistent
insistently
insobriety
insolent
insolence
insolently
insoluble
insolubility
insolubly
insolvent
insolvence
insomnia
insomniac

insouciant
insouciance
inspect
inspection
inspector
inspectorate
inspector's
          (of the inspector)
inspectors'
          (of the inspectors)
inspire
inspiration
inspiring
instability
install
installed
installing
installation
instalment
installment
instance
instancing
instant
instantaneous
instantaneously
instantly
instead
instep
instigate
instigating
instigation
instigator
instil
instill
instilled
instilling
instils
instills
instinct
instinctive
instinctively
institute
instituting
institution
institutional

institutionalise
institutionalize
institutionalising
institutionalizing
instruct
instruction
instructional
instructive
instructor
instructor's
          (of the instructor)
instructors'
          (of the instructors)
instrument
instrumental
instrumentalist
instrumentality
instrumentation
insubordinate
insubordinately
insubordination
insubstantial (unreal)
insufferable
insufferably
insufficient
insufficiency
insufficiently
insular
insularity
insulate
insulating
insulation
insulator
insulin
insult
insuperable
insuperably
insupportable
insure
insurability
insurable
insurance
insurer
insuring
insurgent

insurgence
insurgency
insurmountable
insurmountably
insurrection
insurrectionary
intact
intake
intangible
intangibly
integer
integral
integrally
integrate
integrating
integration
integrity
intellect
intellectual
intellectualise
intellectualize
intellectualising
intellectualizing
intellectualism
intellectually
intelligent (clever)
intelligence
intelligently
intelligentsia
intelligible
(understandable)
intelligibility
intelligibly
intemperate
intemperance
intemperately
intend
intention
intense
intensely
intensify
intensification
intensified
intensifies
intensifying

intensity
intensities (*pl.*)
intensive
intensively
intent (purpose)
intention
intentional
intentionally
intent (earnest)
intently
inter (to bury)
interment (burial)
interred
interring
inters
inter alia
interact
interaction
interbreed
interbred
intercalate (to insert)
intercalary
intercalating
intercalation
intercede
interceding
intercession
intercept
interception
interceptor
interchange
interchangeable
interchanging
intercommunicate
intercom.
intercommunicating
intercommunication
interconnect
interconnection
intercontinental
intercourse
interdenominational
interdepartmental
interdependence
interdependent

interdependently
interdict
interdiction
interdisciplinary
interest
interested
interface
interfere
interference
interfering
interim
interior
interiorly
interject
interjection
interlace
interlacing
interleave
interleaving
interline
interlining
interlock
interlope
interloper
interloping
interlude
intermarry
intermarriage
intermarried
intermarries
intermarrying
intermediary
intermediaries (*pl.*)
intermediate
intermediately
interment (burial)
intermezzo
intermezzos, intermezzi
(*pl.*)
intermezzi (pl.)
interminable
interminably
intermingle
intermingling
intermission

intermittent
intermittently
intern, interne (doctor)
intern (to confine)
  internee
  internment
internal
  internally
international
  internationalisation
  internationalization
  internationalise
  internationalize
  internationalised
  internationalized
  internationalism
  internationally
internecine
interpellate
      (to ask questions)
  interpellating
  interpellation
interplanetary
Interpol
interpolate (to insert)
  interpolating
  interpolation
interpose
  interposing
  interposition
interpret
  interpretation
  interpreter
interracial
interregnum
interrelated
  interrelating
  interrelation
interrogate
  interrogating
  interrogation
  interrogative
  interrogator
interrupt
  interrupter

interruption
interruptor
intersect
  intersection
intersperse
  interspersion
  interspersing
interstellar
interstice
interstitial
interval
intervene
  intervening
  intervention
interview
  interviewee
  interviewer
interweave
  interweaving
  interwove
  interwoven
intestate (without a Will)
  intestacy
intestine
  intestinal
intimate (to suggest)
  intimating
  intimation
intimate (friendly)
  intimacy
  intimately
intimidate (to frighten)
  intimidating
  intimidation
intolerable (unbearable)
  intolerably
intolerance (impatience)
  intolerant
  intolerantly
intonation (pitch of voice)
intone (to chant)
  intoning
intoxicate
  intoxicant
  intoxicated

intoxicating
intoxication
intractable
  intractableness
  intractably
intramuscular
intransigent
  intransigence
  intransigently
intransitive
intrauterine
intravenous
intrepid
  intrepidity
  intrepidly
intricate
  intricacy
  intricacies (*pl.*)
  intricately
intrigue
  intriguer
  intriguing
intrinsic
  intrinsically
introduce
  introducing
  introduction
  introductory
introspection
  introspective
introvert
  introversion
intrude
  intruder
  intruding
  intrusion
  intrusive
intuition
  intuitive
  intuitively
inundate
  inundating
  inundation
inure
  inured

invade
invader
invading
invasion
invalid (ill person)
invalidism
invalid's (of the invalid)
invalids'
(of the invalids)
invalid (not valid)
invalidate
invalidating
invalidation
invaluable (very valuable)
invariable
invariably
invasion
invective
inveigh (to abuse)
inveighed
inveigle (to entice)
inveigling
invent
invention
inventive
inventiveness
inventor
inventor's
(of the inventor)
inventors'
(of the inventors)
inventory (list)
inventories (pl.)
inverse
inversely
inversion
invert
inverter
invertebrate
invest
investment
investor
investor's
(of the investor)

investors'
(of the investors)
investigate
investigating
investigation
investigator
investiture
inveterate
inveteracy
inveterately
invidious (causing offence)
invidiously
invigilate
invigilating
invigilation
invigilator
invigorate
invigorating
invigoration
invincible
invincibility
invincibly
inviolable (sacred)
inviolate (unbroken)
invisible
invisibility
invisibly
invite
invitation
inviting
invocation (from invoke)
invoice
invoicing
invoke
invocation
invoking
involuntary
involuntarily
involuted (complicated)
involve
involvement
involving
invulnerable
invulnerability
inward

inwardly
inwardness
inwards
iodine
iodide
ion
ionic
ionisation
ionization
ionise
ionize
ionising
ionizing
ionosphere
iota
ipecacuanha
ipso facto
irascible
irascibility
irascibly
irate
irately
ire (anger)
ireful
iridescence
iridescent
iris
irises (pl.)
irk
irksome
iron
ironmonger
ironmonger's
(of the ironmonger)
ironmongers'
(of the ironmongers)
ironmongery
iron ore
irony
ironies (pl.)
ironic
ironical
ironically
irradiate
irradiating

irradiation
irrational
  irrationality
  irrationally
irreconcilable
  irreconcilability
  irreconcilableness
  irreconcilably
irrecoverable
  irrecoverably
irredeemable
  irredeemably
irreducible
  irreducibly
irrefutable
  irrefutably
irregular
  irregularity
  irregularities (*pl.*)
  irregularly
irrelevance
  irrelevant
      (not to the point)
  irrelevantly
irreligious
irremediable
  irremediably
irremissible
irremovable
  irremovably
irreparable
  irreparably
irreplaceable
irrepressible
  irrepressibly
irreproachable
  irreproachably
irresistible
  irresistibly
irresolute
  irresolutely
irrespective
  irrespectively
irresponsible
  irresponsibility

irresponsibly
irretrievable
  irretrievably
irreverent (not pious)
  irreverence
  irreverently
irreversible
  irreversibility
  irreversibly
irrevocable
  irrevocability
  irrevocably
irrigate
  irrigating
  irrigation
  irrigator
irritable
  irritability
  irritably
irritate
  irritant
  irritating
  irritation
irrupt (to break in)
  irruption
  irruptive
isinglass
island
  islander
  island's (of the island)
  islands' (of the islands)
  isle
  islet
isn't (is not)
isobar
isochronous
isolate
  isolating
  isolation
isometric
  isometrically
isosceles
isotherm
  isothermal
isotope

issue
  issuance
  issuing
isthmus
  isthmuses, isthmi (*pl.*)
italic
  italicise
  italicize
  italicising
  italicizing
itch
  itched
  itches
  itching
  itchy
item
  itemise
  itemize
  itemising
  itemizing
iterate (to repeat)
  iterating
  iteration
  iterative
itinerant
itinerary
  itineraries (*pl.*)
it's (it is)
its (of it)
  itself
I've (I have)
ivory
  ivories (*pl.*)
ivy
  ivies (*pl.*)
  ivy's (of the ivy)
  ivies' (of the ivies)

J

jab
  jabbed

jabbing
jabs
jabber
 jabbered
 jabbering
jack
 jackanapes
 jack-knife
 jack-knives (pl.)
 jack-knifed
 jack-knifing
jackal
jackass
 jackasses (pl.)
jackdaw
jacket
Jacobean
       (of James I's time)
Jacobin
     (French revolutionary)
 Jacobinic
 Jacobinical
Jacobite
        (loyal to James II)
jade
 jaded
jag
 jagged
jaguar
jail, gaol
 jailer, gaoler, jailor
jam
 jammed
 jamming
 jammy
jamb (of door)
jamboree
jangle
 jangling
janitor
January
japan (to varnish)
 japanned
 japanning
japonica

jar
 jarred
 jarring
jardinière
jargon
jasmine, jasmin,
                jessamine
jasper
jaundice
 jaundiced
jaunt (short walk)
jaunty (sprightly)
 jauntily
 jauntiness
javelin
jaw
 jawbone
jay
jazz
 jazzy
jealous
 jealously
 jealousy
jeans
jeep
jeer
 jeered
 jeering
jejune (scanty)
jelly
 jellies (pl.)
 jellied
 jellified
 jellifies
 jellifying
jemmy
 jemmies (pl.)
jeopardy
 jeopardise
 jeopardize
 jeopardising
 jeopardizing
jeremiad (lamentation)
jeroboam (large bottle)
jerk

 jerkily
 jerkiness
 jerky
jerkin (jacket)
jerry
 jerry-builder
 jerry-building
 jerry-built
jersey
 jerseys (pl.)
jessamine, jasmine
jest
 jester
jet
 jet-propelled
 jetting
jetsam
jettison
 jettisoned
jetty
 jetties (pl.)
jewel
 jewelled
 jeweled
 jeweller
 jeweler
 jeweller's
        (of the jeweller)
 jewellers'
        (of the jewellers)
 jewellery, jewelry
 jewelry
jib
 jibbed
 jibbing
jibe (to agree, fit)
jibe (see gibe, gybe)
jiffy
jig
 jiggered
 jigsaw
jilt
jingle
 jingling
jingo

136

jingoes (*pl.*)
jingoism
jinx
jitter
jittery
jiu-jitsu
    (Japanese wrestling)
        jiu-jutsu, ju-jitsu
jive
  jiving
job
  jobber
  jobbery
  jobless
jockey
  jockeys (*pl.*)
  jockey's (of the jockey)
  jockeys'
      (of the jockeys)
  jockeyed
jocose (playful)
  jocosely
  jocosity
jocular (humorous)
  jocularity
  jocularly
jocund (cheerful)
  jocundity
  jocundly
jodhpurs
jog
  jogged
  jogging
  jogs
joggle
  joggling
joie de vivre
join
  joiner
  joinery
  joiner work
joint
  jointer
  jointly
jointure (inheritance)

joist
joke
  joker
  joking
  jokingly
jolly
  jollier
  jolliest
  jollification
  jollify
  jollifying
  jollily
  jollity
jolt
jonquil
josser (fellow)
jostle
  jostling
jot
  jotted
  jotting
joule (unit of energy)
journal
  journalese
  journalism
  journalist
journey
  journeys (*pl.*)
  journeyed
  journeying
  journey's
      (of the journey)
  journeys'
      (of the journeys)
jovial
  joviality
  jovially
jowl
joy
  joyful
  joyfully
  joyless
  joyous
  joyously
  joy-ride

joy-riding
jubilant
  jubilantly
  jubilation
jubilee
judder
  juddered
  juddering
judge
  judgement
  judging
  judgment
judicature (jurisdiction)
judicial (lawful)
  judicially
judiciary
  (all judges in a country)
judicious (reasonable)
  judiciously
judo (ju-jitsu)
jug
  jugged
juggernaut
juggle
  juggler
  jugglery
  juggling
jugular (vein)
juice
  juicier
  juiciest
  juicily
  juiciness
  juicy
ju-jitsu
jujube
juke-box
julep
julienne
jumble
  jumble sale
  jumbling
jumbo
jump
  jumper

jumpily
jumpiness
jumpy
junction
juncture
jungle
junior
juniority
juniper
junk
junket
  junketed
  junketing
junta
juridical (relating to law)
jurisconsult (legal expert)
jurisdiction (legal power)
  jurisdictional
jurisprudence
     (science of law)
  jurisprudent
jurist (legal expert)
juror
  juror's (of the juror)
  jurors' (of the jurors)
jury
  juries (*pl.*)
  juryman
  jurymen (*pl.*)
just
  justly
justice
justiciary
    (legal administrator)
  justiciaries (*pl.*)
justify
  justifiable
  justifiably
  justification
  justified
  justifying
jut
  jutted
  jutting
  juts

jute
juvenile
juxtapose
  juxtaposing
  juxtaposition

K

kale (cabbage)
kaleidoscope
  kaleidoscopic
kalends, calends
kamikaze
kangaroo
  kangaroos (*pl.*)
  kangaroo's
    (of the kangaroo)
  kangaroos'
    (of the kangaroos)
kaolin
kapok
karate
kata- (down)
  katabolism
kayak
kebab
kedgeree
keel
keen
  keener
  keenly
  keenness
keep
  keeper
  keepsake
  kept
keg
kelp
kempt
ken
kennel
  kennelled

  kenneled
  kennelling
  kenneling
kept (*from* keep)
kerb, curb (road edge)
  curb
  kerbstone
  curbstone
kerchief
  kerchiefs (*pl.*)
kernel (centre)
kerosine, kerosene
kestrel
ketch
ketchup
  catsup
kettle
  kettledrum
key
  keyboard
  keyhole
  keynote
khaki
khan (Oriental title)
kibbutz
  kibbutzim (*pl.*)
  kibbutznik
kibosh
kick
  kick-off
kid (to deceive)
  kidded
  kidding
  kids
kid (child)
  kid's (of the kid)
  kids' (of the kids)
kidnap
  kidnapped
  kidnaped
  kidnapper
  kidnaper
  kidnapping
  kidnaping
  kidnaps

kidney
  kidneys (*pl.*)
kill
  killer
kiln
kilo- (thousand)
  kilocycle
  kilogram, kilogramme
  kilohertz
  kilolitre
  kiloliter
  kilometre
  kilometer
  kiloton
  kilotonne (metric)
  kilowatt
kilt
kimono
  kimonos (*pl.*)
kin
  kindred
  kinsfolk
  kinship
  kinsman
  kinsmen (*pl.*)
  kinswoman
  kinswomen (*pl.*)
kind
  kinder
  kind-hearted
  kindliness
  kindly
  kindness
kindergarten
  kindergartens (*pl.*)
kindle
  kindling
kinetic
king
  kingdom
  king's (of the king)
  kings' (of the kings)
kink
  kinky
kiosk

kipper
  kippered
kirk
kiss
  kisses (*pl.*)
  kissed
  kisses
kit
kitchen
  kitchenette
kite
kith
kitten
  kittenish
kitty (fund of money)
klaxon
kleptomania
  kleptomaniac
knack
  knacker
  knapsack
knave
  knavery
  knavish
knead (to mix dough)
knee
  kneecap
kneel
  kneeled
  knelt
knell (sound of bell)
knew (*from* know)
knickers
  knickerbockers
knick-knack
knife
  knives (pl.)
knight
  knighted
  knight-errant
  knight-errantry
  knighthood
  knightly (chivalrous)
knit
  knits

knitted
knitter
knitting
knob
  knobby
knock
  knocker
  knock-kneed
  knock out (to disable)
  knock-out (disablement)
knoll (small hill)
knot
  knotted
  knotting
knout (to flog)
know
  knew
  know-how, knowhow
  known
knowledge
  knowledgeable
  knowledgeably
knuckle
  knuckling
koala
  koala bear
Kodak
kohlrabi
Koran
kosher
kowtow
krona (Swedish money)
  kronor (*pl.*)
krone (Danish, Norwegian)
  kroner (*pl.*)
kudos

L

laager (encampment)
label
  labelled

labeled
labelling
labeling
labels
labial (of the lips)
laboratory
laboratories (*pl.*)
laborious
laboriously
labour
labor
labourer
laborer
labourer's
   (of the labourer)
labourers'
   (of the labourers)
laburnum
laburnums (*pl.*)
labyrinth
labyrinthine
lace
lacing
lacerate (to tear)
lacerating
laceration
lachrymal
lachrymose (tearful)
lack
lackadaisical
lackadaisically
lackey
lackeys (*pl.*)
lack-lustre
laconic
laconically
lacquer (varnish)
lacquered
lacquering
lacrosse
lactation
lactic
lad
lad's (of the lad)
lads' (of the lads)

laddie (young fellow)
ladder
laden (loaded)
lading
ladle
ladling
lady
ladies (*pl.*)
ladies' (of the ladies)
ladylike
lady's (of the lady)
ladyship
lady's-maid
lag
lagged
lagging
lager (beer)
laggard
lagoon
laid (*see* Appendix)
lain (*see* Appendix)
lair (den)
laird
laird's (of the laird)
lairds' (of the lairds)
laissez-faire
laity
lake
lama (priest)
lamb
lamb's (of the lamb)
lambs' (of the lambs)
lambkin (baby lamb)
lambskin
lambda (Greek letter L)
lambent (softly radiant)
lambast, lambaste
    (to beat)
lame
lamely
lameness
lamé (fabric)
lament
lamentable
lamentably

lamentation
lamented
lamina
laminae (*pl.*)
laminated
lamination
lamp
lamplight
lampoon
lampooner
lampoonist
lamprey
lampreys (*pl.*)
lance
lancing
lancer (soldier)
lancers (dance)
lancet (knife)
land
landfall
landlady
landladies (*pl.*)
landlady's
   (of the landlady)
landladies'
   (of the landladies)
landlocked
landlord
landlord's
   (of the landlord)
landlords'
   (of the landlords)
landlubber
landlubberly
landmark
landowner
landscape
landscaping
landslide
lane
language
languid (slack)
languidly
languidness
languish (to fade)

languor (feebleness)
  languorous
lank
  lankiness
  lanky
lanolin
lantern
lanyard
lap
  (to drink with tongue)
  lapped
  lapping
  laps (it)
lap (of a person)
  lap-dog
lapel
  lapelled
lapidary
        (like stone, heavy)
lapis lazuli
lapse
  lapsing
lapsus linguae
        (slip of tongue)
larboard
larceny
  larcenies (pl.)
larch
lard
larder
large
  largely
  larger
  largish
largesse (gifts)
  largess
largo (very slow)
  larghetto (rather slow)
lark (joke)
lark (bird)
larva
  larvae (pl.)
  larval
larynx
  larynges (pl.)

laryngeal
laryngitis
lascivious
  lasciviously
  lasciviousness
laser
  lase
  lasing
lash
lass
  lasses (pl.)
  lassie
lassitude
lasso
  lassos, lassoes (pl.)
  lassoed
  lassoing
last
  lastly
latch
  latches (pl.)
  latchkey
late
  lately
  later
latent
  latency
lateral
  laterally
lath (strip of wood)
lathe (machine)
lather
  lathered
  lathering
latitude
latrine
latter
  latter-day
  latterly
lattice
laud (to praise)
  laudable
  laudably
laudanum
laugh

laughable
laughed
laughing-stock
laughs
laughter
launch
  launches (pl.)
  launched
  launches
launder
  laundered
  launderette
  laundress (fem.)
  laundrette
  laundry
  laundries (pl.)
laureate
  Poet Laureate
laurel
  laurel wreath
lava (from volcano)
lavatory
  lavatories (pl.)
lavender
laver (kind of seaweed)
lavish
  lavishly
  lavishness
law
  law-abiding
  lawful
  lawfully
  lawfulness
  lawless
  lawlessly
  lawlessness
  lawsuit
  lawyer
  lawyer's (of the lawyer)
  lawyers'
        (of the lawyers)
lawn
  lawn-mower
lax
  laxity

141

laxative

laxly
laxative
lay (person)
  laity
  layman
lay (*see* Appendix)
  laid
  layer (of eggs)
layby
  lay-bys (*pl.*)
layer
  layered
layette
layoff
laze
  lazier
  lazily
  laziness
  lazy
leach (to filter)
lead
  leader
  leadership
  led
lead (metal)
  leaded
  leaden (very heavy)
leaf
  leaves (*pl.*)
  leafage
  leafiness
  leafless
  leafy
leaflet
league
leak (hole in pipe)
  leakage
  leaky
lean (to slope)
  leaned
  leant
lean (thin)
  leanness
leaning (aptitude)
lean-to

leap
  leaped
  leapt
  leap-year
learn
  learned
  learned (very clever)
  learner
  learnt
lease
  leasing
  leasehold
leash
least
  leastways
  leastwise
leather
  leatherette
  leathery
leave
  leaving
  left
leaven (to add yeast)
  leavened
leaves (*from* leaf)
lecher
  lecherous
  lechery
lectern
lecture
  lecturer
  lecturing
led (*from* to lead)
ledge
ledger
lee
  leeward
  leeway
leech (sucking worm)
leek (vegetable)
leer
  leered
  leering
leery (sly)
left

left-handed
leftward
left wing
left-winger
left (*from* leave)
leg
  legged
  legging
  leggy
  leg-pull
legacy
  legacies (*pl.*)
legal
  legalisation
  legalization
  legalise
  legalize
  legalising
  legalizing
  legality
  legally
legate (Papal envoy)
legation
  (diplomat's residence)
legato
  (in music, smoothly)
legend
  legendary
legerdemain
legible
  legibility
  legibly
legion
  legionary
  legionaries (*pl.*)
legislate
  legislating
  legislation
  legislator
  (maker of laws)
  legislature
  (legal assembly)
legitimate
  legitimacy
  legitimately

legitimation
legitimatise
legitimatize
legitimise
legitimize
legitimising
legitimizing
legume (vegetable)
leguminous
Leicester
leisure
leisurely
leitmotiv, leitmotif
lemming (animal)
lemon
lemonade
lend
lender
lent
length
lengthen
lengthily
lengthways
lengthwise
lengthy
lenience
leniency
lenient
leniently
lens
lent (*from* lend, lean)
Lent
Lenten
lentil
leonine (lion-like)
leopard
leopardess
leopard's
(of the leopard)
leopards'
(of the leopards)
leotard
leper
leprosy
leprous

leprechaun
lesbian
lèse-majesté
lesion
less
lessen (to make less)
lessened
lessening
lesser
lessee (tenant)
lessor (granter of lease)
lesson
let
lettable
letting
lethal
lethally
lethargy
lethargic
lethargically
let's (let us)
letter
lettering
lettuce
leucocyte
leukaemia
leukemia
level
level-headed
levelled
leveled
leveller
leveler
levelling
leveling
lever
leverage
leviathan
levis (jeans)
levitate
levitating
levitation
levity (humour)
levy (payment)
levies (*pl.*)

levied
levying
lewd
lewdly
lewdness
lexicographer
lexicography
lexicon
liable
liability
liabilities (*pl.*)
liaison
liaise
liaising
liar (*see* Appendix)
libation
libel
libelled
libeled
libeller
libeler
libelling
libeling
libellous
libelous
libels
liberal (generous)
liberality
liberally
Liberal (politics)
liberate
liberating
liberation
liberator
libertine
(licentious person)
liberty
liberties (*pl.*)
libido
libidinal
libidinous
library
libraries (*pl.*)
librarian
libretto (text of opera)

143

libretti, librettos (*pl.*)
   librettos (*pl.*)
lice (*pl.* of louse)
licence (permission)
   license
licence
(freedom from restraint)
   license
license
   (to grant permission)
licensed
licensee
   (holder of licence)
licenser
   (granter of licence)
licensing
licentiate (graduate)
licentious (lewd)
licentiousness
lichen
lick
licorice, liquorice
   licorice
lid
   lidded
lido
   lidos (*pl.*)
lie
   linearityepl.)ry)))R).)R))
   lain
   lay
   lying
lie (to fib, *see* Appendix)
   liar
   lied
   lying
lied (song)
   lieder (*pl.*)
lien (right to property)
lieu (instead of)
lieutenant
   lieutenancy
life
   lives (*pl.*)
   lifebuoy

life-guard
lifeless
lifelessly
lifelike
lifelong
life-size
life-sized
lift
lift-off
ligament (bone binding)
ligature (cord)
light
   lighted
   lighter
   light-hearted
   light-heartedly
   lighthouse
   lightly
   lightness
   light-weight
   lit
lighten
   lightened
   lightening
      (making lighter)
lighter (boat)
   lighterage
lightning
      (in thunderstorm)
lignite
like
   likeable, likable
   likable
   likelihood
   likely
   likeness
   likewise
   liking
liken
lilac
lilliputian
lilt
lily
   lilies (*pl.*)
   lilies' (of the lilies)

lily-livered
lily's (of the lily)
limb
   limbless
limber
   limbered
   limbering
limbo
   limbos (*pl.*)
lime
   limelight
   limerick
limit
   limitation
   limited
limousine
limp
   limpness
limpet
limpid
linage, lineage
      (number of lines)
linchpin
line
lineage (ancestry)
lineal
linear
linearity
   lining
lineament
linen
   linen-draper
liner
linger
   lingered
   lingering
lingerie
lingo
   lingoes (*pl.*)
lingua (tongue)
   lingual
linguist
   linguistic
lining
liniment

link
linkage
linked
links (Golf)
linnet
lino
 linocut
 linoleum
 linotype
linseed
lint
lintel (over door)
lion
 lion's (of the lion)
 lions' (of the lions)
 lioness
 lionesses (*pl.*)
 lion-hearted
 lionisation
 lionization
 lionise
 lionize
 lionising
 lionizing
lip
 lipped
 lip-read
 lip-reader
 lip-reading
 lipstick
liquefy
 liquefaction
 liquefiable
 liquefied
 liquefies
 liquefying
 liquescent
liqueur
 (strong, sweet alcohol)
liquid
 liquidate
 liquidating
 liquidation
 liquidator
 liquidity

liquor (liquid)
liquorice, licorice
 licorice
lira (Italian money)
 lire (*pl.*)
 liras (*pl.*)
lisle
lisp
lissom (agile)
 lissome
list
list (of a ship, to lean)
listen
 listened
 listener
 listening
listless
 listlessly
 listlessness
lit (*from* light)
litany
 litanies (*pl.*)
literal (exact)
 literally
literary (learned)
literate (able to read)
 literacy
literature (books etc.)
lithe
litho- (stone)
 lithograph
 lithography
litigate
 litigant
 litigating
 litigation
 litigious
litmus
 litmus-paper
litre (measure)
 liter
litter (rubbish)
 littered
little
littoral (near the sea)

liturgy
 liturgies (*pl.*)
 liturgical
live
 liveable
 livable
 livelihood
 living
lively
 livelier
 liveliness
liven (to cheer up)
 livened
 livening
liver
 liverish
livery (costume)
 liveries (*pl.*)
livestock
living (clergyman's)
livid
lizard
llama (kind of camel)
load
loaf (bread)
 loaves (*pl.*)
loaf (to be idle)
 loafer
loam
 loamy
loan
loath, loth (unwilling)
loathe (to hate)
 loathing
 loathsome
lob
 lobbed
 lobbing
 lobs
lobby
 lobbies (*pl.*)
 lobbied
 lobbies
 lobbying
lobe (of the ear)

lobster
local
  localisation
  localization
  localise
  localize
  localising
  localizing
  locally
locale (locality of events)
locality
  localities (*pl.*)
locate
  locating
  location
locative (*grammar*)
loch (lake)
lock
  locked out
  locker
  lockjaw
  lockout
  lockouts (*pl.*)
lock (of hair)
lock (on river or canal)
locket
locksmith
locomotion
  locomotive
locum
  locum tenens
          (substitute)
locus
  loci (*pl.*)
locust
lode (of metal ore)
lodge
  lodgement
  lodger
  lodging
  lodgment
loft
  loftier
  loftily
  loftiness

lofty
loft (attic)
log
  log-book
  logged
  logging
loganberry
  loganberries (*pl.*)
logarithm
  logarithmic
  logarithmically
loggerhead
  loggerheads
  loggia
logic
  logical
  logically
  logician
logistics
logotype, logo
          (business symbol)
loin
loiter
  loitered
  loiterer
  loitering
loll
  lolled
  lolling
lollipop
lone
  lonelier
  loneliness
  lonely
  lonesome
long (extensive)
  longer
  long-suffering
  longways
  longwise
long (to wish for)
  longing
longevity
longitude
  longitudinal

longitudinally
loo (lavatory)
loofah
  loofa
look
  looker-on
  lookers-on (*pl.*)
loom (for weaving)
loom
  (to appear threatening)
loop
  loophole
loose
  loose-leaf
  loosely
  looseness
  looser
loosen
  loosened
  loosening
loot
  looter
lop
  lopped
  lopping
  lops
  lopsided
lope (to run)
  loping
loquacious
  loquaciously
  loquaciousness
  loquacity
lord
  lordly
  lord's (of the lord)
  lords' (of the lords)
  Lord Mayor
  lordship
lore (tradition)
lorgnette
lorry
  lorries (*pl.*)
lose
  loser

losing
lost
loss
lot
loth, loath (unwilling)
Lothario
lotion
lottery
  lotteries (*pl.*)
lotus
  lotuses (*pl.*)
loud
  louder
  loudly
  loud-mouthed
  loudness
  loud-speaker
lounge
  lounging
lour, lower (to frown)
  lower
  loured, lowered
  lowered
  louring, lowering
  lowering
louse
  lice (*pl.*)
  lousy
lout
  loutish
louvre
  louver
  louvred
  louvered
love
  lovable, loveable
  lover
  lovelorn
  loving
lovely
  lovelier
  loveliness
low
  lower
  lowliness

lowly
lowness
low (to moo)
lower
(to make lower, reduce)
  lowered
  lowering
loyal
  loyalism
  loyalist
  loyally
  loyalty
  loyalties (*pl.*)
lozenge
lubber
  lubberly
lubricate
  lubricant
  lubricating
  lubrication
lucid
  lucidity
  lucidly
  lucidness
luck
  luckier
  luckily
  lucky
lucre
  lucrative
  lucratively
ludicrous
  ludicrously
  ludicrousness
luff
lug (to drag)
  lugged
  lugging
  lugs
lug (projection)
luggage
lugger (small ship)
lugubrious
  lugubriously
lukewarm

lull
  lullaby
  lullabies (*pl.*)
lumbago
lumbar (of the loin)
lumber (rubbish)
  lumber-room
lumberjack
lumen (unit of light)
luminary
  luminaries (*pl.*)
luminescence
  luminescent
luminous
  luminosity
lump
  lumpiness
  lumpy
luna- (moon)
  lunar
  lunacy
  lunatic
lunch
  luncheon
lung
lunge (to thrust forward)
  lunging
lurch
lure
  luring
lurid
  luridly
lurk
luscious
  lusciousness
lush
lust
  lustful
lustre
  luster
  lustrous
lusty
  lustier
  lustily
  lustiness

lute
luxury
  luxuries (*pl.*)
  luxuriance
  luxuriant
  luxuriate
  luxuriating
  luxurious
  luxuriously
lying (see Appendix)
lymph
  lymphatic
lynch (to murder)
lynx (animal)
lyre (harp)
lyric
  lyrical
  lyrically
  lyricism

M

ma'am (madam)
macabre
macadam
  macadamise
  macadamize
  macadamised
  macadamized
macaroni
macaroon
macassar (hair-oil)
macaw
mace
  mace-bearer
macerate
  macerating
  maceration
Mach (speed ratio)
machiavellian
machination
machine

machinery
machining
machinist
mackerel
mackintosh
macramé
macro- (large)
  macrobiotic
  macrocosm
  macroscopic
macula (spot on skin)
  maculae (*pl.*)
mad
  madder
  madding
  madly
  madman
  madmen (*pl.*)
  madness
madam
Madame (French for Mrs)
  Mesdames (*pl.*)
madden
  maddening
madder
      (plant or red dye)
made (*from* make)
Madeira
Mademoiselle
  Mesdemoiselles (*pl.*)
madonna
madrigal
maelstrom
maestro
  maestros, maestri (*pl.*)
Mafia
magazine
magenta
maggot
  maggoty
magic
  magical
  magically
  magician

magician's
      (of the magician)
magicians'
      (of the magicians)
magisterial
magisterially
magistrate
magistrate's
      (of the magistrate)
magistrates'
      (of the magistrates)
magistracy
  magistracies (*pl.*)
magistral
magistrature
magnanimous
magnanimity
magnanimously
magnate (great man)
magnesia
magnesium
magnet
magnetic
magnetically
magnetisable
magnetizable
magnetisation
magnetization
magnetise
magnetize
magnetising
magnetizing
magnetism
magneto
  magnetos (*pl.*)
magnificent
magnificence
magnificently
magnify
magnification
magnified
magnifier
magnitude
magnolia
magnum

magnum opus
  magna opera (*pl.*)
magpie
maharajah, maharaja
maharani, maharanee
mah-jong, mah-jongg
mahogany
Mahomet, Mohammed,
        Muhammad
  Mahometan,
      Mohammedan,
      Muhammadan
maid
  maiden
  maidenly
  maid's (of the maid)
  maids' (of the maids)
mail (letters or armour)
maim
  maimed
main
  mainly
maintain
  maintenance
maisonette, maisonnette
maître d'hôtel
maize (corn)
majestic
  majestically
  majesty
  majesties (*pl.*)
  Majesty's
     (of Her Majesty)
  Majesties'
     (of Their Majesties)
majolica
major
  majority
  majorities (*pl.*)
major-domo
make
  made
  maker
  makeshift
  make-up

makeweight
making
maladjusted
  maladjustment
maladminstration
maladroit
  maladroitness
malady
  maladies (*pl.*)
malaise
malapropos
  malapropism
malaria
malcontent
male (masculine)
malediction
malefactor
  malefaction
malevolence
  malevolent
malformation
malfunction
malice
  malice aforethought
malicious
  maliciously
malign (to slander)
  maligned
  maligner
  maligning
  malignity
malignant (very bad)
  malignancy
malinger (to feign illness)
  malingerer
  malingering
mall (shady walk)
mallard
malleable
  malleability
mallet
mallow
malnutrition
malodorous
malpractice

malt
maltreat
  maltreatment
mamma, mama (mother)
mammal
  mammalian
  mammary
mammon
mammoth
man
  men (*pl.*)
  manful
  manfully
  manhole
  manliness
  manly
  manned
  manning
  man's (of the man)
  men's (of the men)
  mans (he, she)
  manslaughter
manacle
manage
  manageable
  managed
  management
  manager
  managerial
  manager's
     (of the manager)
  managers'
     (of the managers)
  managing
mandarin
mandate
  mandatary (person)
  mandatory (compulsory)
mandible (lower jaw)
mandolin, mandoline
  mandolin
mandrel (part of lathe)
mandrake (plant)
mandrill (baboon)
mane (of horse)

manège (horsemanship)
manganese
mange
  mangy
mangel-wurzel,
      mangold-wurzel
  mangel-wurzel
manger
mangle
  mangling
mango
  mangoes, mangos (*pl.*)
mangrove
manhandle
manhood
mania
  maniac
  maniacal
  maniac's
      (of the maniac)
  maniacs'
      (of the maniacs)
manicure
  manicuring
  manicurist
manifest
  manifestation
  manifesto
  manifestos,
      manifestoes(*pl.*)
manifold
manikin (little man)
manilla
  manila
manipulate
  manipulating
  manipulation
  manipulative
  manipulator
mankind
manna (miraculous food)
mannequin (model)
manner
  mannered
  mannerism

mannerly
manoeuvre
  maneuver
manoeuvrability
  maneuverability
manoeuvrable
  maneuverable
manoeuvring
  maneuvering
manometer
      (pressure gauge)
manor (estate)
  manorial
manse
mansion
manslaughter
mantel
  mantelpiece
mantle (cloak)
manu- (hand)
  manual
  manually
  manufacture
  manufacturer
  manufacturing
  manuscript
manure
  manuring
many
map
  mapped
  mapping
maple
mar
  marred
  marring
marathon
maraud
  marauder
marble
march
  marcher
marchioness
      (*fem.* of marquess)
Marconi

Mardi Gras
      (Shrove Tuesday)
mare (horse)
margarine
margin
  marginal
  marginally
marguerite
marigold
marijuana, marihuana
marina (harbour)
marinade (pickle solution)
  marinading
marinate (to pickle)
  marinating
marine
  mariner
  mariner's
      (of the mariner)
  mariners'
      (of the mariners)
marionette
marital
maritime
marjoram
mark
  marked
  markedly
  marker
  marksman
market
  marketability
  marketable
  marketeer
  marketing
marl
marlinspike
  marline-spike
marmalade
marmoreal (of marble)
marmoset (monkey)
marmot (kind of squirrel)
maroon
  marooned
marquee (large tent)

marquetry, marqueterie
marquis, marquess
marrow
marry
  marriage
  marriageable
  married
  marries
  marrying
marsh
  marsh-mallow
marshal
  marshalled
  marshaled
  marshalling
  marshaling
  marshals
marsupial
mart (market place)
marten (weasel)
martial
  martial law
  martially
Martian
martin (bird)
martinet (tyrant)
martyr
  martyrs (*pl.*)
  martyrdom
  martyrise
  martyrize
  martyrising
  martyrizing
marvel
  marvelled
  marveled
  marvelling
  marveling
  marvellous
  marvelous
  marvellously
  marvelously
  marvels
Marylebone
Marx (Karl)

Marxism
  Marxist
marzipan
mascara
mascot
masculine
  masculinity
mash
mask (face cover)
masochism
  (pleasure from pain)
  masochist
mason
  masonic
  masonry
masque (entertainment)
masquerade
  masquerading
mass
massacre
  massacred
  massacring
massage
  massaging
  masseur
  masseuse (*fem.*)
massif (mountain tops)
massive (very large)
  massively
  massiveness
mast
  mast-head
master
  mastered
  masterful
  masterfully
  mastering
  masterpiece
  master's (of the master)
  masters'
    (of the masters)
  mastery
masticate
  masticating
  mastication

mastiff
  mastiffs (*pl.*)
mastoid
masturbate
  masturbating
  masturbation
mat
  matted
  matting
mat, matt (dull surface)
matador
match
  matchless
matchmaker
mate
  matey
  mating
mater- (mother)
  maternal
  maternally
  maternity
material
  materialism
  materialist
  materially
materialise
  materialize
  materialisation
  materialization
  materialising
  materializing
mathematics, maths
  mathematical
  mathematician
matinée
matins
matriarch
  matriarchal
  matriarchy
matriculate
  matriculating
  matriculation
matrimonial
  matrimony
matrix

matrices, matrixes (*pl.*)
matrixes (*pl.*)
matron
matt, mat (dull surface)
matter
  mattered
  matter-of-fact
mattock
mattress
mature
  maturely
  maturing
  maturity
matutinal
     (in the morning)
maudlin
maul (hammer)
maul (to treat roughly)
mausoleum
mauve
maverick
mawkish
  mawkishness
maxim
maximum
  maxima (*pl.*)
  maximums (*pl.*)
  maximal
  maximisation
  maximization
  maximise
  maximize
  maximising
  maximizing
may
  maybe
  mayn't (may not)
May (month)
may (tree)
mayhem
mayonnaise
mayor
  mayoral
  mayoralty
  mayor's (of the mayor)

mayors' (of the mayors)
maypole
maze (tangle of paths)
mazurka
mead
meadow
meagre
  meager
  meagrely
  meagreness
meal (grain)
  mealy
  mealy-mouthed
meal (repast)
  mealtime
mean
  meaning
  meaningful
  meaningfully
  meaningless
  meant
mean (mid-point)
  meantime
  meanwhile
mean (miserly)
  meaner
  meanly
  meanness
meander
  meandered
means (money, etc.)
  means test
measles
  measly
measure
  measurable
  measureless
  measurement
  measuring
meat (food)
  meatless
mechanic
  mechanical
  mechanically
  mechanician

mechanic's
    (of the mechanic)
mechanics'
    (of the mechanics)
mechanisation
mechanization
mechanise
mechanize
mechanising
mechanizing
mechanism
medal (for bravery, etc.)
  medalled
  medaled
  medallion
  medallist
  medalist
meddle (to interfere)
  meddler
  meddlesome
  meddling
media (newspapers, etc.)
mediaeval, medieval
median
  medial
  medially
mediate
  mediating
  mediation
  mediator
Medicaid
medical
  medically
Medicare
medicate
  medicament
  medicating
  medication
medicine
  medicinal
  medicinally
medieval, mediaeval
mediocre
  mediocrity
  mediocrities (*pl.*)

meditate
meditating
meditation
meditator
Mediterranean
medium (newspapers, etc.)
media (*pl.*)
medium (spiritualist)
mediums (*pl.*)
medlar (fruit)
medley (mixture)
meek
meekly
meekness
meet (to encounter)
meeting
met
meet (proper)
mega- (great)
megahertz
(million cycles)
megalith (large stone)
megalithic
megaphone
megatonne
(million tonnes)
megaton (million tons)
megavolt
megawatt
megohm (million ohms)
megalo- (great)
megalomania
megalomaniac
melancholy
melancholia
melancholic
mélange
mêlée
mellifluous
mellow
melodrama
melodramatic
melodramatically
melody
melodies (*pl.*)

melodic
melodically
melodious
melon
melt
melted
molten (melted state)
member
member's
(of the member)
members'
(of the members)
membership
membrane
membraneous
membranous
memento
mementoes, mementos
(*pl.*)
memo
memos (*pl.*)
memoir
memorabilia
memorable
memorably
memorandum
memoranda,
memorandums(*pl.*)
memorandums (*pl.*)
memorial
memory
memories (*pl.*)
memorise
(to learn by heart)
memorize
memorising
memorizing
memsahib
menace
menacing
ménage
menagerie
mend
mended
mendacious (lying)

mendaciously
mendacity
mendicant (beggar)
mendicity
menhir (prehistoric stone)
menial
menially
meningitis
menopause
menopausal
menstrual
menstruate
menstruating
menstruation
mensuration
mental
mentality
mentally
menthol
mention
mentor (adviser)
menu
menus (*pl.*)
mercantile
mercenary
mercenaries (*pl.*)
mercerise
mercerize
merchandise
merchant
merchant's
(of the merchant)
merchants'
(of the merchants)
mercury
mercurial
mercy
mercies (*pl.*)
merciful
mercifully
merciless
mercilessly
mere (only)
merely
merest

153

mere (lake)
meretricious (showy)
merge
 merger
 merging
meridian
 meridional (southern)
meringue
merit
 merited
 meritorious
 meritoriously
 meritocracy
mermaid
 mermaid's
  (of the mermaid)
 mermaids'
  (of the mermaids)
merry
 merrier
 merrily
 merriment
mésalliance
  (inferior marriage)
Mesdames
  (*pl. of* Madame)
 Mesdemoiselles
  (*pl. of* Mademoiselle)
mesh
mesmerism
 mesmerise
 mesmerize
 mesmerising
 mesmerizing
mess
 messier
 messily
 messiness
 messy
message
messenger
 messenger's
  (of the messenger)
 messengers'
  (of the messengers)

Messiah
 Messianic
Messieurs
  (*pl. of* Monsieur)
Messrs. (*pl. of* Mister)
messuage
  (house property)
met (*from* meet)
metabolism
 metabolic
metal
 metalled
 metaled
 metallic
 metallurgical
 metallurgist
 metallurgy
metamorphose
 metamorphosis
 metamorphoses (*pl.*)
metaphor
 metaphorical
 metaphorically
metaphysical
 metaphysically
 metaphysics
mete (to apportion)
 meting
meteor
 meteoric
 meteorically
 meteorite
 meteoroid
 meteorological
 meteorologist
 meteorology
meter (gas, etc.)
 metered
methane
method
 methodical
 methodically
 methodology
methyl
 methylated

meticulous
 meticulously
 meticulousness
métier
metre (measure of length)
 meter
 metric
metricate
 metricating
 metrication
metricize
 metricizing
metronome
metropolis
 metropolitan
mettle (temperament)
mews (stabling)
mezzanine
mezza voce (softly)
mezzo- (half)
 mezzo-forte
 mezzo-soprano
 mezzotint
miaow, miaou
miasma
 miasmal
mica
mice (*pl.* of mouse)
mickle, muckle
  (large amount)
micro- (small)
microbe
 microbial
microbiology
 microbiologist
microcosm
microfarad
micrometer
microphone
 microphonic
microscope
 microscopic
 microscopical
 microscopy
microtome

microwave
micturition
midday
midden (dunghill)
middle
  middleman
  middlemen (*pl.*)
  middleweight
  middling
  middy (midshipman)
  middies (*pl.*)
  middy's (of the middy)
  middies'
     (of the middies)
midge
midget
midinette
midnight
midriff
midshipman
  midshipmen (*pl.*)
midst
midsummer
midway
Midwest
  Midwesterner
midwife
  midwives (*pl.*)
  midwife's
     (of the midwife)
  midwives'
     (of the midwives)
  midwifery
mien (appearance)
miffed
might
  mightier
  mightily
  mightiness
  mighty
might (*from* may)
mignonette
migraine
migrant (migrator)

migrant's
    (of the migrant)
migrants'
    (of the migrants)
migrate
migrating
migration
migrator
mikado
mike (to idle)
  miking
milch-cow
mild
  milder
  mildly
  mildness
mildew
  mildewy
mile
  mileage
milieu (surroundings)
  milieus (*pl.*)
  milieux (*pl.*)
militant (aggressive)
  militancy
military
  militarily
  militarisation
  militarization
  militarise
  militarize
  militarised
  militarized
  militarising
  militarizing
  militarism
  militarist
militate (to influence)
  militating
militia
milk
  milker
  milkiness
  milkmaid
  milksop

milky
mill
miller
  miller's (of the miller)
  millers' (of the millers)
millstone
mille- (thousand)
mille-feuille
millenium
    (thousand years)
millepede, millipede
millipede
millet
milli- (thousandth part)
  milliampere
  milliamp
  milligram
  millilitre
  milliliter
  millimetre
  millimeter
  millivolt
  milliwatt
milliard (thousand million)
milliner
  millinery
million
  millionaire
  millionaire's
    (of the millionaire)
  millionaires'
    (of the millionaires)
  millionth
mime
  miming
mimic
  mimicked
  mimicker
  mimicking
  mimicry
mimosa
minaret
minatory (threatening)
mince
  mincemeat

mincepie
mincer
mincing
mind
  minder
  mindful
  mindless
mine
  miner (for coal)
  mining
mine (*from* my)
mineral
  mineralogist
  mineralogy
minestrone
mingle
  mingling
mingy (stingy)
mini- (small)
  miniature
  minim
  minimal
  minimally
  minimum
  minima (*pl.*)
  minimums (pl.)
  miniskirt
minimise
  minimize
  minimised
  minimized
  minimising
  minimizing
minion
minister
  ministered
  ministerial
  ministerially
  ministering
  minister's
  (of the minister)
  ministers'
  (of the ministers)
  ministrant
  ministration

ministry
  ministries (*pl.*)
mink
minnow
minor (smaller)
  minority
  minorities (*pl.*)
minster (church)
minstrel (singer)
mint
  mint sauce
minuet
minus
  minus sign
minuscule
minute (to make notes)
  minutes
  (notes of meeting)
  minuting
minute (of time)
minute (very small)
  minutely
  minuteness
  minutiae (small details)
minx
mirabile dictu
  (wonderful to relate)
miracle
  miraculous
  miraculously
mirage
mire
  miry (muddy)
mirror
  mirrored
  mirroring
mirth
  mirthful
misadventure
misalliance
misanthrope (man hater)
  misanthropic
  misanthropist
  misanthropy
misapply

misapplication
misapplied
misapplying
misapprehend
  misapprehension
misappropriate
  misappropriating
  misappropriation
misbehave
  misbehaving
  misbehaviour
  misbehavior
miscalculate
  miscalculating
  miscalculation
miscarry
  miscarriage
  miscarried
  miscarries
  miscarrying
miscast
miscegenation
miscellaneous
  miscellany
  miscellanies (*pl.*)
mischance
mischief
  mischievous
  mischievously
miscible (mixable)
misconceive
  misconceiving
  misconception
misconduct
misconstrue
  misconstruction
  misconstruing
miscount
miscreant
misdeed
misdemeanour
  misdemeanor
mise-en-scène
miser
  miserliness

miserly
miser's (of the miser)
misers' (of the misers)
miserable
miserably
misery
miseries (*pl.*)
misfire
misfiring
misfit
misfortune
misgiving
misgovern
misgovernment
misguide
misguidance
misguiding
mishandle
mishandling
mishap
mishmash
misinform
misinterpret
misinterpretation
misjudge
misjudgement
misjudging
misjudgment
mislay
mislaid
mislead
misleading
misled
mismanage
mismanagement
mismanaging
mismatch
misnomer
misogyny
misogynist
misplace
misplacement
misplacing
misprint
mispronounce

mispronouncing
mispronunciation
misquote
misquotation
misquoting
misread
misreading
misrepresent
misrepresentation
misrule
miss
missed
missing
Miss
Misses (*pl.*)
missal (book of prayer)
missel (thrush)
misshapen
missile
mission
missionary
missionaries (*pl.*)
missionary's
(of the missionary)
missionaries'
(of the missionaries)
Mississippi
missive
misspell
misspelling
misspelt
misspelled
misspend
misspent
misstate
misstatement
misstating
mist
mistier
mistily
mistiness
misty
mistake
mistaken
mistakenly

mistaking
mistook
Mister, Mr
Messrs. (*pl.*)
mistime
mistiming
mistletoe
mistral
mistranslate
mistranslating
mistranslation
mistress
mistresses (*pl.*)
mistress's
(of the mistress)
mistresses'
(of the mistresses)
mistrust
mistrustful
misunderstand
misunderstood
misuse
misusing
mite (small insect)
mitigate
mitigating
mitigation
mitre
miter
mitten
mix
mixed
mixer
mixture
mizen, mizzen (sail)
mnemonic
moan
moaner
moat (ditch)
moated
mob
mobbed
mobbing
mobile
mobility

mobilise
mobilize
  mobilisation
  mobilization
  mobilising
  mobilizing
moccasin
Mocha (coffee)
mock
  mockery
  mock-heroic
mode
  modal
  modish
model·
  modelled
  modeled
  modelling
  modeling
  models
  model's (of the model)
  models' (of the models)
moderate
  moderately
  moderating
  moderation
  moderator
modern
  modernisation
  modernization
  modernise
  modernize
  modernising
  modernizing
  modernism
  modernity
modest
  modestly
  modesty
modicum
  modicums (*pl.*)
modify
  modifiable
  modification
  modified

modifies
modifying
modulate
  modulating
  modulation
  modulator
module
  (unit of measurement)
  modular
modulus
  moduli (*pl.*)
modus operandi
mogul
mohair
Mohammed
    (*see* Mahomet)
moiety
moire, moiré (fabric)
moist
  moisten
  moistened
  moistening
  moistness
  moisture
moisturise
  moisturize
  moisturising
  moisturizing
molar
molasses
mole
  molehill
  moleskin
molecule
  molecular
molest
  molestation
mollify
  mollified
  mollifies
  mollifying
mollusc
  mollusk
mollycoddle
  mollycoddling

molten (*from* melt)
molybdenum
moment
  momentarily
  momentary
momentous
momentum
monachal (like a monk)
  monachism
monarch
  (king or emperor)
  monarchical
  monarchy
  monarchies (*pl.*)
  monarch's
    (of the monarch)
  monarchs'
    (of the monarchs)
monastery
  monasteries (*pl.*)
  monastic
  monasticism
Monday
monetary
  monetarism
  monetarist
money
  moneys, monies (*pl.*)
  moneyless
Mongol
  Mongolian
  mongolism
mongoose
  mongooses (*pl.*)
mongrel
monitor
  monitored
  monitoring
monk
monkey
  monkeys (*pl.*)
  monkey's
    (of the monkey)
  monkeys'
    (of the monkeys)

mono- (single)
monochrome
　　　(single colour)
　monochromatic
monocle
monogamy
　monogamist
　monogamous
monogram
monograph
monolith
　monolithic
monologue
monomania
　monomaniac
monoplane
monopoly
　monopolies (*pl.*)
　monopolisation
　monopolization
　monopolise
　monopolize
　monopolising
　monopolizing
　monopolist
　monopolistic
monorail
monosyllable
　monosyllabic
monotheism
monotony
　monotonous
　monotonously
monotype
monoxide
Monseigneur
Monsieur
　Messieurs (*pl.*)
monsoon
monster
　monstrosity
　monstrosities (*pl.*)
　monstrous
montage
month

monthly
month's (of the month)
months' (of the months)
monument
monumental
monumentally
moo
　mooed
　mooing
　moos
mooch
mood
　moodily
　moodiness
　moody
moon
　moonless
　moonlight
　moonlighting
　moonlit
　moonshine
moon (to mope)
moor (a boat)
　moorage
　moored
moor (hill)
moose
moot (not yet decided)
　moot point
mop (to wipe)
　mopped
　mopping
　mops
mope (to feel sad)
　moping
moppet
moral
　morale (state of mind)
　morality
　morally
moralise
　moralize
　moralising
　moralizing
　morally

morass
moratorium
　moratoriums,
　　　　moratoria(*pl.*)
　moratoria (*pl.*)
morbid
　morbidity
　morbidness
mordant
more
　moreover
morganatic
　morganatically
morgue
moribund
morn
　morning
Morocco
　Moroccan
moron
　moronic
morose
　morosely
　moroseness
Morpheus
　　　(god of dreams)
　morphia
　morphine
　morphinism
morphology
　morphological
morris dance
morrow
Morse (code)
morsel
mortal
　mortality
　mortally
mortar
　mortar-board
mortgage
　mortgagee
　(receiver of mortgage)
　mortgaging

159

mortify

mortgagor
  (giver of mortgage)
mortify
  mortification
  mortified
  mortifies
  mortifying
mortise, mortice
mortuary
  mortuaries (*pl.*)
mosaic
  Moslem, Muslim
mosque
mosquito
  mosquitoes (*pl.*)
moss
  mossy
most
  mostly
mote (speck)
motel
motet (hymn)
moth
  moth-eaten
  moth's (of the moth)
  moths' (of the moths)
mother
  mothered
  mother-in-law
  mothers-in-law (*pl.*)
  mother-in-law's
   (of the mother-in-law)
  mothers-in-law's
  (of the mothers-in-law)
  mothering
  motherless
  motherly
  mother's
      (of the mother)
  mothers'
      (of the mothers)
  mother tongue
motif
  motifs (*pl.*)
motion

motionless
motive
  motivate
  motivating
  motivation
motley
motor
  motorboat
  motored
  motoring
  motorise
  motorize
  motorist
  motorway
mottled
motto
  mottoes (*pl.*)
moujik, muzhik
      (Russian peasant)
  muzhik
mould (small fungi)
  mold
  moulder
  molder
  mouldered
  moldered
  mouldering
  moldering
  mouldiness
  moldiness
  mouldy
  moldy
mould (to shape)
  mold
  moulded
  molded
  moulding
  molding
mould (pattern)
  mold
mould (soil)
  mold
moult
  molt
mound

mount
mountain
  mountaineer
  mountainous
mountebank
mourn (to grieve)
  mourned
  mourner
  mournful
  mournfully
  mourning (for the dead)
mouse
  mice (*pl.*)
  mouser
  mousy
moussaka (Greek food)
mousse (fruit cream)
moustache
  mustache
mouth
  mouthed
  mouthful
  mouthfuls (*pl.*)
  mouthing
  mouthpiece
move
  movable
  moveable
  movement
  moving
movie
mow
  mowed
  mower
  mown
  mowed
Mr (mister)
Mrs (missis)
much
mucilage
  mucilaginous
muck
  mucky
muckle, mickle
      (large amount)

mucus (phlegm)
  mucous (slimy)
mud
  muddied
  muddier
  muddy
muddle
  muddle-headed
  muddler
  muddling
mudslinging
muff
muffin
muffle
  muffler
  muffling
mufti
mug
  mugged
  mugger
  mugging
  mugs
mug (large cup)
muggy
mugwump
mulatto
  mulattos, mulattoes (pl.)
  mulattoes (pl.)
mulberry
  mulberries (pl.)
mulch
mulct
mule
  muleteer
  mulish
mulligatawny
mullion (of a window)
  mullioned
multi- (many)
multifarious
multiform
multilateral
  multilaterally
multiple
multiplex

multiplicity
multiply
  multiplication
  multiplied
  multiplier
  multiplying
multiracial
multitude
  multitudinous
mum (silent)
mumble
  mumbling
mumbo-jumbo
mummery
mummy
  mummies (pl.)
  mummified
munch
mundane
municipal
  municipality
  municipalities (pl.)
munificence
  munificent
munition
mural
murder
  murdered
  murderer
  murderer's
    (of the murderer)
  murderers'
    (of the murderers)
  murderess (fem.)
  murdering
  murderous
  murderously
murk
  murkily
  murkiness
  murky
murmur
  murmured
  murmuring
  murmurs

murrain (cattle disease)
muscat
  muscatel
muscle
  muscular
muse (goddess)
muse (to meditate)
  musing
museum
  museums (pl.)
mush
  mushy
mushroom
music
  musical
  musically
  musician
  musician's
    (of the musician)
  musicians'
    (of the musicians)
musk
musket
  musketry
Muslim, Moslem
muslin (cotton cloth)
musquash
mussel (mollusc)
must
  mustn't (must not)
mustang
mustard
muster
  mustered
  mustering
musty
  mustiness
mutable
  mutability
mutation
  mutant
mute
  mutely
mutilate
  mutilating

mutilation
mutilator
mutiny
  mutinies (*pl.*)
  mutineer
  mutinied
  mutinies
  mutinous
  mutinying
mutter
  muttered
  muttering
  mutters
mutton
mutual
  mutually
Muzak
muzzle
  muzzling
muzzy
  muzzily
  muzziness
my
  myself
mycelium
mycology
myelitis
myo- (muscle)
  myocarditis
  myocardium
        (heart muscle)
myo- (shut)
  myopia
  myopic (short-sighted)
myriad
myrmidon
myrrh
myrtle
myself
mystery
  mysteries (*pl.*)
  mysterious
  mysteriously
mystic
  mystical

mysticism
mystify
  mystification
  mystified
  mystifies
mystique
myth
  mythical
mythology
  mythologies (*pl.*)
  mythological
  mythologist
myxomatosis

N

nab
  nabbed
  nabbing
  nabs
nabob
nadir
nag (to scold)
  nagged
  nagger
  nagging
  nags
nag (horse)
naiad
naïve, naïf
  naïveté
nail
naked
  nakedly
  nakedness
namby-pamby
name
  nameable
  namable
  name-dropper
  nameless
  namesake

namely
naming
nanny
  nannies (*pl.*)
  nanny's (of the nanny)
  nannies'
      (of the nannies)
nap
  napping
nape (of neck)
naphtha
  naphthalene
napkin
nappy
  nappies (*pl.*)
narcissus
  narcissi, narcissuses (*pl.*)
  narcissus (*pl.*)
  narcissism
narcosis
narcotic
narrate
  narrating
  narration
  narrative
  narrator
narrow
  narrower
  narrowly
  narrow-minded
  narrowness
nasal
  nasally
nascent
  nascency
nasturtium
  nasturtiums (*pl.*)
nasty
  nastier
  nastily
  nastiness
natal
  natality
natation (swimming)
nation

national
nationalisation
nationalization
nationalise
nationalize
nationalising
nationalizing
nationalism
nationalist
nationalistic
nationality
nationalities (*pl.*)
nationally
nation's (of the nation)
nations' (of the nations)
native
nativity
NATO, N.A.T.O.
natter
  nattered
  natterer
  nattering
  natters
natty (smart)
  nattier
natural
  naturalism
  naturalist
  naturalistic
  naturally
naturalise
  naturalize
  naturalisation
  naturalization
  naturalising
  naturalizing
nature
naught (nothing)
naughty
  naughtier
  naughtily
  naughtiness
nausea
  nauseate
  nauseating

nauseous
nautical
nautilus
  nautiluses, nautili (*pl.*)
naval
  (of ships, navy, etc.)
nave (of church)
navel (umbilicus)
navigate
  navigability
  navigable
  navigating
  navigation
  navigator
navvy (labourer)
  navvies (*pl.*)
  navvying
navy (ships)
  navies (*pl.*)
  navy's (of the navy)
  navies' (of the navies)
nay (no)
N.B. (nota bene)
near
  nearly
  nearby
  nearer
  nearness
  near-sighted
neat
  neater
  neatness
  neatly
nebula
  nebulae, nebulas (*pl.*)
nebulous (vague)
  nebulosity
necessary
  necessarily
necessitate
  necessitating
  necessitous
necessity
  necessities (*pl.*)
neck

neckerchief
necklace
necktie
necros (corpse)
necromancy
necrosis
nectar
nectarine
né (born)
  née (*fem.*)
need
  needful
  needless
  needlessly
  needy
needle
  needlework
  needling
ne'er (never)
ne'er-do-well
nefarious
  nefariously
negate
  negating
  negation
negative
  negatively
neglect
  neglectful
negligé, negligée
negligence
negligent
negligently
negligible
negligibly
negotiate
  negotiable
  negotiating
  negotiation
  negotiator
Negro
  Negroes (*pl.*)
  Negro's (of the Negro)
  Negroes'
    (of the Negroes)

neigh

Negress (*fem.*)
Negresses (*pl.*)
Negress's
        (of the Negress)
Negresses'
        (of the Negresses)
Negroid
neigh (horse's cry)
    neighing
neighbour
    neighbor
    neighbourhood
    neighborhood
    neighbouring
    neighboring
    neighbourliness
    neighborliness
    neighbourly
    neighborly
    neighbour's
        (of the neighbour)
    neighbours'
        (of the neighbours)
neither
Nemesis
neo- (new)
    neoclassic
    neolithic
    neologism
    neology
    neon (gas)
    neophyte (novice)
nephew
    nephew's
        (of the nephew)
    nephews'
        (of the nephews)
nephritis
    nephritic
nepotism
nerve
    nerve-racking
    nerving
    nervy
nervous

nervously
nervousness
nest
nestle
nestling
net
netting
net, nett (weight or price)
net
nether (lower)
nettle
nettlerash
network
neuro- (nerve)
neural
neuralgia
neurasthenia
neurasthenic
neuritis
neurological
neurologist
neurology
neurosis
neurotic
neuter
neutered
neutral
neutralisation
neutralization
neutralise
neutralize
neutralising
neutralizing
neutrality
neutron
never
nevermore
nevertheless
new
new-born
newcomer
newer
newfangled
new-laid
newly

newness
newel
news
    newsagent
    newspaper
    newsworthy
newt
next
nib
nibble
    nibbling
nice
    nicely
    niceness
    nicer
    nicety
    niceties (*pl.*)
niche
nick
nickel
    nickelled
    nickeled
nickname
nicotine
niece
    niece's (of the niece)
    nieces' (of the nieces)
niggard
    niggardly
niggle
    niggling
nigh
night
    nightdress
    nightdresses (*pl.*)
    nightfall
    nightlight
    nightly (every night)
    night porter
    night shift
    night-time
    night watchman
nightingale
nightmare
    nightmarish

nihilism
  nihilistic
nil
nimble
  nimbler
  nimbly
nimbus
  nimbi, nimbuses (*pl.*)
nincompoop
nine
  nineteen
  nineteenth
  ninetieth
  ninety
  nineties (*pl.*)
  ninth
  ninthly
ninny
  ninnies (*pl.*)
nip
  nipped
  nipper
  nipping
  nips
nipple
nirvana
nisi (unless)
nit
  nit-picking
  nitwit
  nitwitted
nitre
  niter
  nitrate
    (salt of nitric acid)
  nitric
  nitrite
    (salt of nitrous acid)
nitrogen
  nitro-glycerine
  nitro-glycerin
  nitrous
nitty-gritty
nob
Nobel prize

noble
  nobility
  nobleman
  nobleman's
    (of the nobleman)
  noblemen's
    (of the noblemen)
  nobler
  nobly
noblesse oblige
nobody
  nobodies (*pl.*)
  nobody's (of nobody)
  nobodies' (of nobodies)
nocturnal
  nocturnally
  nocturne
nod
  nodded
  nodding
  nods
noddle (head)
node
  nodal
nodule (lump)
  nodular
Noel, Noël
noes (those saying no)
noggin (mug)
nogging (brickwork)
nohow (by no means)
noise
  noiseless
  noiselessly
  noisier
  noisily
  noisiness
  noisy
noisome (disgusting)
nomad
  nomadic
nom de plume
nomenclature
nominal
  nominally

nominate
  nominating
  nomination
  nominator
  nominee
  nominative (*grammar*)
nonage
nonagenarian
nonce
  nonce-word
nonchalance
nonchalant
nonchalantly
non-combatant
non-commissioned
non-committal
  non-committally
non compos mentis
non-conductor
nonconformist
non-contributory
non-cooperation
  non-cooperative
nondescript
none
none the less,
                nonetheless
  nonetheless
nonentity
  nonentities (*pl.*)
non-essential
non-existent
nonpareil
nonplussed
  nonplused
nonsense
  nonsensical
  nonsensically
non sequitur
nonsuch, nonesuch
  nonesuch
noodle
nook
noon
no one

noose
normal
 normalisation
 normalization
 normalise
 normalize
 normalising
 normalizing
 normality
 normally
north
 northerly
 northern
 northward
 northwards
nose
 nosey
 nosiness
 nosing
 nosy
nosegay
nostalgia (homesickness)
 nostalgic
nostril
nostrum
 nostrums (*pl.*)
notable
 notability
 notabilities (*pl.*)
 notably
notary
 notaries (*pl.*)
 notary's (of the notary)
 notaries'
  (of the notaries)
notation
notch
 notches (*pl.*)
 notched
 notching
note
 noteworthiness
 noteworthy
 noting
nothing

notice
 noticeable
 noticeably
 noticing
notify
 notifiable
 notification
 notified
 notifies
 notifying
notion
 notional
 notionally
notorious
 notoriety
 notoriously
notwithstanding
nougat
nought (zero)
noun
nourish
 nourishment
nouveau riche
 nouveaux riches (*pl.*)
novel
 novelette
 novelist
 novelist's
  (of the novelist)
 novelists'
  (of the novelists)
novelty
 novelties (*pl.*)
novice
noviciate, novitiate
 novitiate
now
 nowadays
 nowhere
 nowise
noxious
nozzle
nuance
nubile
 nubility

nucleus
 nuclei (*pl.*)
 nuclear
nude
 nudism
 nudist
 nudity
nudge
 nudging
nugatory
nugget
nuisance
null
 nullification
 nullified
 nullifies
 nullify
 nullifying
numb
 numbness
number
 numbered
 numbering
numeral
numerator
numerical
 numerically
numerous
numismatic
 numismatist
numskull
nun
 nunnery
 nunneries (*pl.*)
 nun's (of the nun)
 nuns' (of the nuns)
nuncio
 nuncios (*pl.*)
nuptial
nurse
 nurseling
 nursemaid
 nurse's (of the nurse)
 nurses' (of the nurses)
 nursery

nurseries (*pl.*)
nurseryman
nurserymen (*pl.*)
nursing
nursling
nurture
nurturing
nut
nutcracker
nutty
nutmeg
nutrient
nutriment
nutrition
nutritious
nutritive
nuzzle
nuzzling
nylon
nymph
nymphomania
nymphomaniac

oaf
oafs (*pl.*)
oafish
oak
oaken
oakum (fibre)
oar (of boat)
oasis
oases (*pl.*)
oast
oast-house
oat
oatmeal
oath
oaths (*pl.*)
obbligato
obdurate

obduracy
obdurately
obedient
obedience
obediently
obeisance (bowing)
obelisk
obese (fat)
obesity
obey
obeyed
obituary
obituaries (*pl.*)
object
objection
objectionable
objector
object (thing)
objective
objectively
objectivity
objet d'art
objets d'art (*pl.*)
oblation
oblige
obligation
obligatory
obliging
oblique
obliquely
obliquity
obliterate
obliterating
obliteration
oblivion
oblivious
oblong
obloquy
obloquies (*pl.*)
obnoxious
obnoxiously
obnoxiousness
oboe
oboes (*pl.*)
oboist

obscene
obscenely
obscenity
obscenities (*pl.*)
obscure
obscurely
obscurity
obscurities (*pl.*)
obsequious
(over-respectful)
obsequiously
obsequiousness
obsequy (funeral)
obsequies (*pl.*)
observatory
observatories (*pl.*)
observe
observable
observance
observant
observation
observer
observer's
(of the observer)
observers'
(of the observers)
observing
obsess
obsessed
obsession
obsessive
obsolete
obsolescence
obsolescent
obstacle
obstetric
obstetrician
obstetrics
obstinate
obstinacy
obstinately
obstreperous
obstreperously
obstreperousness
obstruct

obstruction
obstructive
obstructively
obtain
obtainable
obtrude
obtruder
obtruding
obtrusion
obtrusive
obtuse
obtusely
obtuseness
obverse
obviate
obviating
obvious
obviously
occasion
occasional
occasionally
occident (west)
occidental
occlude
occluding
occlusion
occult (to conceal)
occultation
occult (mysterious)
occupant
occupancy
occupation
occupational
occupy
occupied
occupier
occupier's
(of the occupier)
occupiers'
(of the occupiers)
occupies
occupying
occur
occurred
occurrence

occurring
occurs
ocean
oceanic
ocelot (animal)
ochre
ocher
o'clock
oct- (eight)
octagon
octagonal
octane
octave
octavo
octet
October
octogenarian
octopus
octopuses, octopodes
(pl.)
octoroon
ocular
oculist
oculist's (of the oculist)
oculists' (of the oculists)
odd
odder
oddity
oddities (pl.)
oddly
oddment
odds
odds-on
ode
odious (hateful)
odiously
odiousness
odium
odour (smell)
odor
odoriferous
odorous
odourless
odorless
oecumenical, ecumenical

ecumenical
oedema
edema
oesophagus
esophagus
oesophageal
off
offing
off-licence
offal
offence
offense
offend
offender
offensive
offensively
offensiveness
offer
offered
offering
offers
offertory
offhand
offhanded
offhandedly
offhandedness
office
officer
officer's (of the officer)
officers' (of the officers)
official
officialese
officially
officiate
officiating
officious
officiously
officiousness
offprint
offset
offsetting
offshoot
offside
offspring
oft

often
oftener
ogle (to make eyes at)
ogling
ogre (giant)
ogress (*fem.*)
ohm
ohmic
ohmmeter
Ohm's Law
oil
oily
ointment
OK, O.K., okay
old
olden
older
old-fashioned
old maid
old maid's
    (of the old maid)
old maids'
    (of the old maids)
old-maidish
oleander (shrub)
olfaction
olfactory
olig- (few)
oligarch
oligarchy
oligarchies (*pl.*)
oligopoly
oligopolies (*pl.*)
olive
Olympia
Olympian
Olympic
Ombudsman
omega
omelette
omelet
omen
ominous
ominously
omicron

omit
omission
omits
omitted
omitting
omni- (all)
omnibus
omnibuses (*pl.*)
omnipotence
omniscience
omniscient
omnivorous
once
once-over
oncoming
one
oneness
one's (of one)
oneself
onerous
onerousness
one-up
one-upmanship
ongoing
onion
on-line, online
onlooker
only
onomatopoeia
onomatopoeic
onrush
onset
onslaught
onus
onward
onyx
oolite
oolitic
ooze
oozing
opacity
opal
opalescence
opalescent
opaque

opacity
opaquely
open
open-and-shut
opened
open-ended
opener
opening
openly
openness
opera
operatic
operatically
operetta
operate
operability
operable
operating
operation
operational
operationally
operative
operator
ophthalmia
ophthalmic
ophthalmologist
ophthalmology
opiate (drug)
opine
opining
opinion
opinionated
opium
opossum
opossums (*pl.*)
opponent
opportune
opportunely
opportuneness
opportunism
opportunist
opportunity
opportunities (*pl.*)
oppose
opposer

opposing
opposite
opposition
oppress
  oppression
  oppressive
  oppressively
  oppressor
opprobrious
  opprobrium
opt (to choose)
  optative
optic (of the eye)
  optical
  optically
  optician
optimum
  optimisation
  optimization
  optimise
  optimize
  optimising
  optimizing
  optimism
  optimist
  optimistic
  optimistically
option
  optional
  optionally
opulence
  opulent
opus
  opera (*pl.*)
oracle
  oracular
oral
  orally
orange
  orangeade
orang-utan, orang-utang
orate
  orating
  oration
  oratio obliqua

oratio recta
orator (speaker)
oratory (speech-making)
oratorio (sacred opera)
  oratorios (*pl.*)
oratory (chapel)
  oratories (*pl.*)
orb
orbit
  orbital
  orbited
  orbiting
  orbits
orchard
orchestra
  orchestras (*pl.*)
  orchestra's
      (of the orchestra)
  orchestras'
      (of the orchestras)
  orchestrate
  orchestrating
  orchestration
  orchestrator
orchid
ordain
  ordination
ordeal
order
  ordered
  ordering
  orderliness
  orderly
  orders
ordinal (number)
ordinance (decree)
ordinary
  ordinarily
ordinate (*maths.*)
ordination
ordnance (military stores)
  Ordnance Survey
ordure
ore (mineral)
oregano (herb)

organ
  organist
organic
  organically
organise
  organize
  organisation
  organization
  organiser
  organizer
  organising
  organizing
  organism
orgasm
orgy
  orgies (*pl.*)
  orgiastic
oriel (window)
orient (east)
  oriental
  orientally
  orientate
  orientating
  orientation
orifice
origami (paper-folding)
origin
  original
  originality
  originally
originate
  originating
  originator
orison
ormolu
ornament
  ornamental
  ornamentation
ornate
  ornately
ornitho- (bird)
  ornithologist
  ornithology
orotund
orphan

orphanage
orphaned
orphan's
            (of the orphan)
orphans'
            (of the orphans)
orrery
  orreries (*pl.*)
ortho- (right or straight)
  orthodontics
  orthodontist
  orthodox
  orthodoxy
  orthographic
  orthography
  orthopaedic
  orthopedic
ortolan
oscillate
  oscillating
  oscillation
  oscillator
  oscillatory
  oscillogram
  oscillograph
  oscilloscope
osculate (to kiss)
  osculating
  osculation
osier
osmosis
osprey
  ospreys (*pl.*)
  osprey's (of the osprey)
  ospreys'
            (of the ospreys)
oss- (bone)
  osseous
  ossification
  ossified
  ossify
  ossifying
  ossuary
  ossuaries (*pl.*)
ostensible

ostensibly
ostensive
  ostensively
ostentation
  ostentatious
  ostentatiously
osteo- (bone)
  osteo-arthritis
  osteology
  osteopath
  osteopathic
  osteopathy
ostler
ostracise
  ostracize
  ostracising
  ostracizing
  ostracism
ostrich
  ostriches (*pl.*)
  ostriches'
            (of the ostriches)
  ostrich's (of the ostrich)
other
  otherwise
otiose (lazy)
otitis (ear disease)
otter
ottoman
oubliette
ought
  oughtn't (ought not)
ounce
our
  ours
  ourself
  ourselves (*pl.*)
out
  outage
  outer
  outermost
  outing
outbid
  outbidding
outboard

outbound
outbreak
outburst
outcast
outclass
  outclassed
outcome
outcry
  outcries (*pl.*)
outdo
  outdoing
  outdone
outdoors
outerspace, outer space
outfit
  outfitter
  outfitting
outflank
  outflanked
outgoing
outgrow
  outgrew
  outgrown
  outgrowth
outing
outlandish
outlast
outlaw
  outlawry
outlay
outlet
outline
  outlining
outlive
  outliving
outlook
outlying
outmanoeuvre
  outmaneuver
  outmanoeuvring
  outmaneuvring
outmoded
outmost
outnumber
  outnumbered

outnumbering
out-patient
  out-patient's
    (of the out-patient)
  out-patients'
    (of the out-patients)
outpost
outpouring
output
  outputting
outrage
  outrageous
  outrageously
  outraging
outreach
outrider
outrigger
  outrigged
outright
outrun
  outran
  outrunning
outset
outshine
  outshining
  outshone
outside
  outsider
  outsider's
    (of the outsider)
  outsiders'
    (of the outsiders)
outsize
outskirts
outspoken
  outspokenness
outstanding
outstare
  outstaring
out-station
outstay
  outstayed
outstretched
outstrip
  outstripped

outstripping
outstrips
outvote
  outvoting
outward
  outward-bound
  outwardly
outweigh
outwit
  outwits
  outwitted
  outwitting
outworn
oval
ovary
  ovaries (*pl.*)
ovation
oven
over
  overall
overact
overarm
overawe
  overawing
overbalance
  overbalancing
overbearing
overboard
overburden
  overburdened
overcast
overcharge
  overcharged
  overcharging
overcoat
overcome
  overcame
  overcoming
over-confident
overcrowded
overdo
  overdoes
  overdoing
  overdone
  overdid

overdose
  overdosing
overdraft
overdraw
  overdrew
overdress
  overdressed
overdrive
overdue
overeat (to eat too much)
  overate
  overeaten
  overeating
overflow
  overflowed
overground
overgrow
  overgrew
  overgrown
  overgrowth
overhang
  overhanging
  overhung
overhaul
overhead
overhear
  overheard
overheat
  overheated
over-indulgence
overjoy
  overjoyed
overland
overlap
  overlapped
  overlapping
  overlaps
overlay
  overlaid
overleaf
overload
  overloaded
overlook
overnight
overpay

over-paid
over-populate
overpower
  overpowered
  overpowering
overrate (to over-value)
  overrated
  overrating
overreach
over-react
override
  overridden
  overriding
  overrode
overripe
overrule
  overruled
  overruling
overrun
  overran
  overrunning
overseas
oversee
  overseeing
  overseen
  overseer
  overseer's
      (of the overseer)
  overseers'
      (of the overseers)
over-sexed
overshadow
  overshadowed
overshoot
  overshot
oversight
over-simplify
  over-simplification
oversleep
  overslept
overspend
  over-spent
overstate
  overstatement
  overstating

overstay
overstep
  overstepped
  overstepping
over-subscribe
overt
  overtly
overtake
  overtaking
  overtook
overtax
  overtaxing
overthrow
  overthrew
  overthrown
overtime
overtire
  overtired
  overtiring
overtone
overture
overturn
  overturned
overweening
overweight
overwhelm
overwork
overwrought
oviduct
oviparous
ovoid (egg-shaped)
ovulate
  ovulation
ovum (egg cell)
  ova (*pl.*)
owe
  owing
owl
own
  owned
  owner
  owner's (of the owner)
  owners' (of the owners)
  ownership
ox

oxen (*pl.*)
oxalic
  oxalic acid
oxide
oxidise
  oxidize
  oxidisation
  oxidization
  oxidising
  oxidizing
oxtail
oxtongue
oxy-acetylene
oxygen
  oxygenate
  oxygenating
  oxygenation
oyster
  oyster's (of the oyster)
  oysters' (of the oysters)
ozone

P

pace
  pacing
pachyderm
  pachydermatous
pacific (peaceful)
  pacifically
Pacific
pacify
  pacifiable
  pacification
  pacified
  pacifier
  pacifies
  pacifism
  pacifist
  pacifying
pack
  package

packaging
packed
packet (parcel)
pact (treaty)
pad
  padded
  padding
  pads
paddle
  paddler
  paddling
paddock
padlock
  padlocked
padre
  padre's (of the padre)
  padres' (of the padres)
padrone (boss)
paean (thanksgiving)
paed- (child)
  paediatrician
  pediatrician
  paediatrics
  pediatrics
pagan
  paganism
page
  pagination
  paging
pageant
  pageantry
  pageantries (*pl.*)
pagoda
  pagodas (*pl.*)
paid (*from* pay)
  paid-up
pail (bucket)
pain
  painful
  painfully
  painless
  painlessly
  painstaking
paint
  painter

painter's (of the painter)
painters'
  (of the painters)
pair
  paired
paisley
pal (friend)
  pally
  pal's (of the pal)
  pals' (of the pals)
palace
  palatial
palaeo- (ancient)
  palaeographic
  paleographic
  palaeography
  palaeolithic
  paleolithic
  palaeozoic
palate (of mouth)
  palatable (tasting good)
palatial (*from* palace)
palaver
  palavered
  palavering
  palavers
pale (whitish)
  palely
  paleness
  pallor
pale (stake *or* post)
  paling
palette (artist's)
palindrome
palisade
pall (cloth over coffin)
  pall-bearer
pall (to be boring)
  palled
  palling
Palladium
pallet (tool)
pallet (mattress)
palliasse
  paillasse

palliate
  (to ease pain, etc.)
  palliating
  palliation
  palliative
pallid (pale)
pallor (paleness)
palm
  palmist
  palmistry
palm (tree)
palmy (flourishing)
palomino
  palominos (*pl.*)
palpable (obvious)
  palpably
palpate
  (to feel with the hand)
  palpating
  palpation
palpitate (to throb)
  palpitating
  palpitation
palsy
  palsied
paltry
  paltrier
  paltriness
pamper
  pampered
  pampering
pamphlet
  pamphleteer
pan
  pancake
Pan (god of nature)
pan- (all)
  panacea
  panchromatic
  pancreas
  pandemic
  pandemonium
  panegyric
  panoply
  panorama

panoramic
pantechnicon
Pantheon
pantomime
panache (swagger)
panda (animal)
pander (to indulge)
  pandered
  pandering
pane (of glass)
panel
  panelist
  panelled
  paneled
  panelling
  paneling
pang
panic
  panicked
  panicking
  panicky
  panics
  panic-stricken
pannier
panorama
  panoramas (*pl.*)
  panoramic
  panoramically
pansy
  pansies (*pl.*)
  pansy's (of the pansy)
  pansies' (of the pansies)
pant (to breathe quickly)
pantaloon
pantechnicon
pantheism
  pantheistic
Pantheon
panther
  panther's
      (of the panther)
  panthers'
      (of the panthers)
pantile (curved tile)
pantomime

pantry
  pantries (*pl.*)
pants (clothes)
papacy
  papal
paper
  paperback
  papered
  papering
  paperweight
papier mâché
papist
  papistry
paprika
papyrus
  papyri (*pl.*)
par (nominal value)
parable (story)
parabola (curve)
  parabolic
  parabolically
parachute
  parachute's
      (of the parachute)
  parachutes'
      (of the parachutes)
  parachuting
  parachutist
parade
  parading
paradise
paradox
  paradoxical
  paradoxically
paraffin
paragon
paragraph
parakeet, parrakeet
parallax
parallel
  paralleled
  paralleling
  parallelism
  parallelogram
  parallelepiped

paralyse
  paralyze
  paralysing
  paralyzing
  paralysis
  paralytic
parameter
paramilitary
paramount (supreme)
paramour (lover)
paranoia
  paranoiac
  paranoid
parapet
paraphernalia
paraphrase
  paraphrasing
paraplegia (paralysis)
parasite
  parasitic
  parasitical
parasol
paratroops
  paratrooper
paratyphoid
parboil
parcel
  parcelled
  parceled
  parcelling
  parceling
parched (thirsty)
parchment
pardon
  pardonable
  pardoned
  pardoning
pare (to cut)
  paring
paregoric (pain-killer)
parent
  parentage
  parental
  parentally
  parent's (of the parent)

parents' (of the parents)
parenthesis
  parentheses (*pl.*)
  parenthetic
par excellence
pariah (outcast)
parish
  parishes (*pl.*)
  parishioner
Parisian
  Parisienne (*fem.*)
parity
  parities (*pl.*)
park
parka
parlance
    (choice of words)
parley (to discuss)
  parleyed
  parleying
  parleys
parliament
  parliamentarian
  parliamentary
parlour (room)
  parlor
parlous (perilous)
parochial
  parochialism
  parochially
parody
  parodies (*pl.*)
  parodied
  parodies
  parodist
  parodying
parole
paroxysm
  paroxysmal
parquet
  parqueted
  parquetry
parrakeet, parakeet
parricide
  parricidal

parrot
  parrot's (of the parrot)
  parrots' (of the parrots)
parry
  parried
  parries
  parrying
parse
  parsing
parsimonious
parsimony
parsley
parsnip
parson
  parsonage
  parson's (of the parson)
  parsons'
    (of the parsons)
part
  partly
partake
  partaken
  partaker
  partaking
  partook
parterre
parthenogenesis
  parthenogenetic
  parthenogenetically
Parthenon
partial
  partiality
  partially
participate
  participant
  participating
  participation
  participator
participle
  participial
particle
particular
  particularise
  particularize
  particularising

  particularizing
  particularity
  particularly
partisan
partition
  partitioned
  partitioning
partner
  partnered
  partnering
  partner's
    (of the partner)
  partners'
    (of the partners)
  partnership
partridge
part-time
parturition (giving birth)
  parturient
party
  parties (*pl.*)
parvenu
  parvenus (*pl.*)
  parvenue (*fem.*)
  parvenues (*pl.*)
paschal (of Easter)
pass
  passable
  passably
  passed
  passer-by
  passers-by (*pl.*)
  passes
passage
passé
passenger
  passenger's
    (of the passenger)
  passengers'
    (of the passengers)
passim (at various places)
passion
  passionate
  passionately
passive

passively
passiveness
passivity
passport
password
past
past master
paste
pasteboard
pasting
pastel (picture)
pasteurise
pasteurize
pasteurisation
pasteurization
pasteurised
pasteurized
pasteurising
pasteurizing
pastille (lozenge)
pastime
pastor (minister)
pastoral
pastorate
pastor's (of the pastor)
pastors' (of the pastors)
pastry
pastries (*pl.*)
pasture (grazing land)
pasturage
pasty
pasties (*pl.*)
pat
pats
patted
patting
patch
patched
patching
patchwork
patchy
pate (head)
pâté de foie gras
patent (open)
patently

patent (invention, etc.)
patentable
patentee
(holder of patent)
pater- (father)
paterfamilias
paternal
paternalistic
paternally
paternity
paternoster
path
pathless
pathway
path- (suffering)
pathetic
pathetically
pathogenic
pathological
pathologically
pathologist
pathology
pathos
patient (ill person)
patient's (of the patient)
patients'
(of the patients)
patience (calmness)
patient
patiently
patina
patio (open courtyard)
patisserie
patois (dialect)
patriarch
patriarchal
patriarchy
patrician
patricide
patrimony
patrimonies (*pl.*)
patrimonial
patriot
patriotic
patriotically

patriotism
patrol
patrolled
patrolling
patrols
patron
patronage
patroness (*fem.*)
patronise
patronize
patroniser
patronizer
patronising
patronizing
patron's (of the patron)
patrons'
(of the patrons)
patronymic
patten (kind of shoe)
patter (to chatter)
pattered
pattering
patter (to tap)
pattered
pattering
pattern (design)
patterned
patty
patties (*pl.*)
paucity
paunch
paunchy
pauper
pauperism
pauper's (of the pauper)
paupers'
(of the paupers)
pause
pausing
pave
pavement
paving
paviour
pavior
pavilion

paw
  pawed
pawn
  pawnbroker
pay
  paid
  payable
  payee
   (one who gets paid)
  payer (one who pays)
  paying
  paymaster
  payment
  payoff
  payroll
pea
  peas (*pl.*)
  peanut
  pease-pudding
peace
  peaceable
  peaceably
  peaceful
  peacefully
  peacefulness
peach
  peaches (*pl.*)
peacock
  peacock's
   (of the peacock)
  peacocks'
   (of the peacocks)
  peahen (*fem.*)
peak
  (projecting part of cap)
  peaked
peak (top)
  peak-load
peak (to waste away)
  peaky
peal (of bells)
pear
pearl
  pearly
  pearlies (*pl.*)

peasant
  peasantry
  peasant's
   (of the peasant)
  peasants'
   (of the peasants)
peat
pebble
  pebbly
peccadillo
  peccadilloes (*pl.*)
  peccadillos (*pl.*)
peccant (sinning)
pêche Melba
peck
  pecked
  pecking
  peckish (hungry)
pectoral
peculation (embezzlement)
  peculator
peculiar (odd)
  peculiarity
  peculiarities (*pl.*)
  peculiarly
pecuniary (financial)
peda- (boy, child)
  pedagogue (teacher)
  pedagogy
pedal (of bicycle etc.)
  pedalled
  pedaled
  pedalling
  pedaling
  pedals
pedant
  pedantic
  pedantry
peddle (to sell trifles)
  peddling
  pedlar (hawker)
  peddler
  pedlar's (of the pedlar)
  pedlars' (of the pedlars)
pedestal

pedestrian
pedicure
pedigree
pediment
pedlar (hawker)
  peddler
pedometer
peek (to peep)
  peeked
peel (to remove skin)
peep
peer (to stare)
peer (nobleman)
  peerage
  peeress (*fem.*)
  peeress's
   (of the peeress)
  peeresses'
   (of the peeresses)
  peer's (of the peer)
  peers' (of the peers)
peer (equal)
  peer group
  peerless
peeved
  peevish
  peevishness
peewit, pewit
  pewit
peg
  pegged
  pegging
  pegs
pejorative
  pejoratively
Pekinese, Pekingese
pelagic (of open sea)
pelican
pellet
pell-mell
pellucid (clear)
pelmet
pelt (to rain hard)
pelt (animal skin)
pelt (to throw)

pelvis
  pelvic
pen (for cattle)
  penned
  penning
pen (for writing)
penal
  penalisation
  penalization
  penalise
  penalize
  penalised
  penalized
  penalising
  penalizing
  penalty
  penalties (*pl.*)
penance
penchant
pencil
  pencilled
  penciled
  pencilling
  penciling
pendant (hanging jewel)
pendent (hanging)
pending
pendulous (drooping)
pendulum
  pendulums (*pl.*)
penetrate
  penetrability
  penetrable
  penetrating
  penetration
  penetrative
penguin
  penguin's
    (of the penguin)
  penguins'
    (of the penguins)
penicillin
peninsula
  peninsulas (*pl.*)

peninsular
    (of a peninsula)
penis
penitence
  penitent
  penitential
  penitentiary
  penitentiaries (*pl.*)
penknife
  penknives (*pl.*)
pennant
penniless
  pennilessness
pennon
penny
  pennies, pence (*pl.*)
penology (study of crime)
pension
  pensionable
  pensioner
pensive
  pensively
  pensiveness
penta- (five)
  pentagon
  pentagonal
  pentameter
  Pentateuch
  pentathlon
penultimate
  penultimately
penumbra
  penumbrae, penumbras
    (*pl.*)
penury (poverty)
  penurious
peon (labourer)
peony (plant)
  peonies (*pl.*)
people
pep (energy)
pepper
  peppered
  peppering
  peppery

peppermint
pepsin
  peptic
Pepys
  Pepysian
peradventure
perambulate
  perambulating
  perambulation
  perambulator
per annum
per capita
perceive
  perceivable
  perceiving
per cent
  percentage
perception
  perceptible
  perceptibly
  perceptive
perch
perchance
percipience
  percipient
percolate
  percolating
  percolation
  percolator
percuss
  percussed
  percussion
  percussive
perdition
peregrinate (to wander)
  peregrinating
  peregrination
  peregrine
peremptory
  peremptorily
  peremptoriness
perennial
  perennially
perfect
  perfection

perfidy

perfectionist
perfidy
perfidious
perforate
perforating
perforation
perforator
perforce
perform
performance
performer
performer's
(of the performer)
performers'
(of the performers)
perfume
perfumery
perfumeries (*pl.*)
perfuming
perfunctory
perfunctorily
perfunctoriness
pergola
pergolas (*pl.*)
perhaps
peri- (around)
pericardial
pericardium
perimeter
peripatetic
peripheral
periphery
periphrasis
periscope
peritoneum
peritonitis
peril
perilous
perilously
period
periodic
periodical
periodically
periodicity

peripatetic
(walking about)
periphery
peripheral
periscope
perish
perishable
peritonitis
periwinkle
perjure
perjurer
perjuring
perjurious
perjury
perk
perkiness
perky
perks (perquisites)
permafrost
permalloy
permanence
permanency
permanent
permanently
permanganate
permeable
permeability
permeate
permeating
permeation
permission
permissible
permissive
permissiveness
permit
permits
permitted
permitting
permutation
pernicious (injurious)
perniciously
perniciousness
pernickety (fussy)
perorate
(to end a speech)

perorating
peroration
peroxide
perpendicular
perpendicularity
perpendicularly
perpetrate
(to commit crime, etc.)
perpetrating
perpetration
perpetrator
perpetual
perpetually
perpetuate
(to make permanent)
perpetuating
perpetuity
perplex
perplexity
perquisite
per se
persecute
persecuting
persecution
persecutor
persevere
perseverance
persevering
persiflage
persimmon
persist
persistence
persistency
persistent
persistently
person
personable (handsome)
personage
personal
personality
personalities (*pl.*)
personally
person's (of the person)
persons'
(of the persons)

persona grata
  persona non grata
personate
  personating
  personation
  personator
personify
  personification
  personified
  personifies
  personifying
personnel (staff)
perspective
perspicacious (intelligent)
  perspicacity
perspicuous
      (clearly expressed)
  perspicuity
perspire
  perspiration
  perspiring
persuade
  persuadable
  persuader
  persuading
  persuasion
  persuasive
  persuasively
pert
  pertly
  pertness
pertain
pertinacious (persevering)
  pertinaciously
  pertinacity
pertinent (to the point)
  pertinence
perturb
  perturbation
  perturber
peruke (wig)
peruse
  perusal
  perusing
pervious (permeable)

pervade
  pervaded
  pervading
  pervasion
  pervasive
  pervasively
perverse (obstinate)
  perversely
  perversity
pervert (to lead astray)
  perversion
  perverter
  perverting
peseta (Spanish money)
peso (S.American money)
pessary
  pessaries (*pl.*)
pessimism
  pessimist
  pessimistic
  pessimistically
pest
  pesticide
  pestiferous
  pestilence
  pestilent
  pestilential
pester (to annoy)
  pestered
  pesterer
  pestering
pestle
pet
  pets
  pet's (of the pet)
  pets' (of the pets)
  petted
  petting
petal
  petalled
  petaled
petard
peter (to give out)
  petered
  petering

  peters out
petite (small)
petit four (small cake)
petition
  petitioner
petit mal (slight epilepsy)
petit point (embroidery)
petrel (sea-bird)
petr- (stone)
  petrifaction
  petrified
  petrifies
  petrify
  petrifying
petrol
petroleum
petticoat
pettifog
  pettifogged
  pettifogger
  pettifoggery
  pettifogging
pettish (sulky)
petty
  pettier
  pettiest
  pettily
  pettiness
petulance
  petulant
  petulantly
pew
pewit, peewit
  pewit
pewter
pfennig (German money)
phagocyte
phalanx
  phalanges, phalanxes
          (*pl.*)
phallus
  phallic
phantasm
  phantasmagoria
  phantasmal

181

phantasmic
phantom
pharisee
pharisaic
pharmacy
  pharmacies (*pl.*)
  pharmaceutical
  pharmacist
  pharmacologist
  pharmacology
  pharmacopoeia
pharynx
  pharyngeal
  pharyngitis
phase
  phasing
pheasant
  pheasant's
    (of the pheasant)
  pheasants'
    (of the pheasants)
phenacetin
phenobarbitone
  phenobarbital
phenol (type of benzene)
phenomenon
  phenomena (*pl.*)
  phenomenal
  phenomenally
phenyl
  (formed from benzene)
phial, vial (small bottle)
phil-, philo- (loving)
  philander
  philanderer
  philanthropic
  philanthropically
  philanthropist
  philanthropy
  philatelist
  philately
  philharmonic
  philologist
  philology
  philosopher

philosopher's
  (of the philosopher)
philosophers'
  (of the philosophers)
philosophical
philosophically
philosophy
Philistine
philistinism
philtre (love-potion)
  philter
phlebitis
phlegm
  phlegmatic
  phlegmatically
phlox
phobia
phoenix
phon- (voice)
  phone (telephone)
  phonetic
  phonetically
  phoning
  phonograph
phoney (sham)
  phony
phos- (light)
  phosgene
  phosphate
  phosphorescence
  phosphorescent
  phosphoric
  phosphorus
phot- (light)
  photocopier
  photocopy
  photocopies (*pl.*)
  photocopying
  photogenic
  photograph
  photographer
  photographic
  photography
  photometer
  photometric

photometry
photostat
photosynthesis
phrase
  phraseology
  phrasing
phrenetic, frenetic
phrenology
  phrenologist
phthisis
  phthisical
phylactery
  phylacteries (*pl.*)
phylloxera
phylum
  phyla (*pl.*)
phys- (nature)
  physical
  physically
  physician
  physicist
  physics
  physiognomist
  physiognomy
  physiological
  physiologically
  physiologist
  physiology
  physiotherapist
  physiotherapy
  physique
piano
  pianos (*pl.*)
  pianist
  pianoforte
  pianola
  piano's (of the piano)
  pianos' (of the pianos)
  piano (softly)
  pianissimo (very softly)
piastre (Turkish money)
  piaster
piazza
picador (bull-fighter)
picaresque (literary style)

Piccadilly
piccalilli (pickle)
piccaninny (small child)
  pickaninny
  piccaninnies (*pl.*)
  pickaninnies (*pl.*)
piccolo (flute)
  piccolos (*pl.*)
pick
  pickaxe
  pickax
  picker
pick-a-back, piggyback
picket (of strikers)
  picketed
  picketing
picket (long stick)
picket (soldiers or police)
pickle
  pickling
pickpocket
picnic
  picnicked
  picnicker
  picnicking
picric (acid)
pictorial
  pictorially
picture
  picturesque
  picturesquely
  picturesqueness
  picturing
piddle
  piddling
pidgin English
pie
piebald
piece
  piecemeal
  piece-work
  piecing
pièce de résistance
pied-à-terre
pier (at seaside)

pier-head
pierce
  piercing
pierrot
  pierrot's (of the pierrot)
  pierrots'
      (of the pierrots)
  pierrette (*fem.*)
piety
  pietism
  pietist
piezo-electric
  piezo-electricity
piffle
  piffling
pig
  pigged
  piggery
  piggeries (*pl.*)
  pigging
  piggish
  pig-iron
  piglet
  pig's (of the pig)
  pigs' (of the pigs)
  pigsty
  pigsties (*pl.*)
pigeon
  pigeon-hole
  pigeon-holing
  pigeon-toed
piggyback, pick-a-back
pigheaded
  pigheadedness
pigment
  pigmentation
pigtail
  pigtailed
pike (long stick)
  pikestaff
pike (fish)
pilaff, pilaf
pilchard
pile
  pile up

piling
pilfer
pilferage
pilfered
pilferer
pilfering
pilgrim
pilgrimage
pilgrim's
      (of the pilgrim)
pilgrims'
      (of the pilgrims)
pill
pillage
pillager
pillaging
pillar
  pillar-box
pillion
pillory
  pilloried
  pillorying
pillow
pilot
  pilotage
  piloted
  piloting
  pilot's (of the pilot)
  pilots' (of the pilots)
pimpernel
pimple
  pimply
pin
  pinhead
  pinned
  pinning
pinafore
pince-nez
pincers
pinch
  pinched
  pinch-hit (*baseball*)
  pinch-hitter
  pinch-hitting
pincushion

pine (tree)
pine (to waste away)
 pining
pineapple
ping-pong
pinion
 pinioned
 pinioning
pink
pinnace
pinnacle
pinpoint
pint
pin-up
pioneer
 pioneered
 pioneering
 pioneers
pious
 piously
pip
 pipped
 pip-squeak
pipe
 piper
 pipette
 piping
pippin (apple)
piquant
 piquancy
pique (vexation)
piquet (card-game)
pirate
 piracy
 pirate's (of the pirate)
 pirates' (of the pirates)
 piratical
 pirating
pirouette
 pirouetted
 pirouetting
pisc- (fish)
 piscatorial
 piscina (fish pond)
 piscine (bathing pool)

pistachio (nut)
 pistachios (*pl.*)
pistil (of flower)
pistol (fire-arm)
piston (of engine)
pit
 pitted
 pitting
pitch
 pitches (*pl.*)
pitcher (jug)
piteous
 piteously
pitfall
pith
 pithily
 pithiness
 pithy
pittance
pituitary
pity
 pities (*pl.*)
 pitiable
 pitied
 pities
 pitiful
 pitifully
 pitiless
 pitilessly
 pitying
pivot
 pivotal
 pivoted
 pivoting
pixy, pixie
 pixies (*pl.*)
pizza
 pizzeria
pizzicato
placard
placate
 placability
 placable
 placating
 placation

place
 placement
 placing
placebo
 placebos (*pl.*)
placenta
placid
 placidity
 placidly
placket
plage (beach)
plagiarise
 plagiarize
 plagiarising
 plagiarizing
 plagiarism
 plagiarist
plague
 plaguing
plaice (fish)
plaid
plain
 plainclothed
 plainclothes
 plainer
 plainly
 plainness
 plainsong
 plain-spoken
plaint
 plaintiff (prosecutor)
 plaintiffs (*pl.*)
 plaintiff's
  (of the plaintiff)
 plaintiffs'
  (of the plaintiffs)
plaintive (sad)
 plaintively
 plaintiveness
plait (of hair)
plan
 planned
 planner
 planning
 plans

planchette
plane
  planing
planet
  planetarium
  planetaria,
      planetariums(*pl.*)
  planetary
plank
plankton
plant
  planter
plantain
plantation
plaque
plasma
plaster
  plastered
  plasterer
  plastering
plastic
  plastically
  plasticine
  plasticity
plate
  plateful
  platefuls (*pl.*)
  plate-glass
  plating
plateau
  plateaus, plateaux (*pl.*)
platform
platinum
platitude
  platitudinous
platonic
  platonically
platoon
platter
platypus
  platypuses (*pl.*)
plaudit
plausible
  plausibility
  plausibly

play
  player
  playfellow
  playful
  playfully
  playfulness
  playgoer
  playgoing
  playmate
  play off
  playwright
  playwright's
      (of the playwright)
  playwrights'
      (of the playwrights)
plaza
plea
plead
  pleader
pleasant
  pleasantly
  pleasantness
  pleasantry (joke)
  pleasantries (*pl.*)
please
  pleased
  pleasing
pleasure
  pleasurable
  pleasurably
pleat
plebeian
plebiscite
pledge
  pledging
Pleistocene
plenary
plenipotentiary
  plenipotentiaries (*pl.*)
plenitude
plenteous
  plenteously
plenty
  plentiful
  plentifully

  plentifulness
plethora
  plethoric
pleura
  pleural
  pleurisy
pliable
  pliability
pliant
  pliancy
pliers
plight
Plimsoll line
plimsolls (canvas shoes)
plinth
Pliocene
plod
  plodded
  plodder
  plodding
  plods
plonk (cheap wine)
plop
  plopping
plot
  plots
  plotted
  plotter
  plotting
plough
  plow
plover
ploy
pluck
  pluckier
  pluckily
  plucky
plug
  plugged
  plugging
  plugs
plum
  plummy
  plum-pudding
  plumage

plumb (to measure depth)
plumbago
plumber
  plumbing
plume
plummet
  plummeted
  plummeting
plump
  plumper
  plumpness
plunder
  plundered
  plunderer
  plundering
plunge
  plunger
  plunging
pluperfect
plural
  pluralism
  plurality
plus
plush
  plushy
plutocracy
  plutocracies (*pl.*)
  plutocrat
  plutocratic
plutonium
ply
  plied
  plies
  plying
  plywood
pneum- (wind, lung)
  pneumatic
  pneumonia
poach (to steal game)
  poached
  poacher
  poacher's
      (of the poacher)
  poachers'
      (of the poachers)

poaches
poach (to cook)
  poached
  poaches
  poaching
pock
  pockmark
  pock-marked
pocket
  pocket-book (wallet)
  pocketed
  pocketing
pod
podge
  podgy
podium
  podia (*pl.*)
  podiums (*pl.*)
poem
poesy
poet
  poetic
  poetical
  poetically
  poetry
  poet's (of the poet)
  poets' (of the poets)
pogrom
poignant
  poignancy
  poignantly
poinsettia
point
  point-blank
  pointed
  pointedly
  pointless
  pointlessly
poise
poison
  poisoned
  poisoner
  poisoning
  poisonous
poke

poker
poking
poky
polar
  polarisation
  polarization
  polarise
  polarize
  polarising
  polarizing
  polarity
pole
polemic
  polemical
  polemically
police
  policing
  policeman
  policemen (*pl.*)
  policeman's
      (of the policeman)
  policemen's
      (of the policemen)
  policewoman
  policewomen (*pl.*)
  policewoman's
      (of the policewoman)
  policewomen's
      (of the policewomen)
policy
  policies (*pl.*)
poliomyelitis
polish
polite
  politely
  politeness
  politer
politic
  political
  politically
  politician
  politician's
      (of the politician)
  politicians'
      (of the politicians)

polity
polka
poll
  polled
  polling
  polls
  pollster
pollard
pollen
pollinate
  pollinating
  pollination
  pollinator
pollute
  pollutant
  polluting
  pollution
polo
polonaise
polonium
polony
  polonies (*pl.*)
poltergeist
poltroon
poly- (many)
  polyandrous
  polyandry
  polyanthus
  polychrome
  polychromatic
  polyester
  polygamist
  polygamous
  polygamously
  polygamy
  polyglot
  polygon
  polymer
  polymerisation
  polymerization
  polymerise
  polymerize
  polyp
  polyphonic
  polyphony

polypus
polystyrene
polysyllabic
polytechnic
polythene
polyunsaturated
pomade
pomatum
pomegranate
pommel (of saddle)
pomp
  pomposity
  pompous
  pompously
Pompeii
  Pompeian
poncho
  ponchos (*pl.*)
pond
ponder (to consider)
  pondered
  pondering
  ponderous (heavy)
poniard
pontiff
  pontiffs (*pl.*)
  pontifical
pontificate
  pontificating
  pontification
pontoon
pony
  ponies (*pl.*)
  ponies' (of the ponies)
  pony's (of the pony)
  pony-tail
poodle
  poodle's (of the poodle)
  poodles'
    (of the poodles)
pooh-pooh
pool
  pooled
poop
poor

poorer
poorly
poorness
pop
popcorn
pop-eyed
popped
popper
popping
pops
pope
popery
pope's (of the pope)
popes' (of the popes)
poplar (tree)
poplin
poppet
poppy
  poppies (*pl.*)
populace
popular
  popularisation
  popularization
  popularise
  popularize
  popularising
  popularizing
  popularity
  popularly
populate
  populating
  population
  populous
porcelain
porch
  porches (*pl.*)
porcupine
pore
(to look, think intently)
  poring
pore (of skin)
pork
  porker
pornography
  pornographer

pornographic
pornographically
porous
  porosity
porphyry
porpoise
  porpoise's
      (of the porpoise)
  porpoises'
      (of the porpoises)
porridge
  porringer
port (harbour)
port (wine)
portable
  portability
portal (gateway)
portcullis
portend (to foreshadow)
portent (omen)
  portentous
porter (for luggage)
  porterage
porter (beer)
portfolio
  portfolios (*pl.*)
porthole
portico
  porticoes, porticos (*pl.*)
portion
portly
  portlier
  portliness
portmanteau
  portmanteaus,
      portmanteaux(*pl.*)
portrait
  portraiture
portray
  portrayal
  portrayed
Portugal
  Portuguese
pose
  poser

posing
posh
position
  positioned
  positioning
positive
  positively
  positivism
  positivist
positron
posse
possess
  possession
  possessive
  possessively
  possessiveness
  possessor
possible
  possibility
  possibilities (*pl.*)
  possibly
post (letters, etc.)
  postage
  postal order
  poste restante
  post-haste
  postman
  postmen (*pl.*)
  postman's
      (of the postman)
  postmen's
      (of the postmen)
  postmark
  postmaster
  postmaster's
      (of the postmaster)
  postmasters'
      (of the postmasters)
  post office
  post-paid
post- (after)
  post-date
  post-dating
posterior
posterity

postgraduate
posthumous
posthumously
post-impressionism
post-impressionist
post-mortem
post-natal
postpone
postponement
postponing
postscript
poster
postulate
  postulant
  postulating
  postulation
posture
  postural
  posturer
  posturing
posy
  posies (*pl.*)
pot
  potted
  potter
  potting
potable (drinkable)
  potation
potash
  potassium
potato
  potatoes (*pl.*)
pot-belly
  pot-bellied
pot-boiler
potency
potent
  potently
potentate
potential
  potentiality
  potentially
potentiometer
pother
pot-hole

pot-holer
pot-holing
potion (drink)
pot-pourri
pottage
potter
  pottered
  potterer
  putterer
  pottering
pottery
  potteries (*pl.*)
potty (crazy)
  pottier
  pottily
pouch
  pouches (*pl.*)
pouffe (hassock)
  pouf
poultice
  poulticing
poultry
  poulterer
pounce
  pouncing
pound
  poundage
pound (to beat)
poundal (unit)
pour
  poured
  pouring
pourboire (tip)
pourparler (discussion)
pout
  pouter
poverty
powder
  powdered
  powdering
  powdery
power
  powered
  powerful
  powerfully

powerless
powerlessness
powwow
pox
practicable (possible)
  practicability
practical (ingenious)
  practicality
  practicalities (*pl.*)
  practically (almost)
practice (doctor's, etc.)
  practitioner
practise (piano, etc.)
  practice
  practising
  practicing
pragmatic
  pragmatical
  pragmatically
  pragmatism
prairie
praise
  praiseworthy
  praising
praline
prance
  prancing
prank
prate
  prating
prattle
  prattler
  prattling
prawn
pray (to say prayers)
  prayed
  prayer
  praying
preach
  preached
  preacher
  preacher's
      (of the preacher)
  preachers'
      (of the preachers)

preaches
preamble
prearrange
  prearrangement
  prearranging
prebend
  prebendary
  prebendaries (*pl.*)
precarious
  precariously
  precariousness
precaution
  precautionary
precede (to go before)
  precedence
  precedent
  preceding
precentor
precept
precession (*from* precede)
precinct
precious
precipice
precipitate
  precipitant
  precipitately
  precipitating
  precipitation
  precipitous
  precipitously
précis (shortened version)
  précis (*pl.*)
precise (exact)
  precisely
  precision
preclude
  precluding
  preclusive
precocious
  precociousness
  precocity
precognition
preconceived
  preconception
precursor

precursory
predator
  predacious
  predatory
predecease (to die before)
  predeceasing
predecessor
predestine
  predestination
predetermined
predicament
predicate (to confirm)
  predicating
  predication
predicate (*grammar*)
predict (to prophesy)
  predictable
  predictably
  prediction
predigest
  predigestion
predilection
predispose
  predisposing
  predisposition
predominant
  predominance
  predominantly
predominate
  predominating
pre-eminent
  pre-eminently
  pre-eminence
pre-empt
  pre-emption
  pre-emptive
preen
pre-exist
  pre-existence
  pre-existent
  pre-existing
prefab
prefabricate
  prefabricating
  prefabrication

preface
  prefacing
  prefatory
prefect
  prefectorial
  prefect's (of the prefect)
  prefects'
      (of the prefects)
  prefecture
prefer
  preferable
  preferably
  preference
  preferential
  preferentially
  preferment
  preferred
  preferring
  prefers
prefix
  prefixes (*pl.*)
  prefixed
pregnant
  pregnancy
  pregnancies (*pl.*)
prehensile
  prehension
prehistoric
  prehistorically
  prehistory
prejudge
  prejudgement
  prejudging
  prejudgment
prejudice
  prejudicial
  prejudicially
  prejudicing
prelate
  prelate's (of the prelate)
  prelates'
      (of the prelates)
  prelacy
  prelacies (*pl.*)
preliminary

preliminaries (*pl.*)
preliminarily
prelude
  preluding
premarital
premature
  prematurely
  prematurity
premeditate
  premeditating
  premeditation
premier (prime minister)
  premiership
premier (most important)
première (first night)
premise, premiss
    (statement in logic)
  premises, premisses (*pl.*)
premises (houses, etc.)
premium
premonition
  premonitory
prenatal
prentice
preoccupy
  preoccupation
  preoccupied
  preoccupying
prepare
  preparation
  preparative
  preparatorily
  preparatory
  preparedness
  preparing
prepay
  prepaid
  prepayable
  prepayment
  prepays
preponderance
  preponderant
  preponderantly
  preponderate
  preponderating

preposition
prepossess
  prepossessing
preposterous
  preposterously
prerequisite
prerogative
presage
  presaged
  presaging
presbyter
  Presbyterian
prescience
  prescient
prescribe (medicine, etc.)
  prescribing
  prescription
  prescriptive
present (gift)
present (to give)
  presentation
present (being there)
  presence
present (now)
  presently
present (to introduce)
  presentable
presentiment (expectation)
preserve
  preservation
  preservative
  preserver
  preserving
preside
  presidency
  presidencies (*pl.*)
  president
  presidential
  president's
    (of the president)
  presidents'
    (of the presidents)
  presidial
  presiding
  presidium

press
  pressed
  pressure
  pressurisation
  pressurization
  pressurise
  pressurize
  pressurising
  pressurizing
prestidigitator (conjurer)
  prestidigitation
prestige
  prestigious
presto (fast)
  prestissimo (very fast)
pre-stress
  pre-stressed
presume
  presumably
  presuming
  presumption
  presumptive
  presumptuous
presuppose
  presupposing
  presupposition
pretence
  pretense
pretend
  pretender
  pretension
  pretentious
  pretentiously
preterite
  preterit
preternatural
pretext
pretty
  prettier
  prettily
  prettiness
prevail
  prevailing
  prevalence
  prevalent

prevaricate
  prevaricating
  prevarication
  prevaricator
prevent
  preventable,
            preventible
  prevention
  preventive,
            preventative
preview
previous
  previously
pre-war
prey (plunder)
  preyed
  preying
price
  priceless
  pricing
prick
  pricker
prickle
  prickling
  prickly
pride
priest
  priesthood
  priestly
  priest's (of the priest)
  priests' (of the priests)
prig
  priggish
prim
  primly
  primmer
  primmest
primacy
prima donna
  prima donnas (*pl.*)
  prima donna's
    (of the prima donna)
  prima donnas'
    (of the prima donnas)
prima facie

primary
  primarily
primate
  primacy
prime
  prime minister
  priming
primeval
primitive
  primitively
primogeniture
      (being first-born)
  primogenitor
      (earliest ancestor)
primordial
  primordially
primrose
primula
  primulas (*pl.*)
primus (stove)
prince
  princely
  prince's (of the prince)
  princes' (of the princes)
  princess
  princesses (*pl.*)
  princess's
      (of the princess)
  princesses'
      (of the princesses)
  principality
  principalities (*pl.*)
principal (chief)
  principally
principle (moral code)
print
  printable
  printer
  printer's (of the printer)
  printers'
      (of the printers)
prior (before)
  priority
  priorities (*pl.*)
prior (monk)

prioress (*fem.*)
priory
priories (*pl.*)
prise, prize
      (to force open)
prize
prising, prizing
prizing
prism
  prismatic
prison
  prisoner
  prisoner's
      (of the prisoner)
  prisoners'
      (of the prisoners)
pristine
private
  privacy
  privateer
  privately
privation
privative
privet (hedge)
privilege
  privileged
privy
  Privy Council
  Privy Councillor
prize (reward)
  prize fight
  prize fighter
prize (to value)
  prizing
probable
  probability
  probably
probate
probation
  probationer
probe
  probing
probity (integrity)
problem
  problematic

problematical
problematically
proboscis
  proboscises,
      proboscides(*pl.*)
proceed
  procedural
  procedure (method)
  proceeding
process
  processes (*pl.*)
  processor
procession
  processional
proclaim
  proclaimed
  proclamation
proclivity
  proclivities (*pl.*)
procrastinate
  procrastinating
  procrastination
  procrastinator
procreate
  procreating
  procreative
  procreator
proctor
  proctorial
  proctor's
      (of the proctor)
  proctors'
      (of the proctors)
procure
  procurable
  procuration
  procurator
  procuring
prod
  prodded
  prodding
  prods
prodigal
  prodigality
  prodigally

prodigy
  prodigies (*pl.*)
  prodigious
  prodigiously
  prodigiousness
produce
  producer
  producing
product
  production
  productive
  productively
  productiveness
  productivity
profane
  profanation
  profanely
  profanity
  profanities (*pl.*)
profess
  professed
  professes
  professing
  profession
  professional
  professionalism
  professionally
  professor
  professor's
      (of the professor)
  professors'
      (of the professors)
  professorial
proffer
  proffered
  proffering
proficiency
  proficient
  proficiently
profile
profit
  profitability
  profitable
  profitably
  profited

profiteer
  profiteered
  profiteering
  profiting
  profitless
  profits
profligate
  profligacy
  profligately
pro forma
profound
  profounder
  profundity
  profoundly
profuse
  profusely
  profusion
progenitor (ancestor)
  progenitrix (*fem.*)
  progeniture
progeny
prognosis
  prognoses (*pl.*)
  prognostic
  prognosticating
  prognostication
program (for a computer)
programm
        (usual spelling)
  programmed
  programmer
  programming
progress
  progresses
  progression
  progressive
  progressively
prohibit
  prohibited
  prohibiting
  prohibition
  prohibitionist
  prohibitive
  prohibitively
project

projection
  projector
projectile
prolapse
proletarian
  proletariat
proliferate
  proliferating
  proliferation
prolific
  prolifically
  prolification
prolix (long-winded)
  prolixity
prologue
prolong
  prolongating
  prolongation
promenade
  promenader
  promenading
prominence
  prominent
  prominently
promiscuous
  promiscuity
  promiscuously
promise
  promising
  promissory
promontory
  promontories (*pl.*)
promote
  promoter
  promoter's
      (of the promoter)
  promoters'
      (of the promoters)
  promoting
  promotion
prompt
  prompter
  promptitude
  promptly
  promptness

promulgate
  promulgating
  promulgation
  promulgator
prone
prong
  pronged
pronoun
pronounce
  pronounceable
  pronouncement
  pronouncing
  pronunciation
proof
  proof-reader
  proof-reader's
    (of the proof-reader)
  proof-readers'
    (of the proof-readers)
  proof-reading
prop
  propped
  propping
  props
propaganda
  propagandist
propagate
  propagating
  propagation
  propagator
propel
  propellant (rocket fuel)
  propellent
  propelled
  propeller
  propelling
  propels
propensity
  propensities (*pl.*)
proper
  properly
property
  properties (*pl.*)
  propertied
prophecy (prediction)

prophecies (*pl.*)
prophesy (to predict)
  prophesied
  prophesies
  prophesying
prophet
  prophetic
  prophetically
prophylactic
  prophylaxis
propinquity
propitiate
  propitiating
  propitiator
  propitiatory
  propitious
  propitiously
proponent
proportion
  proportional
  proportionally
  proportionate
propose
  proposal
  proposer
  proposing
  proposition
propound
proprietary
    (legally owned)
proprietor (owner)
  proprietor's
    (of the proprietor)
  proprietors'
    (of the proprietors)
  proprietress (*fem.*)
  proprietress's
    (of the proprietress)
  proprietresses'
    (of the proprietresses)
propriety (decency)
  proprieties (*pl.*)
propulsion
  propulsive
pro rata

prorogue
  prorogation
  proroguing
prosaic
  prosaically
proscenium
proscribe (to outlaw)
  proscribing
  proscription
  proscriptive
prose
  prosily
  prosiness
  prosy
prosecute
  prosecution
  prosecutor
  prosecutor's
    (of the prosecutor)
  prosecutors'
    (of the prosecutors)
proselyte
  proselytise
  proselytize
  proselytiser
  proselytizer
  proselytising
  proselytizing
  proselytism
prosody
prospect
  prospective
  prospector
  prospectus
  prospectuses (*pl.*)
prosper
  prospered
  prospering
  prosperity
  prosperous
prostate (gland)
prostitute
  prostituting
  prostitution
prostrate (lying flat)

prostration
protagonist
protean (variable)
protect
  protection
  protective
  protector
  protectorate
protégé
protein (food chemical)
pro tempore, pro tem
protest
  protestation
  protester, protestor
Protestant
  Protestantism
  Protestant's
    (of the Protestant)
  Protestants'
    (of the Protestants)
proto- (first)
  protocol
  proton
  protoplasm
  prototype
  protozoon
  protozoa (pl.)
protract
  protractor
protrude
  protruding
  protrusion
protuberance
  protuberant
proud
  prouder
  proudly
prove
  provable
  proved
  proven (in Law)
  proving
provenance
provender
proverb

proverbial
proverbially
provide
  provider
  providing
providence
  provident
  providential
  providentially
province
  provincial
  provincialism
provision
  provisional
  provisionally
proviso
  provisos (pl.)
  provisory
provocation
  provocative
  provocatively
provoke
  provoking
provost
prow
prowess
prowl
  prowler
proximate (nearest)
proximity
proxy
  proxies (pl.)
prude
  prudery
  prudish
prudent
  prudence
  prudential
  prudentially
prune
(to trim a plant or tree)
  pruner
  pruning
prune (dried plum)
prurience

prurient
prussic
pry
  pried
  pries
  prying
psalm
  psalmist
  psalter (book of psalms)
pseudo- (false)
  pseudonym
  pseudonymity
  pseudonymous
  pseudonymously
psittacosis (parrot disease)
psych- (soul)
  psyche
  psychedelic
  psychiatric
  psychiatrist
  psychiatry
  psychic
  psychoanalysing
  psychoanalyzing
  psychoanalysis
  psychoanalyst
  psychoanalytic
  psychoanalytical
  psychological
  psychologist
  psychology
  psychopath
  psychopathic
  psychosis
  psychoses (pl.)
  psychosomatic
ptarmigan
pterodactyl
ptomaine
puberty
pubescence
  pubescent
pubis
  pubic
public

publican
publication
publicise
publicize
publicising
publicizing
publicist
publicity
publish
  publisher
  publisher's
    (of the publisher)
  publishers'
    (of the publishers)
puce
puck
  puckish
pucker (to wrinkle)
  puckered
  puckering
pudding
puddle
puerile
  puerilely
  puerility
puerperal
puff
  puffiness
  puffy
puffin (sea-bird)
pug
  pug's (of the pug)
  pugs' (of the pugs)
pugilism
  pugilist
pugnacious
  pugnaciously
  pugnacity
puisne (judge)
pukka
puling (whining)
pull
  pulled
  pulls
pullet

pulley
  pulleys (*pl.*)
pullulate (to sprout)
  pullulating
pulmonary
pulp
pulpit
pulsar (star)
pulsate
  pulsating
  pulsation
pulse
  pulseless
  pulsing
pulverise
  pulverize
  pulverisation
  pulverization
  pulverising
  pulverizing
puma
  pumas (*pl.*)
pumice
pummel
  pummelled
  pummeled
  pummelling
  pummeling
  pummels
pump
pumpernickel
pumpkin
pun
  punned
  puns
  punster
punch
punctilious
  punctiliously
  punctiliousness
punctual
  punctuality
  punctually
punctuate
  punctuating

punctuation
puncture
  punctured
  puncturing
pundit
pungent
  pungency
  pungently
punish
  punishable
  punished
  punishes
  punishment
punitive
punnet (small basket)
punt
  punter
puny
  punier
pup
  puppy
  puppies (*pl.*)
  puppy's (of the puppy)
  puppies'
    (of the puppies)
pupa
  pupae (*pl.*)
  pupate
  pupating
  pupation
pupil (at school)
  pupil's (of the pupil)
  pupils' (of the pupils)
pupil (of the eye)
puppet
  puppeteer
  puppetry
  puppet's (of the puppet)
  puppets'
    (of the puppets)
purblind
purchase
  purchasable
  purchaser

purchaser's
(of the purchaser)
purchasers'
(of the purchasers)
purchasing
purdah
pure
purely
purer
purée (food)
purgatory
purgatorial
purge
purgation
purgative
purged
purging
purify
purification
purified
purifier
purifies
purifying
purism
purist
Puritan
puritanic
puritanical
puritanism
purity
purl (in knitting)
purloin
purple
purport
purpose
purposeful
purposeless
purposely
purr
purred
purse
purser
pursue
pursuance
pursuant

pursuing
pursuit
purulence
purulent
purvey (to provide)
purveyance
purveyor
purview (scope)
pus (from wound)
push
pushed
pusher
pushes
push-over
pusillanimity
pusillanimous
puss (cat)
pussy
pussies (pl.)
pussy's (of the pussy)
pussies' (of the pussies)
pustule
put (to place)
puts
putting
putative
putrefy
putrefaction
putrefied
putrefying
putrescence
putrescent
putrid
putt (in golf)
putted
putter
putting
putts
puttee (leggings)
putty (for glazing)
puzzle
puzzlement
puzzler
puzzling
pyelitis

pygmy
pygmies (pl.)
pyjamas
pajamas
pylon
pyorrhoea
pyorrhea
pyramid
pyramidal
pyr- (fire)
pyre (funeral pile)
pyrites
pyrotechnics
python

quack (charlatan)
quackery
quack (duck's)
quadr- (four)
quadrangle
quadrangular
quadrant
quadratic
quadrature
quadrilateral
quadrille
quadruped
quadruple
quadruplet
quadruplex
quadruplicate
quadruplicating
quadruplication
quadrag- (forty)
quadragenarian
Quadragesima
quaff
quaffed
quaffing
quaffs

quagmire
quail
  quailed
  quailing
quaint
  quainter
  quaintly
  quaintness
quake
  quaking
Quaker
qualify
  qualification
  qualified
  qualifies
  qualifying
qualitative
  qualitatively
quality
  qualities (*pl.*)
qualm
quandary
  quandaries (*pl.*)
quango
  quangos (*pl.*)
quantify
  quantifiable
  quantification
  quantified
  quantifying
quantity
  quantities (*pl.*)
  quantitative
  quantitatively
quantum
  quanta (*pl.*)
quarantine
quarrel
  quarrelled
  quarreled
  quarrelling
  quarreling
  quarrels
  quarrelsome
quarry (excavation)

quarries (*pl.*)
quarrying
quarry (victim)
quart
quarter
  quartered
  quartering
  quarterly
  quartermaster
  quartermaster's
    (of the quartermaster)
  quartermasters'
    (of the quartermasters)
quartet, quartette
quarto
quartz
  quartzite
quasar (star)
quash
quasi- (almost)
Quaternary
quatrain
quaver (to tremble)
  quavered
  quavering
quaver (musical note)
quay
quean (hussy)
queasy
  queasiness
queen (sovereign)
  queenly
  queen's (of the queen)
  queens' (of the queens)
queer
  queered
  queerer
  queering
  queerly
quell
  quelled
quench
querulous
  querulously
  querulousness

query
  queries (*pl.*)
  queries
  queried
  querying
quest
question
  questionable
  questionably
  questioned
  questioner
  questioning
  questionnaire
queue
  queued
  queuer
  queuing
quibble
  quibbler
  quibbling
quick
  quicker
  quickly
  quickness
  quicksand
  quicksilver
quicken
quid pro quo
quiescence
  quiescent
quiet
  quieten
  quietened
  quietening
  quieter
  quietly
  quietude
quietus
quiff
quill
quilt
quince
quinine
quinq- (five)
  quinquennial

quinquennium
quinsy
quint- (fifth)
quintessence
quintet
quintette
quintuple
quintuplet
quip
quipped
quipping
quips
quire (of paper)
quirk
quisling
quit
quits
quitted
quit (he, she)
quitter
quitting
quite
quittance
quiver (to shake)
quivered
quivers
quiver (arrow case)
qui vive
Quixote
quixotic
quixotically
quixotism
quiz
quizzes (*pl.*)
quizzed
quizzes
quizzical
quizzically
quizzing
quod (prison)
quoit
quorum
quorums (*pl.*)
quota
quotas (*pl.*)

quote
quotable
quotation
quoting
quotidian (daily)
quotient

R

rabbi (Jewish preacher)
rabbis (*pl.*)
rabbinical
rabbi's (of the rabbi)
rabbis' (of the rabbis)
rabbit
rabble (mob)
rabid
rabidly
rabies (disease of dogs)
race
racecourse
racehorse
racer
race-track
racily
racing
racy
raceme (of flowers)
racial
racialism
racialist
racially
racism
racist
rack
racket (disturbance)
racket, racquet (tennis)
racket (swindle)
racketeer
raconteur
racoon, raccoon
radar

radial
radially
radiant
radiance
radiantly
radiate
radiating
radiation
radiator
radical
radicalism
radically
radio
radios (*pl.*)
radioactive
radioactivity
radioed
radioes
radiogram
radiographer
radiography
radioisotope
radiologist
radiology
radish
radishes (*pl.*)
radium
radius
radii, radiuses (*pl.*)
raffia
raffish
raffle
raffling
raft
rafter (of a roof)
rag
ragged
rag (to tease)
ragged
ragging
rags
ragamuffin
ragamuffin's
(of the ragamuffin)

ragamuffins'
   (of the ragamuffins)
rage
  raging
raglan
ragout
ragtime
raid
  raider
rail
  railroad
  railway
rail (to scold)
  railing
  raillery (teasing)
raiment
rain (wet weather)
  rainbow
  rain-check
  raincoat
  rainfall
  rainless
  rainy
raise
  raising
raisin (dried grape)
raison d'être
rajah, raja
rake
  raking
  rakish
rallentando
    (becoming slower)
rally
  rallies (pl.)
  rallied
  rallies
  rallying
ram
  rammed
  rammer
  ramming
  ramrod
  rams
ramble

rambler
rambling
ramekin, ramequin
ramify
  ramification
  ramified
  ramifies
ramp
rampage
  rampaging
rampant
  rampancy
rampart
ramshackle
ran (from run)
ranch
  ranches (pl.)
  rancher
rancid
rancour
  rancor
  rancorous
random
  randomly
rang (from ring)
range
  ranging
  rangy
rank
  ranker
rankle
  rankling
ransack
  ransacked
ransom
  ransomed
  ransoming
rant
rap (to knock)
  rapped
  rapping
  raps
rapacious
  rapacity
rape (to violate)

raping
rapist
rape (plant)
rapid
  rapidity
  rapidly
rapier
rapine (robbery)
rapport (close connection)
rapprochement
rapscallion
rapt (enraptured)
rapture
  rapturous
  rapturously
rare
  rarefaction
  rarefied
  rarefy
  rarefying
  rarer
  rarely
  rarity
  rarities (pl.)
rare (underdone)
rarebit (Welsh)
rascal
  rascality
  rascal's (of the rascal)
  rascals' (of the rascals)
rase, raze (to destroy)
  rasing, razing
rash (reckless)
  rashly
rash (on skin)
  rashes (pl.)
rasher (bacon)
rasp
raspberry
  raspberries (pl.)
rat
  rats
  ratted
  ratting
ratchet

rate
  ratable
  rateable
  ratepayer
  rating
rather
ratify
  ratification
  ratified
  ratifies
  ratifying
ratio
  ratios (*pl.*)
ratiocinate
  ratiocinating
  ratiocination
ration
  rationed
  rationing
rational (reasonable)
  rationale (basic reason)
  rationality
  rationally
rationalise
  rationalize
  rationalisation
  rationalization
  rationalising
  rationalizing
  rationalism
rattan
  ratan
rattle
  rattlesnake
  rattling
raucous
  raucously
  raucousness
ravage
  ravager
  ravaging
rave
  raving
ravel
  ravelled

raveled
ravelling
raveling
raven
  raven's (of the raven)
  ravens' (of the ravens)
ravenous
  ravenously
ravine (gorge)
ravioli
ravish
raw
  raw-boned
  rawer
  rawness
ray
rayon
raze, rase (to destroy)
  razing, rasing
razor
  razor's (of the razor)
  razors' (of the razors)
razzle-dazzle
reach
  reached
  reaches
react
  reactance
  reaction
  reactionary
  reactive
  reactor
reactivate
  reactivating
read
  readable
  reader
  reader's (of the reader)
  readers' (of the readers)
readdress
  readdressed
readjust
  readjustment
readmit
  readmission

readmittance
readmitted
readmitting
ready
  readily
  readiness
  ready-made
reagent
real
  realism
  realist
  realistic
  realistically
  reality
  realities (*pl.*)
  really
realise
  realize
  realisable
  realizable
  realisation
  realization
  realising
  realizing
realm
ream (of paper)
reap
  reaped
  reaper
reappear
  reappearance
  reappeared
rear
  rearguard
rear
  (to raise children, etc.)
rearm
  rearmament
rearrange
  rearrangement
  rearranging
reason
  reasonable
  reasonableness
  reasonably

reassemble
  reassembling
reassess
  reassessed
  reassesses
  reassessment
reassure
  reassurance
  reassured
  reassuring
  reassuringly
rebate
rebel
  rebelled
  rebelling
  rebellion
  rebellious
  rebel's (of the rebel)
  rebels' (of the rebels)
  rebels
rebirth
rebound
rebuff
  rebuffed
rebuild
  rebuilt
rebuke
  rebuking
rebut
  rebuts
  rebuttal
  rebutted
  rebutting
recalcitrant
  recalcitrance
recall
  recalled
recant
  recantation
recap
  recapping
recapitulate
  recapitulating
  recapitulation
recapture

recapturing
recede
  receding
receipt
receive
  receivable
  receiver
  receivership
  receiving
recent
  recently
receptacle
reception
  receptionist
  receptive
recess
  recesses (*pl.*)
  recessed
  recession
  recessive
recession
  recessional
  recessive
recharge
  rechargeable
  recharging
recherché
recidivism
  recidivist
recipe
recipient
  recipient's
      (of the recipient)
  recipients'
      (of the recipients)
reciprocal
  reciprocally
reciprocate
  reciprocating
  reciprocation
  reciprocity
recite
  recital
  recitation
  recitative

reciter
  reciting
reckless
  recklessly
  recklessness
reckon
  reckoner
reclaim
  reclamation
recline
  reclining
recluse
  reclusion
recognise
  recognize
  recognisable
  recognizable
  recognisance
  recognizance
  recognising
  recognizing
  recognition
recoil
recollect
  recollection
recommend
  recommendation
recommit
  recommitment
  recommittal
  recommitted
  recommitting
recompense
  recompensing
reconcile
  reconcilable
  reconcilement
  reconciliation
  reconciling
recondite
recondition
  reconditioned
reconnaissance
reconnoitre
  reconnoiter

reconnoitred
reconnoitered
reconnoitring
reconnoitering
reconquer
reconquered
reconquering
reconquest
reconsider
reconsideration
reconsidered
reconsidering
reconstruct
reconstruction
record
recorder
record-player
re-count (to count again)
recount (to tell)
recoup
recouped
recourse
recover (to get better)
recovered
recovering
recovery
recover (to cover again)
recovered
recovering
recreant
re-create (create again)
re-creating
recreation
recreative
recriminate
recriminating
recrimination
recriminatory
recrudescence
recrudescent
recruit
recruit's (of the recruit)
recruits' (of the recruits)
rectangle
rectangular

rectify
rectifiable
rectification
rectified
rectifier
rectifies
rectifying
rectilinear,
rectilineal
rectitude
rector
rectorial
rector's (of the rector)
rectors' (of the rectors)
rectory
rectories (*pl.*)
rectum
rectal
recumbent
recuperate
recuperating
recuperation
recuperative
recur
recurred
recurrence
recurrent
recurring
recurs
recusant
recusancy
recycle
recycling
red
redbreast
redden
reddened
reddening
redder
redeem
redeemable
redeemer
redemption
redeploy
redeployment

redevelop
redeveloped
redevelopment
rediffusion
redirect
redirected
redirection
redistribute
redistributed
redistributing
redistribution
redo
redid
redoing
redone
redolent
redolence
redouble
redoubling
redoubt (type of fortress)
redoubtable (formidable)
redound
redress
redressment
reduce
reducible
reducing
reduction
reductio ad absurdum
redundant
redundancy
redundancies (*pl.*)
reduplicate
reduplicating
reduplication
re-echo
reecho
re-echoed
re-echoes
re-echoing
reed (water plant)
reef
reek (smell)
reel (to stagger)
reel (of cotton, etc.)

reel (dance)
re-elect
  reelect
  re-election
re-enter
  reenter
  re-entered
  re-entering
  re-entrant
  re-entry
re-establish
  reestablish
  re-establishment
re-examine
  reexamine
  re-examination
  re-examining
re-export
  reexport
  re-exportation
refectory (dining-hall)
  refectories (*pl.*)
refer
  referable
  reference
  referred
  referring
  refers
referee
  referees (*pl.*)
  refereed
  refereeing
  referee's (of the referee)
  referees'
    (of the referees)
referendum
  referenda,
    referendums(*pl.*)
refill
  refillable
refine
  refinement
  refinery
  refineries (*pl.*)
  refining

refit
  refits
  refitted
  refitting
reflate
  reflating
  reflation
  reflationary
reflect
  reflection
  reflective
  reflector
reflex
  reflexive (*grammar*)
refloat
reform
  reformation
  reformatory
  reformatories (*pl.*)
  reformed
  reformer
  reformer's
    (of the reformer)
  reformers'
    (of the reformers)
refract
  refraction
    (bending of light)
  refractive
refractory (stubborn)
  refractoriness
refrain
refresh
  refresher
  refreshment
refrigerate
  refrigerant
  refrigerating
  refrigeration
  refrigerator
refuel
  refuelled
  refueled
  refuelling
  refueling

  refuels
refuge
  refugee
  refugee's
    (of the refugee)
  refugees'
    (of the refugees)
refulgence
  refulgent
refund
refurbish
refuse (to say no)
  refusal
  refusing
refuse (rubbish)
refute (to prove wrong)
  refutable
  refutal
  refutation
  refuting
regain
regal (royal)
  regalia
  regally
regale (to entertain)
  regaling
regard
  regardless
regatta
  regattas (*pl.*)
regenerate
  regeneration
  regenerative
  regenerator
regent
  regency
  regencies (*pl.*)
regicide
  regicidal
regime
  (method of government)
  regimen (strict routine)
regiment (soldiers)
  regimental
  regimentation

region
  regional
  regionally
register
  registered
  registering
  register office
  registers
  registration
registrar (of college, etc.)
registry
  registries (*pl.*)
regress
  regression
  regressive
regret
  regretful
  regretfully
  regrets
  regrettable
  regrettably
  regretted
  regretting
regular
  regularity
  regularly
regularise
  regularize
  regularisation
  regularization
  regularising
  regularizing
regulate
  regulating
  regulation
  regulator
regurgitate
  regurgitating
  regurgitation
rehabilitate
  rehabilitating
  rehabilitation
rehearse
  rehearsal
  rehearsing

reign (to rule)
  reigned
  reigning
  reigns
reimburse
  reimbursement
  reimbursing
rein (of horse)
reincarnation
reindeer
reinforce
  reinforceable
  reinforcement
  reinforcing
reinstate
  reinstatement
  reinstating
reiterate
  reiterating
  reiteration
reject
  rejection
rejoice
  rejoicing
rejoinder
rejuvenate
  rejuvenating
  rejuvenation
relapse
  relapsing
relate
  relating
  relation
  relationship
relative (connected with)
  relatively
  relativity
relative (relation)
relax
  relaxation
  relaxed
relay
  relayed
release
  releasing

relegate
  relegating
  relegation
relent
  relentless
  relentlessly
relevance
  relevant
reliable
  reliability
  reliably
  reliance
  reliant
relic
relief
relieve
  relieving
religion
  religious
  religiously
relinquish
reliquary
relish
reluctance
  reluctant
  reluctantly
rely
  reliable
  relied
  relies
  relying
remain
  remainder
  remaindered
remand
remark
  remarkable
  remarkably
remedy
  remedies (*pl.*)
  remediable
  remedial
  remedied
  remedying
remember

remembered
remembering
remembrance
remind
  reminder
reminisce
  reminiscence
  reminiscent
  reminiscing
remiss (careless)
  remissness
remissible
    (may be remitted)
remission
remit (to pardon or pay)
  remits
  remittal
  remittance
  remitted
  remitting
remnant
remonstrate
  remonstrance
  remonstrant
  remonstrating
  remonstration
  remonstrator
remorse
  remorseful
  remorseless
  remorselessly
remote
  remotely
  remotest
remount
remove
  removable
  removal
  remover
  removing
remunerate
  remunerating
  remuneration
  remunerative
Renaissance

rend
  rent (torn)
render
  rendered
  rendering
  rendition
rendezvous
  rendezvous (pl.)
renegade (turncoat)
renege, renegue (to deny)
  renege
  renegation
  reneging, renegueing
renew
  renewable
  renewal
  renewed
rennet
renounce
  renounceable
  renouncement
  renouncing
renovate
  renovating
  renovation
  renovator
renown
  renowned
rent
  rental
  rentier
renunciate
  renunciating
  renunciation
reopen
  reopened
  reopening
reorganise
  reorganize
  reorganisation
  reorganization
  reorganising
  reorganizing
repair
  repaired

repairer
repairs
reparable
reparation
repartee
  repartees (*pl.*)
repast (meal)
repatriate
  repatriating
  repatriation
repay
  repaid
  repayable
  repayment
  repays
repeal
  repealed
repeat
  repeatedly
  repeater
repel
  repelled
  repellent
  repelling
  repels
repent
  repentance
  repentant
repercussion
repertoire (list of plays)
repertory (theatre)
repetition
  repetitious
  repetitive
rephrase
  rephrasing
repine
  repining
replace
  replaceable
  replacement
  replacing
replay
  replayed
replenish

replenishment
replete
  repletion
replica
  replicas (*pl.*)
reply
  replies (*pl.*)
  replied
  replying
report
  reportable
  reportedly
  reporter
  reporter's
      (of the reporter)
  reporters'
      (of the reporters)
  reporting
repose
  reposing
repository
  repositories (*pl.*)
repossess
  repossession
reprehend
  reprehensible
  reprehension
represent
  representation
  representative
repress
  repression
  repressive
reprieve
  reprieving
reprimand
reprint
reprisal
reproach
  reproaches (*pl.*)
  reproached
  reproaches
  reproachful
  reproachfully
reprobate (to condemn)

  reprobating
  reprobation
reprobate (sinner)
reproduce
  reproducible
  reproducing
  reproduction
  reproductive
reproof (blame)
  reproofs (*pl.*)
reprove (to scold)
  reproval
  reproving
  reprovingly
reptile
  reptilian
republic
  republican
  republicanism
republish
  republication
repudiate
  repudiating
  repudiation
repugnance
  repugnant
repulse
  repulsing
  repulsion
  repulsive
repute
  reputable
  reputation
  reputedly
request
requiem
requiescat in pace (R.I.P.)
require
  requiring
requisite
  requisition
requite
  requital
  requited
re-route

re-routeing
rerun
  reran
  rerunning
rescind
  rescission
rescript
rescue
  rescuer
  rescuer's
      (of the rescuer)
  rescuers'
      (of the rescuers)
  rescuing
research
  researches (*pl.*)
  researcher
  researching
resemble
  resemblance
  resembling
resent
  resentful
  resentment
reserve
  reservation
  reservedly
  reserving
  reservist
reservoir
reset
  resets
  resetting
resettle
  resettlement
  resettling
reside
  residence
  residency
  residencies (*pl.*)
  residential
  residing
residue
  residual
  residuary

resign

residuum
        (chem. residue)
resign
resignation
resilience
resilient
resiliently
resin
resinous
resist
resistance
resistant
resister (person)
resistive
resistor (*electr.*)
resit
resat
resitting
resole (shoes)
resoling
resolute
resolutely
resolution
resolve
resolving
resonance
resonant
resonate
resonating
resonator
resort (to turn to)
resort (holiday place)
resound
resource
resourceful
respect
respectability
respectable
respectful
respectfully
respective
respectively
respire
respiration
respirator

respiratory
respiring
respite
resplendence
resplendent
resplendently
respond
respondent
response
responsive
responsible
responsibility
responsibly
rest
restaurant
restaurateur
restful
restfully
restfulness
restitution
restive
restively
restiveness
restless
restlessly
restlessness
restore
restoration
restorative
restorer
restoring
restrain
restraint
restrict
restriction
restrictive
restructure
restructuring
result
resultant
resume
résumé (summary)
resuming
resumption
resurgence

resurgent
resurrect
resurrection
resuscitate
resuscitating
resuscitation
retail
retailer
retailer's (of the retailer)
retailers'
        (of the retailers)
retain
retainer
retention
retentive
retaliate
retaliating
retaliation
retaliatory
retard
retardation
retch (to vomit)
retched
retches
retention
retentive
rethink
rethought
reticence
reticent
reticule
retina (of the eye)
retinue (of people)
retire
retirement
retiring
retort (to answer back)
retort (for distillation)
retouch
retouched
retouches
retrace
retracing
retract
rectractable

retractile
retraction
retractor
retread
retreat
retrench
  retrenchment
retribution
  retributive
retrieve
  retrievable
  retrieval
  retriever
  retrieving
retro- (back)
  retroactive
  retrograde
  retrogression
  retrogressive
  retrospect
  retrospection
  retrospective
  retrospectively
return
  returnable
reunion
reunite
  reuniting
reuse
  reusable
rev (to speed up)
  revs
  revved
  revving
revalue
  revaluation
  revaluing
revamp
  revamping
reveal (to disclose)
  revelation
reveille
revel (to make merry)
  revelled
  reveled

reveller
reveler
revelling
reveling
revelry
revelries (*pl.*)
revels
revenge
revengeful
revenging
revenue
reverberate
reverberating
reverberation
reverberator
revere
reverence
reverend (clergyman)
reverent (respectful)
reverential
revering
reverie
revers (turned back cloth)
reverse
reversal
reversible
reversing
reversion
revert
revetment
review
  (to examine critically)
reviewer
revile
reviling
revise
Revised Version
revising
revision
revitalise
revitalize
revitalising
revitalizing
revive
revival

reviving
revoke
revocable
revocation
revoking
revolt
revolution
revolutionary
revolutionaries (*pl.*)
revolutionise
revolutionize
revolutionising
revolutionizing
revolve
revolver
revolving
revue (entertainment)
review
revulsion
reward
rewrite
rewriting
rewritten
rewrote
rhapsody
rhapsodies (*pl.*)
rhapsodical
rhapsodise
rhapsodize
rhapsodising
rhapsodizing
rheostat
rhesus
rhetoric
rhetorical
rhetorically
rheumatic
rheumatism
rheumatoid
rheumy
rhinoceros
rhinoceroses (*pl.*)
rhinoceros's
  (of the rhinoceros)

rhinoceroses'
  (of the rhinoceroses)
rhizome
rhododendron
  rhododendrons (*pl.*)
rhombus
  rhomboid
rhubarb
rhyme
  rhyming
rhythm
  rhythmic
  rhythmical
  rhythmically
rib
  ribbed
  ribbing
ribald
  ribaldry
ribbon
rice
rich
  riches (*pl.*)
  richer
  richly
  richness
rick (of hay)
rick, wrick (to sprain)
  ricked, wricked
rickets
rickety
rickshaw, ricksha
ricochet
  ricocheted,
        ricochetted
  ricocheted
  ricocheting,
        ricochetting
  ricocheting
rid
  riddance
riddle
ride
  ridable
  ridden

rider
rider's (of the rider)
riders' (of the riders)
riding
rode
ridge
  ridging
ridicule
  ridiculing
  ridiculous
  ridiculously
rife (widespread)
riff-raff
rifle (gun)
rifle (to steal)
  rifling
rift
rig
  rigged
  rigging
right
  right angle
  right-angled
  righteous
  righteousness
  rightful
  rightfully
  rightly
rigid
  rigidity
  rigidly
rigmarole
rigor (stiffness)
  rigor mortis
    (stiffness after death)
rigour (severity)
  rigor
  rigorous
  rigorously
rile
  riling
rim
  rimmed
rime (frost)
rind

ring (to sound)
  rang
  ringer
  rung
ring (jewel)
ring (circle)
ring
  (combine of firms, etc.)
  ringleader
  ringlet (of hair)
rink
rinse
  rinsing
riot
  rioted
  rioter
  riotous
  riotously
  riotousness
rip
  ripped
  rips
ripe
  ripely
  ripen
  ripened
  ripeness
  ripening
  ripens
  riper
R.I.P.
riposte
ripping (excellent)
ripple
  rippling
rise
  risen
  riser
  rising
  rose
risible
risk
  riskier
  riskily
  riskiness

risky
risotto
risqué
rissole
rite (ceremony)
ritual
  ritualism
  ritualist
  ritualistic
  ritually
rival
  rivalled
  rivaled
  rivalling
  rivaling
  rivalry
  rivals
river
  river's (of the river)
  rivers' (of the rivers)
rivet
  riveted
  riveter
  riveting
Riviera
rivulet
roach
  roach (*pl.*)
  roaches (*pl.*)
road
  road-hog
  road sense
  roadway
  roadworthiness
  roadworthy
roam (to wander)
roan
roar
  roared
  roars
roast
rob
  robbed
  robber
  robbery

robberies (*pl.*)
robber's (of the robber)
robbers'
      (of the robbers)
robbing
robs
robe (dress)
  robing
robin
  robin redbreast
  robin's (of the robin)
  robins' (of the robins)
robot
robust
  robustly
  robustness
rock (stone)
  rockery
  rockeries (*pl.*)
  rocky
rock (to swing)
  rock and roll
  rocking-horse
rocket
  rocketed
  rocketing
  rocketry
rococo
rod
rode (*from* ride)
rodent
rodeo
  rodeos (*pl.*)
roe (deer)
roe (of fish)
rogation
rogue
  roguery
  rogue's (of the rogue)
  rogues' (of the rogues)
  roguish
roisterer
role (actor's part)
roll
  roll-call

rolled
roller
roller-skate
rolling
roll (of bread)
rollick
roly-poly
romance
  romancer
  romancing
romantic
  romantically
  romanticise
  romanticize
  romanticising
  romanticizing
  romanticism
romp
  romper
rondo
  rondos (*pl.*)
rood (crucifix)
roof
  roofs (*pl.*)
rook
  rookery
  rookeries (*pl.*)
rookie
room
  roomful
  roominess
  room-mate
  roomy
roost
  rooster (hen)
root
  rootless
rope
  roping
rosary
  rosaries (*pl.*)
rose (flower)
  roseate
  rose-leaf
  rose-leaves (*pl.*)

rosily
rosy
rose (*from* rise)
rosé (wine)
rosemary
rosette
rosin
rosined
roster (list of duties, etc.)
rostrum
rostra, rostrums (*pl.*)
rostra (*pl.*)
rot
rots
rotted
rotten
rottenness
rotter
rotting
rota
rotas (*pl.*)
Rotarian
rotary
rotate
rotatable
rotating
rotation
rote (procedure)
rotisserie
rotor (of electr. motor)
rotund
(round and plump)
rotundity
rotunda (circular building)
rouble (Russian money)
ruble
roué
rouge
rough
roughage
roughen
roughened
roughening
rougher
roughly

roughness
rough-hew
rough-hewed
rough-hewing
rough-hewn
roughshod
roulette
round
roundabout
rounder
roundness
roundelay
rounders
rouse
rousing
rout (to defeat)
route (road taken)
route march
routine (procedure)
rove
rover
roving
row (a boat)
rower
row (line of things, etc.)
row (noise)
rowdy
rowdies (*pl.*)
rowdily
rowdiness
rowdyism
rowlock
royal
royalist
royally
royalty
royalties (*pl.*)
rub
rubbed
rubber
rubbing
rubs
rubbish
rubbishy
rubble (broken bricks)

rubicund
rubric
ruby
rubies (*pl.*)
ruche
ruching
ruck (crease)
rucked
ruckle
ruckling
rucksack
ruction
rudder
ruddy
ruddiness
rude
rudely
rudeness
ruder
rudiment
rudimentary
rue
rueful
ruefully
rueing
ruing
ruff (collar)
ruffian
ruffle
ruffling
rug
rugby, rugger
rugged
ruggedness
ruin
ruination
ruinous
ruinously
rule
ruler
ruler's (of the ruler)
rulers' (of the rulers)
ruling
rum
rumble

rumbling
ruminate
  ruminant
  ruminating
rummage
  rummaging
rummy (game)
rummy (queer)
rumour
  rumor
  rumoured
  rumored
rump
rumple
  rumpling
rumpus
  rumpuses (*pl.*)
run
  ran
  runabout
  runaway
  runner
  runner-up
  running
  runny
  runs
  runway
rune (early Norse letter)
  runic
rung (*from* ring)
rung (of ladder)
rupee (Indian money)
rupture
  rupturing
rural
  rurally
ruse
rush
  rush-hour
rusk
russet
rust
  rustier
  rustiness
  rustless

rust-proof
rust-proofed
rust-proofing
rusty
rustic
  rusticate
  rusticating
  rustication
  rusticity
rustle
  rustler
  rustling
rut (track in ground)
  rutted
rut (of deer)
  ruts
  rutted
  rutting
ruthless (pitiless)
  ruthlessly
  ruthlessness
rye (corn)

sabbath
  Sabbatarian
  sabbatical
sable
sabotage
  sabotaged
  sabotaging
  saboteur
sabre
  saber
sac (pouch)
saccharin
saccrdotal
sachet
sack
  sacked
sacrament

sacramental
sacred
  sacredly
  sacredness
sacrifice
  sacrificial
  sacrificing
sacrilege
  sacrilegious
sacrosanct
sad
  sadden
  saddened
  sadder
  sadly
  sadness
saddle
  saddler
  saddlery
  saddling
sadism
  sadist
  sadistic
safari
  safaris (*pl.*)
safe
  safe conduct
  safe deposit
  safe keeping
  safely
  safer
  safety
safeguard
saffron
sag
  sagged
  sagging
  sags
saga
  sagas (*pl.*)
sagacious
  sagaciously
  sagacity
sage (wise)
  sagely

sage (herb)
sago
sahib
said (*from* say)
sail (of ship)
  sailer (ship)
  sailor (man)
  sailor's (of the sailor)
  sailors' (of the sailors)
saint
  sainthood
  saintliness
  saintly
  saint's (of the saint)
  saints' (of the saints)
sake
salaam (low bow)
  salaamed
salacious
  salacity
salad
salamander
salami (sausage)
salary
  salaries (*pl.*)
  salariat
  salaried
sale (at shop)
  saleability
  salability
  saleable
  salable
  salesman
  salesman's
    (of the salesman)
  salesmen's
    (of the salesmen)
  saleswoman
  saleswomen (*pl.*)
  saleswoman's
    (of the saleswoman)
  saleswomen's
    (of the saleswomen)
salicin
  salicylic

salient
saline
  salinity
saliva
  salivary
  salivate
  salivating
  salivation
salle à manger
    (dining-room)
sallow
  sallowness
sally
  sallies (*pl.*)
  sallied
  sallies
  sallying
salmon
salmonella (bacterium)
salon (drawing-room)
saloon (of pub)
salsify (vegetable)
salt
  salt-cellar
  saltiness
  salty
saltpetre
  saltpeter
salubrious
  salubrity
salutary
salute
  salutation
  saluting
salvation
salve (to save)
  salvage
  salvaging
  salving
salve (ointment)
salver (tray)
salvo (from gun)
  salvoes, salvos (*pl.*)
  salvos (pl.)
sal volatile

Samaritan
same
samovar
sample
  sampler
  sampling
sanatorium
  sanitarium
  sanatoriums,
    sanatoria(*pl.*)
  sanitariums,
    sanitaria(pl.)
sanctify
  sanctification
  sanctified
  sanctifies
sanctimonious
  sanctimoniously
  sanctimoniousness
sanction
sanctity
sanctuary (holy place)
  sanctuaries (*pl.*)
sanctum (private room)
  sanctums, sancta (*pl.*)
sand
  sandbag
  sandbagged
  sandbagging
  sandpaper
  sandpapered
  sandpapering
  sandy
sandal (shoe)
sandalwood
sandwich
  sandwiches (*pl.*)
sane
  sanely
  sanity
sang-froid
sanguinary (bloodthirsty)
sanguine (hopeful)
sanitary
sanitation

sanity (*from* sane)
Santa Claus
sap
  sapped
  sapping
sapience
  sapient
sapling
sapper
sapphire
saprophyte
  saprophytic
saraband
sarcasm
  sarcastic
  sarcastically
sarco- (flesh)
  sarcoma
  sarcophagus
  sarcophagi (*pl.*)
sardine
sardonic
  sardonically
sari, saree
sartorial
sash
  sashes (*pl.*)
Satan
  satanic
satchel
sate
  sated (satisfied)
satellite
satiate
  satiable
  satiated (overfull)
  satiating
  satiation
  satiety
satin
  satinette
  satinet
satire
  satirical
  satirically

satirise
satirize
satirising
satirizing
satirist
satisfy
  satisfaction
  satisfactorily
  satisfactory
  satisfiable
  satisfied
  satisfies
  satisfying
satsuma
saturate
  saturating
  saturation
Saturday
saturnine
satyr (forest god)
sauce (cheek)
  saucier
  saucily
  sauciness
  saucy (cheeky)
sauce (gravy)
  saucepan
  saucer
sauerkraut
sauna (steam bath)
saunter
  sauntered
  sauntering
sauté (fried)
sausage
savage
  savagely
  savagery
  savage's (of the savage)
  savages'
    (of the savages)
savant
save
  saver
  saving

save (except)
saveloy
saviour (rescuer)
  savior
savoir faire
savour (taste)
  savor
savoriness
savouring
  savoring
savoury
  savory
saw (to cut)
  sawed
  sawing
  sawn
saw (*from* see)
saxifrage (rock plant)
saxophone
  saxophonist
say
  said
  saying
  says
scab
scabbard
scabies
scaffold
scald
scale (to climb)
  scaling
scale (of fish)
  scaly
scale (music)
scale (size)
scale (weighing)
scallop, scollop
scallywag
  scalawag
scalp
scalpel
scamp
scamper
  scampered
  scampering

scampi (prawns)
scan (*grammar*)
  scanner
  scanning
  scans
  scansion
scan (to look at)
  scanned
  scanning
  scans
scandal
  scandalise
  scandalize
  scandalising
  scandalizing
  scandalmonger
  scandalous
  scandalously
scant
  scantier
  scantily
  scantiness
  scanty
scapegoat
scapegrace (rascal)
scapula (shoulder-blade)
scar (mark of wound)
  scarred
  scarring
scarce
  scarcely
  scarcity
  scarcities (*pl.*)
scare
  scarecrow
  scaring
scarf
  scarfs, scarves (*pl.*)
scarify
  scarification
  scarified
  scarifying
scarlatina
scarlet
scarp (steep slope)

scat
  scatted
scathe
  scatheless
  scathing
scatter
  scatter-brain
  scattered
  scattering
scavenge
  scavenger
  scavenging
scenario
  scenarios (*pl.*)
scene
  scenery
  scenic
scent (perfume)
  scented
scepsis (doubt)
  sceptic (doubter)
  skeptic
  sceptical
  skeptical
  sceptically
  skeptically
  scepticism
  skepticism
sceptre (ceremonial staff)
  scepter
schedule
  scheduled
  scheduling
scheme
  schematic
  schematically
  schemer
  scheming
scherzo
  scherzos (pl.)
schism
  schismatic
schist (rock)
schizoid
schizophrenia

schizophrenic
schnapps
schnorkel, snorkel
scholar
  scholarly
  scholar's
     (of the scholar)
  scholars'
     (of the scholars)
  scholarship
  scholastic
school
  schoolboy
  schoolboy's
     (of the schoolboy)
  schoolboys'
     (of the schoolboys)
  schoolgirl
  schoolgirl's
     (of the schoolgirl)
  schoolgirls'
     (of the schoolgirls)
  schooling
  schoolmaster
  schoolmistress
  schoolteacher
school (of fish, etc.)
schooner
sciatica
science
  scientific
  scientifically
  scientist
  scientist's
     (of the scientist)
  scientists'
     (of the scientists)
scimitar
scintillate
  scintillating
  scintillation
scion
scission (cutting)
scissors
sclerosis

scoff
scoffer
scold
scollop, scallop
sconce
scone
scoop
scoot
scooter
scope
scorbutic
scorch
scorcher
score
score-board
scorer
scoring
scorn
scornful
scornfully
scorpion
Scot
Scotch
Scotland
Scotsman
Scotsmen (*pl.*)
Scotsman's
(of the Scotsman)
Scotsmen's
(of the Scotsmen)
Scotswoman
Scottish
scot-free
scotch
(to prevent or wedge)
scoundrel
scoundrelism
scour
scourer
scourge
scout
scout's (of the scout)
scouts' (of the scouts)
scowl
scrabble

scrabbling
scrag
scraggy
scramble
scrambling
scrap
scrapped
scrapping
scrappy
scrape
scraper
scraping
scratch
scratches (*pl.*)
scratched
scratches
scrawl
scrawny
scream
screech
screeched
screeches
screech-owl
screed
screen
screened
screenplay
screw
screwdriver
screwy
scribble
scribbler
scribbling
scribe
scrimmage
scrimp
scrip (certificate)
script
script-writer
scripture
scriptural
scrofula
scrofulous
scroll
scrotum

scrounge
scrounger
scrounging
scrub
scrubbed
scrubbing
scrubby
scrubs
scruff (of neck)
scruffy
scruffily
scruffiness
scrum
scrummage
scrumptious
scrunch
scruple
scrupulous
scrupulously
scrupulousness
scrutiny
scrutineer
scrutinise
scrutinize
scrutinising
scrutinizing
scuba
scud
scudded
scudding
scuff
scuffed
scuffle
scuffling
scull
sculler
scullery
sculleries (*pl.*)
scullion
sculpture
sculpt
sculptor
sculptor's
(of the sculptor)

sculptors'
      (of the sculptors)
sculptress
sculptresses (*pl.*)
sculptress's
      (of the sculptress)
sculptresses'
      (of the sculptresses)
scum
  scummy
scupper
  scuppered
scurf
scurrilous
  scurrilously
scurry
  scurried
  scurries
  scurrying
scurvy (mean)
  scurvily
scurvy (deficiency disease)
scutcheon, escutcheon
scuttle (to sink a ship)
  scuttling
scuttle (for coal)
scuttle (to hurry)
  scuttling
scythe
  scything
sea
  seaboard
  sea-borne
  seafarer
  seafaring
  seafood
  seagull
  seagull's (of the seagull)
  seagulls'
      (of the seagulls)
  seakale
  sea-level
  sea-lion
  seaman
  seamen (*pl.*)

seaman's
      (of the seaman)
seamen's
      (of the seamen)
seamanship
seaplane
seascape
sea-serpent
seashore
seasick
seasickness
seaside
seaweed
seaworthiness
seaworthy
seal (to close firmly)
  sealing-wax
seal (animal)
  seal's (of the seal)
  seals' (of the seals)
  sealskin
seam (in sewing)
  seamless
  seamstress, sempstress
  seamy
seance
sear (to scorch)
  seared
search
  searched
  searcher
  searches
  searchlight
season
  seasonable
  seasonably
  seasonal
      (varying by season)
  seasonally
  seasoned
  seasoning
seat
  seat-belt
sebaceous
sec (of wine, dry)

secant, sec (*maths.*)
secateurs
secede
  seceding
secession
seclude
  secluding
  seclusion
  seclusive
second (of time)
  second hand (of watch)
second
   (to support a motion)
  seconded
  seconder
second
   (to transfer an officer)
  secondment
second (after first)
  second-guess
  second-hand (not new)
  second-rate
secondary
  secondaries (*pl.*)
  secondarily
  secondary school
secret
  secrecy
  secretive
  secretively
  secretiveness
  secretly
secretary
  secretaries (*pl.*)
  secretaire (desk)
  secretarial
  secretariat
  secretaries'
      (of the secretaries)
  secretary's
      (of the secretary)
secrete (to hide)
  secreting
secrete (from a gland)
  secreting

secretion
sect
  sectarian
section
  sectional
sector
secular
secure
  securely
  securing
  security
  securities (*pl.*)
sedate (dignified)
  sedately
sedate
  (to use drug to calm)
  sedating
  sedation
  sedative
sedentary
sedge
sediment
  sedimentary
  sedimentation
sedition
  seditious
  seditiously
seduce
  seducer
  seducing
  seduction
  seductive
  seductively
sedulous
  sedulity
see
  saw
  seeing
  seen
  seer
see (bishopric)
seed
  seedling
seed (in tennis)
seedy (unwell)

seediness
seek
  seeker
  sought
seem (to appear)
  seemingly
seemly
  seemliness
seen (*from* see)
seep
  seepage
see-saw
seethe
  seething
segment
  segmentation
segregate
  segregating
  segregation
  segregative
seine (fishing net)
seismic
  seismograph
  seismologist
  seismology
seize
  seizing
  seizure
seldom
select
  selection
  selective
  selectively
  selectivity
  selector
selenium
self
  selves (*pl.*)
  self-addressed
  self-assured
  self-centred
  self-centered
  self-conscious
  self-consciously
  self-consciousness

self-defence
self-defense
self-employed
self-esteem
self-evident
self-explanatory
self-image
self-important
self-interest
selfish
selfishly
selfishness
selfless
self-made
self-portrait
self-possessed
self-raising (flour)
self-regulating
self-righteous
self-righteousness
selfsame
self-satisfied
self-service
self-starter
self-styled
self-sufficient
self-taught
sell
  seller
  sellout
  sold
seltzer
selvage, selvedge
semantic
semaphore
semblance
semen
  seminal
semester
semi- (half)
  semi-automatic
  semibreve
  semicircle
  semicircular
  semicolon

semiconductor
semi-conscious
semi-detached
semifinal
semi-precious
semiquaver
semi-skilled
semitone
semitropical
seminar (study group)
seminary
    (college for priests)
  seminaries (*pl.*)
semolina
sempstress, seamstress
senate
  senator
  senatorial
  senator's
    (of the senator)
  senators'
    (of the senators)
send
  sender
  sent
senile
  senility
senior
  seniority
  senior wrangler
senna
sensation
  sensational
  sensationalism
  sensationally
sense
  senseless
  senselessly
  senselessness
  sensing
sensible
  sensibility
  sensibly
sensitise
  sensitize

sensitising
sensitizing
sensitive
  sensitively
  sensitivity
sensor (detecting device)
sensory
sensual (self-indulgent)
  sensualist
  sensuality
  sensually
sensuous
  (affected by beauty)
  sensuously
  sensuousness
sent (*from* send)
sentence (of words)
sentence
  (to punish for a crime)
  sentencing
sententious (pompous)
  sententiously
  sententiousness
sentience (feeling)
  sentient
sentiment
  sentimental
  sentimentalise
  sentimentalize
  sentimentalising
  sentimentalizing
  sentimentalist
  sentimentality
  sentimentally
sentinel
sentry
  sentries (*pl.*)
  sentries' (of the sentries)
  sentry's (of the sentry)
separate
  separable
  separating
  separation
  scparatism
  separator

sepia
sepoy
  sepoys (*pl.*)
sepsis (infection)
September
septic (infected)
  septicaemia
  septicemia
septuagenarian
septum
sepulchre
  sepulcher
  sepulchral
sequel
sequence
  sequential
sequester (to isolate)
  sequestered
  sequestering
sequestrate (to confiscate)
  sequestrating
  sequestration
  sequestrator
sequin
seraglio
  seraglios (*pl.*)
seraph
  seraphs, seraphim (*pl.*)
  seraphic
serenade
  serenader
  serenading
serendipity
  serendipitous
serene
  serenely
  serenity
serf (land-slave)
  serfdom
sergeant
  sergeant-major
serial
  (story in instalments)
  serialisation
  serialization

serialise
serialize
serialising
serializing
serially
series
  series (*pl.*)
serif
serious
  seriously
  seriousness
serjeant (legal official)
sermon
  sermonise
  sermonize
  sermonising
  sermonizing
serpent
  serpentine
  serpent's
      (of the serpent)
  serpents'
      (of the serpents)
serrated
  serration
serried
serum
  sera, serums (*pl.*)
servant
  servant's
      (of the servant)
  servants'
      (of the servants)
serve
  server
  serving
service
  serviceability
  serviceable
  servicing
serviette
servile
  servility
servitude
sesame

session (academic year)
session (meeting)
set
  setback
  sets
  setter
  setting
settee
settle
  settlement
  settler
  settler's (of the settler)
  settlers' (of the settlers)
  settling
seven
  seventeen
  seventeenth
  seventh
  seventieth
  seventy
  seventies
sever (to cut)
  severance
  severed
  severing
several
  severally
severe (strict)
  severely
  severity
sew (to stitch)
  sewed
  sewing
  sewing-machine
  sewn
sewer (drain)
  sewage
sex
  sexed
  sexier
  sexiness
  sexual
  sexuality
  sexually
  sexy

sexagenarian
sextant
sextet
sexton
sextuple
shabby
  shabbier
  shabbily
  shabbiness
  shabby-genteel
shack
shackle
  shackling
shade
  shading
  shadily
  shady
shadow
  shadowy
shaft
shaggy
shagreen
Shah
  Shah's (of the Shah)
  Shahs' (of the Shahs)
shake
  shaken
  shaker
  shake-up
  shakily
  shakiness
  shaking
  shaky
  shook
shale
shall
  shalt (thou)
  shan't (shall not)
shallot
shallow
  shallower
  shallowness
sham
  shammed
  shammer

shamming
shams
shamble
shambling
shame
shamefaced
shameful
shamefully
shameless
shamelessly
shaming
shampoo
shampooed
shampooing
shamrock
shandy
shandygaff
shanghai
shanghaied
shank
shantung
shanty (hut)
shanties (*pl.*)
shanty town
shanty (song)
shanties (*pl.*)
shape
shapeless
shapeliness
shapely
shaping
shard, sherd (potsherd)
share
shareholder
shareholder's
(of the shareholder)
shareholders'
(of the shareholders)
sharer
sharing
shark
sharp
sharpen
sharpened
sharpener

sharpening
sharper
sharply
sharpshooter
sharp-witted
sharper (cheater at cards)
shatter
shattered
shattering
shatter-proof
shave
shaved
shaven
shaver
shaving
shawl
she
she'd (she had, would)
she's (she is)
she'll (she will)
sheaf
sheaves (*pl.*)
shear (to cut)
sheared
shearer
shearing
shears
shorn
sheath
sheath-knife
sheathe (to encase)
sheathing
shed (hut)
shed (to take off)
shedding
sheds
sheen
sheep
sheep (*pl.*)
sheepish
sheepishly
sheepskin
sheep's (of the sheep)
sheer (absolute)
sheer (to swerve)

sheering
sheer (very steep)
sheet
sheikh, sheik
sheik
shelf
shelves (*pl.*)
shell
shellfish
shellac
shellacked
shellacking
shelter
sheltered
shelterer
sheltering
shelve
shelving
shemozzle
shenanigan
shepherd
shepherded
shepherdess (*fem.*)
shepherdesses (*pl.*)
shepherdess's
(of the shepherdess)
shepherdesses'
(of the shepherdesses)
shepherd's
(of the shepherd)
shepherds'
(of the shepherds)
sherbet
sherd, shard (potsherd)
sheriff
sheriffs (*pl.*)
sheriff's (of the sheriff)
sheriffs' (of the sheriffs)
sherry
sherries (*pl.*)
shield
shift (of workers)
shift (to move)
shifty (deceitful)
shiftily

shiftiness
shilling
shilly-shally
  shilly-shallied
  shilly-shallier
  shilly-shallyer
  shilly-shallies
  shilly-shallying
shimmer
  shimmered
  shimmering
shin
shindy
  shindies (*pl.*)
shine
  shines
  shining
  shiny
  shone
  shined
shingle
  shingled
  shingling
shingles (disease)
ship
  shipmate
  shipment
  shipped
  shipper
  shipping
  ship's (of the ship)
  ships' (of the ships)
  shipshape
  shipwreck
  shipwrecked
  shipwright
shire
shirk
  shirker
shirr
  shirring
shirt
shiver
  shivered
  shivering

shivers
shivery
shoal
shock
  shock-absorber
  shocker
  shocking
shod (fitted with shoes)
shoddy (shabby)
  shoddier
  shoddily
  shoddiness
shoe
  shoes (*pl.*)
  shod
  shoelace
shone (*from* shine)
shoo
  shooed
shook (*from* shake)
shoot
  shot
shop
  shopkeeper
  shoplifting
  shopped
  shopper
  shopping
  shop's (of the shop)
  shops' (of the shops)
shore (to prop up)
  shored
  shoring
shore (seashore)
shorn (cut short)
short
  shortage
  shortbread
  shortcake
  short-change
  short-circuit
  short-circuited
  shortcoming
  short cut
  shorter

short-lived
shortly
shortness
short shrift
short sight
short-sighted
short-sightedness
short-tempered
shorten
  shortened
  shortening
shorthand
shotgun
should (*from* shall)
  shouldn't (should not)
shoulder
  shoulder-blade
  shouldered
  shouldering
shout
shove
  shoving
shovel
  shovelled
  shoveled
  shovelling
  shoveling
show
  showdown
  showed
  showily
  showman
  showmanship
  showmen (*pl.*)
  shown
  show off
  show-piece
  showy
shower
  shower-bath
  showery
shrapnel
shred
  shredded
  shredder

shredding
shrew (witch)
  shrewish
  shrew's (of the shrew)
  shrews' (of the shrews)
shrewd (cunning)
  shrewdly
  shrewdness
shriek
shrift
shrike
shrill
  shriller
  shrilly
  shrillness
shrimp
shrine
shrink
  shrank
  shrinkage
  shrunk
  shrunken
shrivel
  shrivelled
  shriveled
  shrivelling
  shriveling
  shrivels
shroud
shrub
  shrubbery
  shrubberies (*pl.*)
shrug
  shrugged
  shrugging
  shrugs
shudder
  shuddered
  shuddering
shuffle
  shuffling
shun
  shunned
  shunning
  shuns

shunt
shut
  shut-down
  shuts
  shutters
  shutting
shuttle
  shuttlecock
  shuttling
shy (bashful)
  shyer
  shier
  shyly
  shyness
shy (to throw)
  shied
  shies
  shying
shy (of a horse)
  shied
  shies
  shying
sibilant
sibling
sic (thus)
siccative
sick
  sick bay
  sicken
  sickened
  sickening
  sickens
  sickly
  sickness
sickle (for reaping)
side
  sideboard
  sideburns
  sidelight
  sideline
  sidelong
  side-splitting
  side-step
  side-track
  sidewalk

  sideways
  siding
sidle
  sidling
siege
sienna (colour)
siesta
sieve
  sieving
sift
sigh
  sighed
  sighing
sight
  sighted
  sightless
  sightlessness
  sightliness
  sightly
  sightseeing
  sightseer
sign
  signer
  signpost
  sign-writer
  sign-writing
signal
  signalled
  signaled
  signaller
  signaler
  signalling
  signaling
  signally
  signalman
  signalmen (*pl.*)
  signals
signature
signatory
  signatories (*pl.*)
  signatories'
    (of the signatories)
  signatory's
    (of the signatory)
signet (ring)

significance
  significant
  significantly
signify
  signified
  signifies
  signifying
Signor (*Mr.*)
  Signora (*Mrs.*)
  Signorina (*Miss*)
Sikh
silage
silence
  silencer
  silencing
  silent
  silently
silhouette
  silhouetted
  silhouetting
silica (in sand, etc.)
  silicate
  silicon (chem. element)
  silicone
   (compound of silicon)
  silicosis (disease)
silk
  silken
  silkworm
  silky
sill
sillabub, syllabub
      (sweet cream)
silly
  sillier
  sillily
  silliness
silo
  silos (*pl.*)
silt
silvan, sylvan (wooded)
silver
  silvered
  silvering
  silversmith

silver-tongued
silvery
simian
similar (alike)
  similarity
  similarities (*pl.*)
  similarly
simile (comparison)
  similes (*pl.*)
similitude (similarity)
simmer
  simmered
  simmering
simnel
simony
simper
  simpered
simple
  simple-minded
  simpler
  simpleton
  simplex
  simplicity
  simplification
  simplified
  simplifies
  simplify
  simplifying
  simplistic
  simply
simulacrum
  simulacra (*pl.*)
simulate
  simulating
  simulation
  simulator
simultaneous
  simultaneity
  simultaneously
sin
  sinful
  sinfully
  sinfulness
  sinless
  sinned

sinner
sinning
sins
since
sincere
  sincerely
  sincerity
sine (without)
  sinecure
  sine die
  sine qua non
sine, sin (*maths.*)
  sine wave
  sinusoidal
  sinusoidally
sinew
  sinewy
sing
  sang
  singer
  singer's (of the singer)
  singers' (of the singers)
  singing
  singsong
  sung
singe (to scorch)
  singeing
single
  single-minded
  singlet (garment)
  singleton (single thing)
  singling
  singly
singular
  singularity
  singularly
sinister
  sinisterly
sink
  sank
  sinker
  sinking
  sunk (was)
  sunken
sink (in kitchen)

Sino- (Chinese)
  sinologist
  sinology
sinuous (with curves)
  sinuously
sinus (cavity)
  sinuses (*pl.*)
  sinusitis
sip
  sipped
  sips
siphon
  siphoned
sir
  sire
şiren
  siren's (of the siren)
  sirens' (of the sirens)
sirloin
sirocco
  siroccos (*pl.*)
sisal
sister
  sisterhood
  sister-in-law
  sisters-in-law (*pl.*)
  sister-in-law's
    (of the sister-in-law)
  sisters-in-law's
    (of the sisters-in-law)
  sisterly
  sister's (of the sister)
  sisters' (of the sisters)
sit
  sat
  sit-in
  sit-ins (*pl.*)
  sits
  sitter
  sitting
site (location)
situate
  situating
  situation
sitz-bath

six
  sixteen
  sixteenth
  sixth
  sixthly
  sixtieth
  sixty
  sixties (*pl.*)
size
  sizeable
  sizable
  sizeably
size (glue)
  sizing
size up (to estimate)
sizzle
  sizzling
skate
  skater
  skater's (of the skater)
  skaters' (of the skaters)
  skating
skate (fish)
skedaddle
  skedaddling
skein
skeleton
  skeletal
sketch
  sketcher
  sketchier
  sketchily
  sketchiness
  sketchy
skew
  skew-whiff
skewer
ski
  skied
  skier
  skiing
skid
  skidded
  skidding
  skids

skiff
skill
  skilful
  skillful
  skilfully
  skilled
skillet
skim
  skimmed
  skim milk
skimp
  skimpily
  skimpiness
  skimpy
skin
  skin-deep
  skin-diver
  skin-diving
  skinflint
  skinned
  skinning
  skinny
  skin-tight
skip
  skipped
  skipping
  skips
skip (for rubbish)
skipper (captain)
  skipper's
    (of the skipper)
  skippers'
    (of the skippers)
skirl
skirmish
skirt
skit (satire)
skittish
  skittishly
  skittishness
skittle
  skittle alley
skua (sea-bird)
skulk
skulduggery,

skullduggery

skull (of head)
  skull-cap
skunk
sky
  sky-diving
  sky-high
  skylark
  skylight
  skyscraper
slab
slack (lazy)
  slacker
  slacking
slack (coal-dust)
slacken
  slackened
  slackening
  slackness
slag
slain (*from* slay)
slake
  slaking
slalom
slam
  slammed
  slamming
  slams
slander
  slandered
  slanderer
  slandering
  slanderous
  slanders
slang
  slangy
slang (to abuse)
slant
slap
  slapdash
  slapped
  slapping
  slaps
  slapstick
slash

slat
slate
slattern
  slatternly
slaughter
  slaughtered
  slaughter-house
  slaughtering
slave
  slave's (of the slave)
  slaves' (of the slaves)
  slavery
  slavish
  slavishly
  slavishness
slaver
  slavered
  slavering
slay
  slain
  slaying
  slew
sleazy
sled, sledge, sleigh
sledge-hammer
sleek
  sleekness
sleep
  sleeper
  sleepier
  sleepily
  sleepiness
  sleeping
  sleeping-draught
  sleeping partner
  sleepless
  sleeplessness
  sleep-walker
  sleep-walking
  sleepy
  slept
sleet
sleeve
  sleeveless
  sleeving

sleigh (*see* sledge)
sleight (cunning)
  sleight of hand
      (conjuring)
slender
  slenderness
slept (*from* sleep)
sleuth
slew (*from* slay)
slew, slue
    (to swing round)
  slue
  slewed
  slued
  slewing
  sluing
slice
  slicing
slick
  slicker
slide
  slid
  slide-rule
  sliding
slight (small)
  slighter
  slightest
  slightly
slight (to insult)
slim (thin)
  slimmed
  slimmer
  slimming
  slimness
  slims
slime (dirt)
  slimy
sling
  slung
slink
  slunk
slip
  slip-knot
  slipped
  slipperiness

227

slippery
slipping
slips
slipshod
slip-stream
slipper
slit
slitting
slits
slither (to slide)
slithered
slithering
slithers
sliver (to break up)
slivered
slivering
slivers
slobber
slobbered
slobbering
sloe (fruit)
sloe-eyed
sloe gin
slog
slogged
slogger
slogging
slogs
slogan
sloop (ship)
slop
slopped
sloppier
sloppily
sloppiness
sloppy
slops
slope
sloping
slosh
sloshed
sloshes
sloshing
slot
slotted

sloth (laziness)
slothful
sloth (animal)
slouch
slouched
slouches
slough (marsh)
slough (to discard skin)
sloven
slovenliness
slovenly
slow
slower
slowly
sludge
slue, slew
            (to swing round)
slue
slewed
slued
slewing
sluing
slug (animal)
slug (to hit)
slugged
sluggard
sluggish
sluggishly
sluggishness
sluice
sluicing
slum
slumming
slumber
slumbered
slumbering
slumbrous
slumberous
slump
slung (*from* sling)
slunk (*from* slink)
slur
slurred
slurring

slurry
  (liquid mud or cement)
slush
slut
slutish
sly
slyer
slyly
slyness
smack (to hit)
smack (boat)
small
smaller
smallness
smart (neat)
smarten
smartened
smartening
smarter
smartly
smartness
smart (to be painful)
smash
smattering
smear
smeared
smell
smelled
smellier
smelliest
smells
smelly
smelt
smelt (to melt metal)
smelt (fish)
smidgen, smidgin
smile
smiling
smirch (to soil)
smirched
smirk (to grin)
smite
smiting
smitten (was)
smote

smith
smithy
smithies (*pl.*)
smithereens
smock
smocking
smog
smoke
smokable
smokeless
smoker
smokier
smoking
smoky
smooth
smoother
smoothly
smoothness
smorgasbord
smother
smothered
smothering
smoulder
smolder
smouldered
smoldered
smouldering
smoldering
smudge
smudging
smug
smugger
smugly
smugness
smuggle
smuggler
smuggling
smut
smuttiness
smutty
snack
snaffle
snaffling
snag
snail

snail's (of the snail)
snails' (of the snails)
snake
snap
snapdragon
snapped
snapper
snappily
snapping
snappish
snappy
snaps
snapshot
snare
snaring
snarl
snatch
snatched
snatches
sneak
sneer
sneered
sneers
sneeze
sneezing
snicker
snickered
snickering
snickers
snide
sniff
sniffle
sniffling
snifter
snigger
sniggered
sniggering
sniggers
snip (to cut)
snipped
snippet
snipping
snips
snipe (bird)
snipe (to shoot)

sniping
snivel
snivelled
sniveled
sniveller
sniveler
snivelling
sniveling
snivels
snob
snobbery
snobbish
snobbishly
snobbishness
snob's (of the snob)
snobs' (of the snobs)
snooker
snooker pool
snoop
snooper
snooze
snoozing
snore
snorer
snoring
snorkel, schnorkel
snort
snot
snotty
snout
snow
snowball
snowballed
snowballing
snowdrop
snowfall
snowflake
snowmobile
snow-plough
snowplow
snow-shoe
snub
snubbed
snubbing
snub-nosed

snubs
snuff
snuffers
snuffle
  snuffling
snug
  snuggery
  snuggeries (*pl.*)
  snugly
snuggle
  snuggling
soak
soap
  soap-flakes
  soaping
  soap-suds
  soapy
soar (to fly high)
  soared
  soaring
  soars
sob
  sobbed
  sobbing
  sobs
sober
  sobered
  sobering
  sobriety
sobriquet (nickname)
soccer
sociable
  sociability
  sociably
social
  socialisation
  socialization
  socialise
  socialize
  socialising
  socializing
  Socialism
  Socialist
  socialite
  socially

Social Security
society
  societies (*pl.*)
socio-economic
sociology
  sociological
  sociologist
sock
socket
sod (turf)
soda
  soda-water
sodden (wet)
sodium
sodomy
sofa
soft
  softball
  soften
  softened
  softening
  softens
  softer
  softly
  softness
  software
soggy
soil (to dirty)
  soiled
soil (ground)
soirée
sojourn
solace
  solacing
solar
  solarium
  solar system
sold (*from* sell)
solder
  soldered
  soldering iron
soldier
  soldiering
  soldier's (of the soldier)

  soldiers'
     (of the soldiers)
sole (alone)
  solely
sole (fish)
sole (of shoe)
  soling
solecism
solemn
  solemnisation
  solemnization
  solemnise
  solemnize
  solemnising
  solemnizing
  solemnity
  solemnly
solenoid
solicit
  solicitation
  soliciting
  solicitor
  solicitor's
     (of the solicitor)
  solicitors'
     (of the solicitors)
  solicitous (sympathetic)
  solicitously
  solicitude
solid
  solidarity
  solider
  solidification
  solidified
  solidifies
  solidify
  solidifying
  solidity
  solidly
  solid-state
soliloquise
  soliloquize
  soliloquising
  soliloquizing
  soliloquy

soliloquies (*pl.*)
solitaire (single gem)
solitary
  solitarily
  solitariness
solitude
solo
  solos (*pl.*)
  soloist
  soloist's (of the soloist)
  soloists' (of the soloists)
solstice
  solstitial
soluble
  solubility
solution
solve
  solvable
  solving
solvent
  solvency
soma- (body)
  somatic
sombre
  somber
  sombrely
  somberly
  sombreness
  somberness
sombrero
  sombreros (*pl.*)
some
  somebody
  somebody's
    (of somebody)
  somehow
  someone
  somewhat
  somewhere
somersault
somn- (sleep)
  somnambulism
  somnambulist
  somnolence
  somnolent

son
  son-in-law
  sons-in-law (*pl.*)
  son-in-law's
    (of the son-in-law)
  sons-in-law's
    (of the sons-in-law)
  sonny
  son's (of the son)
  sons' (of the sons)
sonar
sonata
  sonatina
song
  songster
sonic
  sonic boom
sonnet
sonorous
  sonorously
  sonority
soon
  sooner
soot
soothe
  soothing
soothsayer
sop
  sopping
soph- (wisdom)
  sophism
  sophist
  sophisticated
  sophistry
  sophomore
soporific
soprano
  sopranos, soprani (*pl.*)
  soprano's
    (of the soprano)
  sopranos'
    (of the sopranos)
sorcerer
  sorceress (*fem.*)
  sorcery

sordid
  sordidly
  sordidness
sore (painful)
  sorely
  soreness
  sorer
sorority
sorrel
sorrow
  sorrowful
  sorrowfully
  sorrowfulness
sorry
  sorrier
sort
  (to arrange in groups)
  sorter
sort (kind)
sortie
sot
  sottish
sotto voce (in a whisper)
soubrette
soufflé
sought (*from* seek)
soul
  soulful
  soulfully
  soulless
sound (low noise)
  sounder
  soundless
  soundlessly
  soundproof
  soundproofed
sound (in good condition)
  soundly
  soundness
sound (to measure depth)
soup
soupçon
sour
  sourer
  sourly

sourness
source (of river)
source (origin)
souse
  sousing
south
  southerly
  southern
  southerner
  southward
  sou'-wester
souvenir
sovereign (ruler, coin)
  sovereign's
      (of the sovereign)
  sovereigns'
     (of the sovereigns)
  sovereignty
sovereign (excellent)
soviet
sow (pig)
sow (to plant seeds)
  sowed
  sown
soya
  soya bean
  soybean
spa
space
  spacecraft
  spaceship
  spacesuit
  spacing
  spacious
  spaciousness
spade
spaghetti
span
  spanned
  spanning
  spans
span (spick and span)
spangle
spaniel
spank

spanner
spar (to box)
  sparred
  sparring
  spars
spar (pole on ship)
spare
  sparing
  sparingly
spark
  sparkle
  sparkler
  sparkling
sparrow
  sparrow's
      (of the sparrow)
  sparrows'
      (of the sparrows)
sparse
  sparsely
spasm
  spasmodic
  spasmodically
spastic
spat (*from* spit)
spate
spatial
spatter
  spattered
spatula
spavin
  spavined
spawn
spay
  spayed
speak
  speaker
  speaker's
      (of the speaker)
  speakers'
      (of the speakers)
  spoke
  spoken
spear
  speared

spearhead
special
  speciality
  specialty
  specialities (*pl.*)
  specialties (pl.)
  specially
specialise
  specialize
  specialisation
  specialization
  specialising
  specializing
  specialist
  specialist's
      (of the specialist)
  specialists'
      (of the specialists)
specie (money in coins)
species
  species (*pl.*)
specify
  specific
  specifically
  specification
  specified
  specifies
  specifying
specimen
specious (plausible)
speck
  speckled
spectacle
  spectacles
  spectacular
  spectacularly
spectator
  spectator's
      (of the spectator)
  spectators'
      (of the spectators)
spectre (ghost)
  specter
  spectral
spectroscope

spectroscopic
spectrum
  spectra (*pl.*)
speculate
  speculating
  speculation
  speculative
  speculatively
  speculator
speech
  speeches (*pl.*)
  speechified
  speechify
  speechifying
  speechless
  speechlessly
speed
  sped
  speeded
  speedier
  speedily
  speedometer
  speedy
spell
  spelled
  speller
  spelling
  spelt
spell (a charm)
  spell-binding
  spellbound
spelt (kind of wheat)
spelter (zinc or pewter)
spend
  spender
  spendthrift
  spent
sperm
  spermaceti
  sperm-whale
spew
sphagnum
sphere
  spherical
  spherically

spheroid
sphincter
sphinx
  sphinxes (*pl.*)
sphygm- (pulse)
  sphygmomanometer
spice
  spicier
  spicily
  spiciness
  spicy
spick and span
spider
  spider's (of the spider)
  spiders' (of the spiders)
  spidery
spigot
spike
  spiking
  spiky
spill (of wood)
  spillikin
spill (to upset)
  spilled
  spillage
  spills
  spilt
spin
  spin-bowler
  spin-drier
  spinner
  spinneret
  spinning
  spinning-wheel
  spin-off
  spins
  spinster
  spun
spinach
spindle
  spindly
spine
  spinal
  spinal column
  spineless

spinet
spinnaker
spinney
  spinneys (*pl.*)
spinster
  spinsterhood
spiraea
spiral
  spiralled
  spiraled
  spiralling
  spiraling
  spirally
spire
spirit
  spirited
  spiritedly
  spiriting
  spiritless
  spirituous
spiritual
  spiritualism
  spiritualist
  spiritualistic
  spiritually
spirt, spurt
spit
  spat
  spitfire
  spits
  spitter
  spitting
  spittle
  spittoon
spit (of earth)
spit (likeness)
spit (promontory)
spite
  spiteful
  spitefully
  spitefulness
spiv
splash
  splash-down
  splashed

233

splatter

splashes
splatter
splay
spleen
 splenetic
splendid
 splendidly
 splendour
 splendor
splice
 splicing
splint
 splinter
 splintered
 splintering
split
 splits
 splitting
splurge
 splurging
splutter
 spluttered
 spluttering
spoil
 spoiled
 spoilt
spoke
 spokeshave
spoke (*from* speak)
 spoken
 spokesman
 spokesmen (*pl.*)
spoliation (*from* spoil)
 spoliator
sponge
 sponger
 sponging
 spongy
sponsor
 sponsored
 sponsoring
 sponsor's
  (of the sponsor)
 sponsors'
  (of the sponsors)

spontaneous
 spontaneity
 spontaneously
spoof
 spoofer
spool
spoon
 spoon-fed
 spoon-feeding
 spoonful
 spoonfuls (*pl.*)
spoonerism
spoor (track)
sporadic
 sporadically
spore
sporran
sport
 sportive
 sportively
 sportsman
 sportsmen (*pl.*)
 sportsman's
  (of the sportsman)
 sportsmen's
  (of the sportsmen)
 sportsmanship
spot
 spot-check
 spotless
 spotlessness
 spotlight
 spotlighting
 spotlit
 spots
 spotted
 spotter
 spotting
 spotty
spouse
spout
sprain
 sprained
sprat
sprawl

spray
 sprayer
spread
 spread-eagle
 spread-eagled
spree
sprig
sprightly
 sprightlier
 sprightliness
spring (to jump)
 sprang
 springboard
 springing
 sprung
spring (season)
 spring-clean
 spring-cleaned
 spring-cleaning
 springtime
spring (of water)
spring (of watch, etc.)
sprinkle
 sprinkler
 sprinkling
sprint
 sprinter
sprite
sprocket
sprout
spruce
 sprucely
 spruceness
sprue
sprung (*from* spring)
spry
 spryer
 spryly
 spryness
spud (potato)
spud (small spade)
spume
spun (*from* spin)
spunk
spur (to encourage)

spurred
spurring
spurs
spur (in horse's side)
spur (side-road)
spurious
spurn
spurt, spirt
sputnik
sputter
  sputtered
  sputtering
  sputters
sputum
spy
  spies (*pl.*)
  spied
  spies' (of the spies)
  spying
  spy's (of the spy)
squabble
  squabbling
squad
  squadron
  squadron-leader
squalid
  squalidly
  squalor
squall (to cry)
  squalled
  squalling
squall (of wind)
  squally
squalor
squander
  squandered
  squandering
square
  squarely
  squaring
squash
squat (dumpy)
squat (to sit down)
  squats
  squatted

squatter
squatting
squaw
squawk
  squawker
squeak
squeal
squeamish
  squeamishness
squeegee
squeeze
  squeezing
squelch
squib (firework)
squid (sea-animal)
squiggle
  squiggling
squill
squint
squire
  squirarchy
  squirearchy
  squireen
  squire's (of the squire)
  squires' (of the squires)
  squiring
squirm
squirrel
  squirrel's
      (of the squirrel)
  squirrels'
      (of the squirrels)
squirt
stab
  stabbed
  stabs
  stabbing
stable (fixed)
  stabilisation
  stabilization
  stabilise
  stabilize
  stabiliser
  stabilizer
  stabilising

  stabilizing
  stability
stable (for horses)
  stabling
staccato
stack
stadium
  stadiums, stadia (*pl.*)
staff (people)
  staffed
  staff officer
staff (rod)
stag
  stag's (of the stag)
  stags' (of the stags)
stage (of theatre)
  stagecraft
  stage fright
  stage manager
  stagey, stagy
  staging
stage (progress)
stagger
  staggered
  staggering
  staggers (sheep disease)
stagnate
  stagnating
  stagnation
  stagnant
staid (steady)
  staidly
  staidness
stain
  stainless
stair (step)
  staircase
stake (post)
stake (to bet)
  stakeholder
  staking
stalactite
    (from roof of cave)
  stalagmite
    (pillar of deposit)

stale (not fresh)
  staleness
stale (to urinate)
  staling
stalemate (in chess)
stalk (to chase)
  stalker
stalk (stem)
stall (of engine, to stop)
  stalled
stall (theatre-seat)
stallion
stalwart
stamen
stamina (strength)
stammer
  stammered
  stammerer
  stammering
stamp (with foot)
  stamped
stamp (postage)
  stamp-album
  stamp book
  stamp-collecting
  stamp-collector
stampede
  stampeding
stance
stanch (to stop bleeding)
stanchion
stand
  stand-by
  stood
stand (for spectators)
standard
  standardisation
  standardization
  standardise
  standardize
  standardising
  standardizing
stanza
staple (most important)
staple (for fixing)

stapler
stapling
star (in the sky)
  starless
  starry
star (famous performer)
  stars
  stardom
  starlet
  starred
  starring
  star-turn
starboard (right-hand side)
starch
stare (to gaze)
  staring
stark
  stark naked
start
  starter
startle
  startling
starve
  starvation
  starveling
  starving
state (country)
  stateless
  statesman
  statesmen (*pl.*)
  statesmanship
state (to say)
  statement
  stating
state (condition)
stately (dignified)
  statelier
  stateliness
static (not moving)
static (*electr.*)
station (position)
  stationary (not moving)
  stationed
  stationing
station (railway)

stationmaster
stationmaster's
  (of the stationmaster)
stationmasters'
  (of the stationmasters)
stationer
stationery (paper)
Stationery Office
statistics
statistical
statistically
statistician
statue (of marble, etc.)
statuary
statuesque
statuette
stature
  (tallness, importance)
status
  status quo
statute (law)
  statutory
staunch (loyal)
  staunchly
  staunchness
stave (to make a hole)
  staved
  staving
  stove
stave (step of ladder)
stave
  staved
  stave-off (to postpone)
stay (support)
stay (to remain)
  stayed
  staying
steadfast
  steadfastly
  steadfastness
steady
  steadied
  steadier
  steadies
  steadily

steadiness
steadying
steak (meat)
steal (to rob)
  stealing
  stole
  stolen
stealth
  stealthily
  stealthiness
  stealthy
steam
  steamed
  steam-engine
  steamer
  steamroller
  steamrollered
  steamrollering
steed
steel (metal)
  steely
steep
  steeper
  steeply
  steepness
steep (to soak)
steeple
  steeplechase
  steeplejack
steer (to guide a boat)
  steerable
  steerage
  steered
  steering
  steersman
steer (bullock)
stele, stela
        (Greek gravestone)
stellar
stem
  stemmed
  stemming
  stems
stench
stencil

stencilled
stenciled
stencilling
stenciling
stenography
  stenographer
  stenographic
stenotype
stentorian
step
  stepfather
  stepmother
step
  stepped
  stepping
  steps
steppe (plain)
stereo- (three-dimensional)
  stereophonic
  stereoscope
  stereoscopic
  stereotype
sterile
  sterilisation
  sterilization
  sterilise
  sterilize
  steriliser
  sterilizer
  sterilising
  sterilizing
  sterility
sterling
stern (strict)
  sternly
  sterner
  sternness
stern (ship's)
sternum (breastbone)
steroid
stertorous
stet (let it stand)
stethoscope
stevedore
stew

stewed
steward
  steward's
        (of the steward)
  stewards'
        (of the stewards)
  stewardess (*fem.*)
  stewardess's
        (of the stewardess)
  stewardesses'
        (of the stewardesses)
stick
  sticker
  sticks
  stuck
stickleback
stickler
sticky
  stickier
  stickily
  stickiness
stiff
  stiffen
  stiffened
  stiffener
  stiffening
  stiffer
  stiffly
  stiff-necked
stifle
  stifling
stigma
  stigmata (*pl.*)
  stigmatise
  stigmatize
  stigmatising
  stigmatizing
stile (over a hedge)
stiletto
  stilettos (*pl.*)
still
  stillbirth
  stillborn
  stillness
still (for distilling)

stilt (pole for walking)
stilted (solemn)
stimulate
  stimulating
  stimulation
  stimulative
  stimulus
  stimuli (*pl.*)
sting (insect's)
  stinger
  stinging
  stingless
  stung
stingy (mean)
  stingier
  stingily
  stinginess
stink
  stank
  stinker
  stunk
stint
stipend
  stipendiary
  stipendiaries (*pl.*)
stipple
  stippling
stipulate
  stipulating
  stipulation
stir
  stirred
  stirring
  stirs
stirrup
stitch
  stitches (*pl.*)
  stitched
  stitches
stoat
stock
  stockbroker
  stockbroker's
    (of the stockbroker)

stockbrokers'
  (of the stockbrokers)
stocked
Stock Exchange
stockholder
stockist
stockpile
stockpiling
stock-still
stocktaking
stockyard
stockade
stocking
  stockinet
  stockinette
stocky (short and fat)
  stockier
  stockiness
stodge
  stodgily
  stodging
  stodgy
stoic
  stoical
  stoically
  stoicism
stoke
  stoker
  stoking
stole (robe)
stole (*from* steal)
  stolen
stolid
  stolidity
  stolidly
stomach
  stomach-ache
stone
  stone-deaf
  stonemason
  stone's throw
  stonewalling
  stonier
  stonily
  stoning

stony
stood (*from* stand)
stooge
  stooging
stook (of corn)
stool
stoop
  stooped
stop
  stopcock
  stopgap
  stopover
  stoppage
  stopped
  stopper
  stopping
  stop-press
  stops
  stop-watch
store
  storage
  storekeeper
  store's (of the store)
  stores' (of the stores)
  storing
storey (of a building)
  story
  storeys (*pl.*)
  stories (*pl.*)
stork (bird)
storm
  storm-bound
  stormiest
  stormily
  stormy
story (tale)
  stories (*pl.*)
  story-teller
stoup (flagon)
stout (beer)
stout (fat, determined)
  stouter
  stout-hearted
  stoutly
  stoutness

stove
stove (*from* stave)
stow
  stowage
  stowaway
straddle
  straddling
strafe
  strafing
straggle
  straggler
  straggling
straight (direct)
  straighten
  straightened
  straightening
  straighter
  straightforward
strain
  strained
strain (to sieve)
  strainer
strait (narrow)
  straiten
  straitened (hard up)
  strait-jacket
  strait-laced
  straits (difficulties)
  Straits of Dover
strand (shore)
strand (thread)
stranded (abandoned)
strange
  strangely
  stranger
strangle
  strangling
  stranglehold
strangulate
  strangulating
  strangulation
strap
  straphanger
  strapped
  strapping

stratagem (trickery)
strategy (war tactics)
  strategies (*pl.*)
  strategic
  strategically
  strategist
stratify
  stratification
  stratified
  stratifying
stratosphere
  stratospheric
stratum (layer)
  strata (*pl.*)
stratus (cloud)
  strati (*pl.*)
straw
  strawberry
  strawberries (*pl.*)
stray
  strayed
streak
  streaky
stream
  streamlined
  streamlining
street
  streetcar
strength
  strengthen
  strengthened
  strengthening
strenuous
  strenuously
  strenuousness
streptococcus
  streptococci (*pl.*)
  streptococcal
streptomycin
stress
stretch
  stretcher
strew
  strewed
  strewn

striate
  striated
  striation
stricken (struck down)
strict
  stricter
  strictness
  strictly
stricture (scolding)
stride
  stridden
  striding
  strode
strident (noisy)
  stridency
  stridently
strife
strike
  strikebound
  strike-breaker
  strike-breaking
  striker
  striking
  struck
string
  stringed (with strings)
  stringy
  strung
stringent (very strict)
  stringency
  stringently
strip
  stripped
  stripper
  stripping
  strip-tease
stripe
stripling
strive
  striven
  striving
  strove
stroboscope
  stroboscopic
stroke

stroking
stroll
stroller
strong
stronger
stronghold
strongly
strontium
strop
stropped
stropping
strops
struck (*from* strike)
structure
structural
structurally
strudel
struggle
struggling
strum
strummed
strummer
strumming
strums
strumpet
strung (*from* string)
strut
struts
strutted
strutting
strychnine
stub
stubbed
stubbing
stubs
stubble
stubborn
stubbornly
stubbornness
stucco
stuccoed
stuck (*from* stick)
stud (for collar)
stud (horses)
stud-farm

student
student's
    (of the student)
students'
    (of the students)
studio
studios (*pl.*)
study
studied
studies
studious
studiously
studying
study (room)
studies (*pl.*)
stuff (fabric)
stuff (to fill tightly)
stuffed
stuffy (lacking fresh air)
stuffier
stuffiness
stultify
stultification
stultified
stultifying
stumble
stumbling
stumbling-block
stump
stumped
stun
stunned
stunning
stung (*from* sting)
stunt (unusual action)
stunted (undersized)
stupefy
stupefaction
stupefied
stupefies
stupefying
stupendous
stupendously
stupid
stupider

stupidity
stupor
sturdy
sturdier
sturdily
sturdiness
sturgeon
stutter
stuttered
stutterer
stuttering
stutters
sty (for pigs)
sties (*pl.*)
sty, stye (on eyelid)
sties (*pl.*)
style (method, elegance)
stylish
stylishly
stylishness
stylist
stylise
stylize
stylised
stylized
stylus
    (gramophone needle)
styluses, styli (*pl.*)
stymie
stymied
styptic
styrene
suave
suavely
suavity
subaltern
subaltern's
    (of the subaltern)
subalterns'
    (of the subalterns)
subcommittee
subconscious
subconsciously
subconsciousness
subcontract

subcontractor

subdivide
  subdividing
  subdivisible
  subdivision

subdue
  subdual
  subdued
  subduing

subedit
  subedited
  subediting
  subeditor
  subeditor's
    (of the subeditor)
  subeditors'
    (of the subeditors)
  subedits

subject (citizen)
  subject's
    (of the subject)
  subjects'
    (of the subjects)

subject
  (matter for discussion)
  subjective
  subjectively
  subjectivity

subject (to subdue)
  subjection

sub judice

subjugate
  subjugating
  subjugation

subjunctive

sublet
  sublets
  subletting

sublime
  sublimity
  sublimely

sublimate (physics)
  sublimating
  sublimation

subliminal

submarine
  submarine's
    (of the submarine)
  submarines'
    (of the submarines)

submerge
  submergence
  submerging
  submersible
  submersion

submit
  submission
  submissive
  submissively
  submissiveness
  submits
  submitted
  submitting

subnormal
  subnormality
  subnormally

subordinate
  subordinating
  subordination

suborn
  subornation (bribing)
  suborner

sub-plot

subpoena
  subpoenaed

sub rosa

subscribe
  subscriber
  subscriber's
    (of the subscriber)
  subscribers'
    (of the subscribers)
  subscribing
  subscription

subsequent
  subsequently

subservient
  subservience

subside
  subsidence

subsiding

subsidiary
  subsidiaries (*pl.*)

subsidise
  subsidize
  subsidising
  subsidizing

subsidy
  subsidies (*pl.*)

subsist
  subsistence

subsoil

subsonic

substance
  substantial
  substantially

substandard

substantiate
  substantiating
  substantiation

substantive (noun)
substantive (permanent)

substation

substitute
  substituting
  substitution

substratum
  substrata (*pl.*)

substructure

subtenant
  subtenancy
  subtenancies (*pl.*)

subtend

subterfuge

subterranean

sub-title

subtle
  subtler
  subtlety (ingenuity)
  subtleties (*pl.*)
  subtly (craftily)

subtract
  subtraction

subtropical

suburb

subvention

suburban	suing	sulkily
suburbanite	suede (kind of leather)	sulkiness
suburbia	suet	sulky
subvention	suet pudding	sullen
subversion	suffer	sullenly
subversive	sufferance	sullenness
subvert	suffered	sully
subverter	sufferer	sullied
subway	suffering	sullying
succeed (to be successful)	suffice	sulphur
succeeded	sufficiency	*sulfur*
success	sufficient	sulphate
successful	sufficiently	*sulfate*
successfully	sufficing	sulphide
succeed (to follow)	suffix	*sulfide*
succeeding	suffixes (*pl.*)	sulphuretted
succession	suffocate	*sulfuretted*
successive	suffocating	sulphuric acid
successively	suffocation	*sulfuric acid*
successor	suffragan (bishop)	sultan (emperor)
succinct	suffrage	sultana (*fem.*)
succour	suffragette	sultanate
succor	suffuse	sultana (dried fruit)
succoured	suffusing	sultry
succored	suffusion	sultrier
succouring	sugar	sultrily
succoring	sugared	sultriness
succulence	sugary	sum
succulent	suggest	summation
succumb	suggestion	summed
succumbed	suggestive	summing
such	suggestively	sums
suck	suicide	summary
sucker	suicidal	(short description)
suckle	suit (to be convenient)	summaries (*pl.*)
suckling	suitability	summarise
sucrose	suitable	*summarize*
suction	suitably	summarising
sudden	suit (clothes)	*summarizing*
suddenly	suitcase	summariness
suddenness	suite (attendants)	summary (without. delay)
suds	suite (of furniture)	summarily
sue	suite (of rooms)	summer
sued	suitor	summertime
sues	sulk	summery (weather)

242

summit
  summitry
summon
  summons
  summonses (pl.)
sump
sumptuary
      (legal expression)
sumptuous (luxurious)
  sumptuously
  sumptuousness
sun
  sunbathe
  sunbathing
  sunbeam
  sunburn
  sunburnt
  Sunday
  sundial
  sunflower
  sunless
  sunlight
  sunned
  sunnier
  sunning
  sunny
  sunrise
  sun's (of the sun)
  sunspot
  sunstroke
  sun-tan
  sun-tanned
sundae (ice-cream)
Sunday
sundry
  sundries (pl.)
sung (from sing)
sunk (from sink)
  sunken
sup
  supped
  supper (meal)
  supping
  sups
super- (above, more, etc.)

superabundance
superabundant
superannuate
superannuated
superannuation
superb
  superbly
supercargo
  supercargoes (pl.)
supercharge
  supercharging
supercilious
  superciliously
  superciliousness
superconductor
  superconductivity
superficial
  superficiality
  superficially
superfluous
  superfluity
  superfluously
superheterodyne
superhuman
superimpose
  superimposing
  superimposition
superintend
  superintendence
  superintendent
  superintendent's
    (of the superintendent)
  superintendents'
    (of the superintendents)
superior
  superiority
superlative
  superlatively
superman
  supermen (pl.)
supermarket
supernatural
  supernaturalism
  supernaturally
supernumerary

supernumeraries (pl.)
superpose
  superposing
  superposition
supersaturate
  supersaturating
  supersaturation
supersede
  supersedence
  superseding
  supersedure
supersonic
superstition
  superstitious
superstructure
supervene
  supervening
  supervention
supervise
  supervising
  supervision
  supervisor
  supervisor's
    (of the supervisor)
  supervisors'
    (of the supervisors)
  supervisory
supine (lying flat)
supine (grammar)
supper
  supperless
supplant
  supplanter
supple
  supplely
  suppleness
supplement
  supplementary
  supplementation
suppliant
supplicate
  supplicating
  supplication
supply
  supplied

supplier
supplier's
    (of the supplier)
suppliers'
    (of the suppliers)
supplies (*pl.*)
supplies
support
supporter
suppose
supposedly
supposing
supposition
suppository
suppositories (*pl.*)
suppress
suppressible
suppression
suppressor
suppurate
suppurating
suppuration
supreme
supremacy
supremely
surcharge
surcharging
sure
surely
surer
surety
sureties (*pl.*)
surf
surf-board
surfer
surface
surfacing
surfeit
surfeited
surge
surging
surgeon
surgeon's
    (of the surgeon)

surgeons'
    (of the surgeons)
surgery
surgeries (*pl.*)
surgical
surgically
surly
surlier
surlily
surliness
surmise
surmising
surmount
surname
surpass
surpasses
surplice (clergyman's)
surplus (excess)
surpluses (*pl.*)
surprise
surprising
surrealism
surrealist
surrender
surrendered
surrendering
surreptitious
surreptitiously
surrogate
surround
surtax
surtaxes (*pl.*)
surveillance
survey
surveyor
surveyor's
    (of the surveyor)
surveyors'
    (of the surveyors)
survive
survival
surviving
survivor
survivor's
    (of the survivor)

survivors'
    (of the survivors)
susceptible
susceptibility
suspect
suspect's
    (of the suspect)
suspects'
    (of the suspects)
suspend
suspender
suspension
suspense
suspicion
suspicious
suspiciously
sustain
sustenance
suture
svelte
swab
swabbed
swabbing
swaddle
swaddling-clothes
swag
swagger
swaggered
swaggerer
swaggering
swain
swallow (food, etc.)
swallow (bird)
swallow's
    (of the swallow)
swallows'
    (of the swallows)
swam (*from* swim)
swamp
swampy
swan
swan's (of the swan)
swans' (of the swans)
swank
swanky

swap, swop (to exchange)
  swapped
  swapping
  swaps, swops
sward (of grass)
swarm
swarthy
  swarthier
  swarthily
  swarthiness
swash
  swashbuckler
swastika
swat (a fly)
  swatted
  swatter
  swatting
swath, swathe (strip)
swathe (to bandage)
  swathing
sway
swear
  swearing
  swore
  sworn
sweat
  sweater
  sweaty
swede (kind of turnip)
Swede
  (person from Sweden)
  Swedish
sweep
  sweeper
  swept
sweeping (comprehensive)
sweepstake
sweet
  sweetbread
  sweeten
  sweetened
  sweetening
  sweeter
  sweetheart
  sweetly

sweetmeat
sweet pea
swell (to get bigger)
  swelled
  swelling
  swollen
swell (dandy)
swelter
  sweltered
  sweltering
swept (*from* sweep)
swerve
  swerving
swift (fast)
  swifter
  swiftly
  swiftness
swift (bird)
swig
  swigged
  swigging
  swigs
swill
  swilled
swim
  swam
  swimmer
  swimmer's
    (of the swimmer)
  swimmers'
    (of the swimmers)
  swimming
  swimmingly
  swims
  swum
swindle
  swindler
  swindling
swine
  swine (*pl.*)
  swinish
swing
  swinging
  swings
  swung

swingeing (huge)
swipe
  swiping
swirl
switch
  switches (*pl.*)
  switchback
  switchboard
  switched
swivel
  swivelled
  swiveled
  swivelling
  swiveling
  swivels
swizzle
  swizzling
swollen (*from* swell)
swoon
swoop
swop, swap (to exchange)
  swopped
  swopping
sword
swore (*from* swear)
  sworn
swot (to study hard)
  swots
  swotted
  swotter
  swotting
sybarite
  sybaritic
sycamore
sycophant
syllable (part of word)
  syllabic
syllabub, sillabub
    (sweet cream)
syllabus (course of study)
  syllabuses, syllabi (*pl.*)
syllogism
sylph
sylvan, silvan
sym- (together)

245

symbiosis
symbol
  symbolic
  symbolical
  symbolically
  symbolise
  symbolize
  symbolising
  symbolizing
  symbolism
symmetry
  symmetrical
  symmetrically
sympathy
  sympathetic
  sympathetically
  sympathise
  sympathize
  sympathiser
  sympathizer
  sympathising
  sympathizing
symphony
  symphonies (*pl.*)
  symphonic
symposium
  symposia (*pl.*)
symptom
  symptomatic
syn- (together)
synagogue
synchromesh
synchronism
  synchronisation
  synchronization
  synchronise
  synchronize
  synchronising
  synchronizing
  synchronous
  synchronously
syncopate
  syncopating
  syncopation
syncope (fainting)

syndic
  syndicalism
  syndicate
  syndication
syndrome
synod
synonym
  synonymous
synopsis
  synopses (*pl.*)
syntax
  syntactic
synthesis
  syntheses (*pl.*)
  synthesise
  synthesize
  synthesising
  synthesizing
  synthetic
  synthetically
syphilis
  syphilitic
syringe
  syringing
syrup
  syrupy
system
  systematic
  systematically
  systematise
  systematize
  systematising
  systematizing
systole (heart function)

T

tab
  tabbed
tabby (cat)
  tabbies (*pl.*)
tabernacle

table
  table d'hôte
  tablespoon
  tablespoonful
  tablespoonfuls (*pl.*)
tableau
  tableaux (*pl.*)
tablet
  tabloid
taboo, tabu
  taboos, tabus (*pl.*)
  tabooed
  tabooing
tabulate
  tabulating
  tabulation
  tabulator
tachycardia
tacit
  tacitly
  taciturn
  taciturnity
tack (nail)
tack
(to change ship's course)
tackle
  tackler
  tackling
tacky (sticky)
  tackiness
tact
  tactful
  tactfully
  tactless
  tactlessly
tactics
  tactical
  tactician
tactile
tadpole
taffeta
tag
  tagged
tagliatelle
tail (of animal)

tailed
tailless
tailor
  tailored
  tailor-made
  tailor's (of the tailor)
  tailors' (of the tailors)
taint
  tainted
take
  taken
  take-off
  take-over
  taker
  takes
  taking
  took
talc
  talcum
tale (story)
talent
  talented
talisman
  talismans (*pl.*)
talk
  talkative
  talkativeness
  talked
  talker
tall
  taller
  tallness
tallow
tally
  tallied
  tallies (*pl.*)
  tallies
  tallying
tally-ho
talon
tambourine
tame
  tameable
  tamable
  tamed

tameness
tamer
taming
tam-o'-shanter
tamp (to plug)
tamper (to interfere with)
  tampered
  tampering
tampon
tan
(to convert into leather)
  tanned
  tanner
  tannery
  tanneries (*pl.*)
  tanning
tan (colour)
tandem
tang
tangent, tan (*maths.*)
  tangential
  tangentially
tangerine
tangible
  tangibility
  tangibly
tangle
  tangling
tango
  tangos (*pl.*)
  tangoed
  tangoing
tank
  tankage
  tanker
  tankful
  tankfuls (*pl.*)
tankard
tannin
  tannic
tantalise
  tantalize
  tantalising
  tantalizing
  tantalisingly

tantalizingly
tantalum (metal)
tantalus (stand for wine)
tantamount
tantrum
tap
  tapped
  tapping
  taproom
  tap-root
  tapster
tape
  tapeworm
  tape-measure
  tape-recorder
  taping
taper
  tapered
  tapering
tapestry
  tapestries (*pl.*)
tapioca
tappet
tar
  tarred
  tarring
tarantella (dance)
tarantula (spider)
tardy
  tardier
  tardily
  tardiness
tare (weight)
target
tariff
  tariffs (*pl.*)
tarmac
tarn
tarnish
  tarnished
tarot (cards)
tarpaulin
tarragon
tarry (to delay)
  tarried

tarries
tarrying
tart (pastry)
tart (bitter)
  tartness
tart (prostitute)
tartan (cloth)
tartar (*chem.*)
  tartaric (acid)
  tartrate
tartar (violent person)
task
  task force
  taskmaster
tassel
  tasselled
  tasseled
taste
  tasteful
  tastefully
  tastefulness
  tasteless
  taster
  tastier
  tasting
  tasty
tatter
  tatterdemalion
  tattered
tattle (chatter)
  tattling
tattoo
  tattooed
  tattooer
  tattooing
tattoo (military display)
taught (*from* teach)
taunt
taupe
taut (tight)
  tauten
  tautened
  tautly
  tautness
tautology

tautologic
tautological
tavern
tawdry
  tawdrily
tawny
tax
  taxable
  taxation
  tax-collector
  tax-deductible
  taxed
  taxpayer
taxi
  taxis (*pl.*)
  taxicab
  taximeter
taxi (to move aircraft)
  taxied
  taxiing
taxidermy
    (stuffing animals)
  taxidermist
tea
  tea-bag
  teacup
  tea-leaf
  tea-leaves (*pl.*)
  tea-party
  tea-parties (*pl.*)
  teapot
  teaspoon
  teaspoonful
teach
  taught
  teacher
  teacher's
    (of the teacher)
  teachers'
    (of the teachers)
  teaches
teak
team (of players, etc.)
  team-mate
  team's (of the team)

  teams' (of the teams)
  teamster
  team-work
tear (from weeping)
  tearful
  tearfully
  tearfulness
  tearless
tear (to pull apart)
  tearing
  tears
  tore
  torn
tease
  teased
  teaser
  teasing
teat
technical
  technicality
  technicalities (*pl.*)
  technically
  technician
  technicolor
  technique
  technocracy
  technocracies (*pl.*)
  technological
  technologically
  technology
  technologies (*pl.*)
Teddy-bear
Te Deum (hymn)
tedium
  tedious
  tediously
  tediousness
tee (in golf)
  teed
  teeing
teem (to be abundant)
  teeming
teens (age)
  teenage
  teenager

teenager's
(of the teenager)
teenagers'
(of the teenagers)
teeth (*from* tooth)
teethe
  teething
teetotal
  teetotaller
  teetotaler
  teetotalism
tele- (far, distant)
telecommunications
telegram
telegraph
  telegraphic
telemeter
telepathy
  telepathic
telephone
  telephonic
  telephoning
  telephonist
  telephony
telephoto
teleprinter
teleprompter
telescope
  telescopic
  telescoping
  telescopy
teletype
televise
  televising
  television
telex
  telexed
  teletex (supertelex)
teletext (data by TV)
tell
  tells
  tell-tale
  told
temerity
temper (to harden metal)

tempered
tempering
temper (anger)
tempera
temperament (chàracter)
temperamental
temperamentally
temperance (soberness)
temperate (mild)
temperature
tempest
  tempestuous
template
temple
  temple's (of the temple)
  temples'
(of the temples)
tempo
  tempi, tempos (*pl.*)
temporal (worldly)
  temporally
temporary
(not permanent)
  temporarily
temporise
  temporize
  temporiser
  temporizer
  temporising
  temporizing
tempt
  temptation
  tempter
  temptress
tempus fugit
ten
  tenfold
  tenth
  tenthly
tenable
  tenability
tenacity
  tenacious
  tenaciously
tenant

tenancy
  tenancies (*pl.*)
tenantry
tenant's (of the tenant)
tenants' (of the tenants)
tend (to be likely)
tend (to look after)
tendency
  tendencies (*pl.*)
  tendentious
tender (soft)
  tenderer
  tender-hearted
  tenderly
tender (to offer)
  tendered
  tenders
tender (small ship)
tenderise
  tenderize
  tenderised
  tenderized
  tenderising
  tenderizing
tendon
tendril
tenement
tenet (belief)
tennis
  tennis-court
  tennis-racket
tenon
  tenon-saw
tenor (procedure)
tenor (singer)
  tenor's (of the tenor)
  tenors' (of the tenors)
tense (tight)
  tensely
  tenseness
tense (*grammar*)
tensile
tension
tent
  tent's (of the tent)

249

tents' (of the tents)
tentacle (of animals)
tentative (experimental)
  tentatively
tenterhook
tenuous (thin)
  tenuously
  tenuity
tenure (holding property)
tepid
  tepidly
tercentenary
  tercentennial
term (of school, etc.)
term (word)
termagant
terminal (final)
  terminally
terminal (at airport)
terminal (*electr.*)
terminate
  terminable
  terminating
  termination
terminology
  terminologies (*pl.*)
  terminological
terminus (end of railway)
  termini, terminuses (*pl.*)
termite (white ant)
tern (bird)
tern (set of three)
terrace
  terracing
terracotta
terra firma
terrain
terrapin
terrestrial
terrible
  terribly
terrier
  terrier's (of the terrier)
  terriers' (of the terriers)
terrify

terrific
terrifically
terrified
terrifies
terrifying
territory
  territories (*pl.*)
  territorial
  territorially
terror
  terrorisation
  terrorization
  terrorise
  terrorize
  terrorising
  terrorizing
  terrorism
  terrorist
terse
  tersely
  terseness
tertian (fever)
Tertiary (third)
test
  test-tube
testament
  testamentary
testate
  testator
  testatrix (*fem.*)
testicle
testify
  testified
  testifies
  testifying
testimony
  testimonial
testy (irritable)
  testily
  testiness
tetanus
  tetany
tetchy (irritable)
  tetchily
  tetchiness

tête-à-tête
tether
  tethered
  tethering
tetra- (four)
  tetragon
  tetragonal
  tetrahedral
  tetrahedron
  tetralogy
  tetrarch
  tetrarchy
  tetrode
Teuton
  Teutonic
text
  textual
  textually
textile (cloth)
texture
than
thank
  thankful
  thankfully
  thankfulness
  thankless
  thank-offering
  thanksgiving
that
  that's (that is)
thatch
  thatcher
thaw
  thawed
theatre
  theater
  theatrical
  theatrically
thee (*from* thou)
theft
their (of them)
  theirs
theism
  theist
them (*from* they)

themselves

theme

  thematic

then

thence

  thenceforth

  thenceforward

theo- (God)

  theocracy

  theologian

  theological

  theologist

  theology

  theosophical

  theosophist

  theosophy

theodolite

theorem

  theoretic

  theoretical

  theoretically

  theoretician

theory

  theories (*pl.*)

  theorise

  theorize

  theorising

  theorizing

therapy

  therapeutic

  therapist

there (at that place)

  thereabouts

  thereafter

  thereby

  therefore

  there's (there is)

  thereupon

therm- (heat)

  therm (unit)

  thermal

  thermally

  thermionic

  thermite

  thermocouple

thermodynamic

thermometer

Thermos

thermostat

thesaurus

  thesauri (*pl.*)

these (*pl.* of this)

thesis

  theses (*pl.*)

they

  them

  they'd

      (they had, would)

  they'll (they will)

  they're (they are)

  they've (they have)

thick

  thicken

  thickened

  thickener

  thickening

  thicker

  thicket

  thick-headed

  thickly

  thickness

  thickset

  thick-skinned

thief

  thief's (of the thief)

  thieves (*pl.*)

  thieves' (of the thieves)

  thieving

thigh

thimble

thin

  thinned

  thinner

  thinning

  thin-skinned

thine

thing

think

  thinker

  thinking

thought

third

  thirdly

thirst

  thirstily

  thirsty

thirteen

  thirteenth

thirty

  thirties (*pl.*)

  thirtieth

this

  these (*pl.*)

thistle

thither

thong

thorax

  thoracic

thorn

  thornless

  thorny

thorough

  thoroughbred

  thoroughfare

  thoroughgoing

  thoroughly

  thoroughness

those

thou (you)

though (in spite of)

thought

  thoughtful

  thoughtfully

  thoughtfulness

  thoughtless

  thoughtlessness

  thought-reader

  thought-reading

thousand

  thousandth

thrash (to beat)

  thrashed

  thrashes

thread

  threadbare

threat
  threaten
  threatened
  threatening
three
  three-cornered
  three-dimensional
  threefold
  three-quarters
  three-ply
  threescore
thresh (corn)
  thresher
threshold
threw (*from* throw)
thrice
thrift
  thriftier
  thriftily
  thriftless
  thrifty
thrill
  thrilled
  thriller
  thrilling
thrive
  thrived
  thriven
  thriving
  throve
throat
throb
  throbbed
  throbbing
  throbs
throe (suffering)
  throes (*pl.*)
thrombosis
throne
throng
  thronged
throttle
  throttling
  throttler

through
    (from end to end)
  throughout
throw (to fling)
  threw
  thrown
thrush
  thrush's (of the thrush)
  thrushes'
    (of the thrushes)
thrust
thud
  thudded
  thudding
thug
  thuggery
thumb
  thumbed
thump
thunder
  thunderbolt
  thundered
  thunderer
  thunderstorm
  thunderstruck
  thundery
Thursday
thus
thwart
  thwarted
thy
  thine
  thyself
thyme (herb)
thyroid
tiara
  tiaras (*pl.*)
tibia
tic (twitch)
tick (like a clock)
  ticked
  ticker
tick (on tick, credit)
tick (insect)
ticker-tape

ticket
  ticket collector
ticking (fabric)
tickle
  tickling
  ticklish
tidbit, titbit
tiddler
tiddly-winks (game)
tide
  tidal
  tideless
tidings
tidy
  tidied
  tidier
  tidies
  tidily
  tidiness
  tidying
tie
  tied
  tying
tie-dye
  tie-dyeing
tier (row of seats)
  tiered
tierce (set of three)
tiff
tiffin (lunch)
tiger
  tiger's (of the tiger)
  tigers' (of the tigers)
  tigress (*fem.*)
  tigresses (*pl.*)
  tigresses'
    (of the tigresses)
  tigress's (of the tigress)
tight
  tighten
  tightened
  tightening
  tighter
  tight-laced
  tight-lipped

tightly
tightrope
tights
tike, tyke (dog)
tile
  tiling
till (for money)
till (to cultivate)
  tillable
  tillage
  tilth
till (until)
tiller (of a boat)
tilt
timber (wood)
  timbered
timbre (quality of sound)
time
  time-honoured
  time-honored
  timekeeper
  timeless
  timely
  timepiece
  timer
  timing
timid
  timider
  timidity
  timidly
timorous
  timorously
  timorousness
timpano (drum)
  timpani (*pl.*)
  timpanist
tin
  tinfoil
  tinned
  tinning
  tinny
  tinplate
  (steel coated with tin)
  tintack
tincture

tinder
tinge
  tingeing
tingle
  tingling
tinker
  tinkered
  tinkering
  tinker's (of the tinker)
  tinkers' (of the tinkers)
tinkle
  tinkling
tinnitus (ringing in ears)
tinsel
  tinselled
  tinseled
tint
  tinted
tiny
  tinier
tip
  tipped
  tipper
  tipping
  tips
tip (top)
  tiptop
tip (suggestion)
  tip-off
  tipped-off
  tipster
tip (for rubbish)
  tipped
tippet
tipple
  tippler
  tippling
tipstaff
  tipstaffs, tipstaves (*pl.*)
tipsy
  tipsily
  tipsiness
tiptoe
  tiptoed
  tiptoes

tiptoeing
tirade
tire
  tired
  tiredness
  tireless
  tirelessly
  tiresome
  tiresomely
  tiring
tiro, tyro (beginner)
  tiros, tyros (*pl.*)
tissue
tit (bird)
tit (nipple)
titan (strong man)
  titanic
titbit
tit for tat
tithe
Titian (painter)
titillate (to stimulate)
  titillating
  titillation
titivate (to smarten)
  titivating
  titivation
title
titmouse
  titmice (*pl.*)
titrate
  titrating
  titration
titter (to giggle)
  tittered
  titters
tittle-tattle
titular (*from* title)
toad
  toadied
  toadstool
  toady
  toadies (*pl.*)
  toadying
to and fro

toast
toaster
tobacco
tobacconist
tobacconist's
(of the tobacconist)
tobacconists'
(of the tobacconists)
toboggan
tobogganed
tobogganer
tobogganist
tobogganing
toccata
tocsin (alarm bell)
today
today's (of today)
toddle
toddler
toddling
toddy (drink)
to-do (fuss)
toe
toe-hold
toeing
toff
toffee
tog
togs (clothes)
togged
togged up (well-dressed)
toggery
together
toggle
toil
toiler
toilet
toiletry
token
tolerate
tolerable
tolerably
tolerance
tolerant
tolerantly

tolerating
toleration
toll
(to ring a church bell)
tolled
toll (tax)
toll call (telephone)
toll (damage)
tomahawk
tomato
tomatoes (*pl.*)
tomato-sauce
tomb
tombstone
tombola
tomboy
tom-cat
tome (volume)
tomfoolery
tomorrow
tomtit
ton (weight)
tonnage
tonne (metric ton)
tone
tonal
tonality
toneless
tongs
tongue
tongue-tied
tonguing
tonic
tonight
tonnage (*from* ton)
tonsil
tonsillectomy
tonsillitis
tonsure
tonsorial
too (also)
tool
tooth
teeth (*pl.*)
toothache

toothless
toothsome
tootle
tootling
top
top-heavy
topknot
topmost
top-notch
topped
topping
top (for spinning)
toper (drinker)
topiary
topic
topical
topically
topography
topographer
topographic
topper (top hat)
topple
toppling
topsy-turvy
toque (small hat)
torch
torches (*pl.*)
toreador
torment
tormentor
tornado
tornadoes (*pl.*)
torpedo
torpedoes (*pl.*)
torpedoed
torpedoing
torpid
torpidity
torpidly
torpidness
torpor
torque (twisting)
torrent
torrential
torrid

torsion
torso
   torsos (*pl.*)
tort (wrong-doing)
tortoise
   tortoise-shell
tortuous
    (not straightforward)
   tortuosity
   tortuously
   tortuousness
torture
   torturer
   torturing
tosh (nonsense)
toss
   tossed
   toss-up
tot
total
   totalisator
   totalizator
   totalitarian
   totality
   totalled
   totaled
   totalling
   totaling
   totally
   tote
totem
totter
   tottered
   tottering
touch
   touched
   touches
   touchier
   touchiness
   touchy
touché
tough
   toughen
   toughened
   toughening

tougher
toughly
toughness
toupee
tour
   tourism
   tourist
   tourist's (of the tourist)
   tourists' (of the tourists)
tour de force
tournedos (beef)
tournament
tourniquet
tousle
   tousling
tout
   touted
   touter
   touting
tow (to pull a boat)
   towage
   towed
   towing
   tow-path
tow (fibre)
toward
   towards
towel
   towelling
   toweling
tower
   towered
   towering
town
   townee
   Town Hall
   township
   townspeople
toxaemia
   toxemia
toxic
   toxicologist
   toxicology
   toxin (poison)
toy

toyed
toying
toyshop
trace
traceable
tracer
tracery
tracing
trachea (windpipe)
tracheitis
trachoma
track
tract
tractable
traction
   traction engine
tractor
trade
   trade mark
   trader
   tradesman
   tradesmen (*pl.*)
   tradesman's
    (of the tradesman)
   tradesmen's
    (of the tradesmen)
   trade unionist
   trading
tradition
   traditional
   traditionally
traduce
   traducer
   traducing
traffic
   trafficker
   trafficking
tragedy
   tragedies (*pl.*)
   tragedian
   tragedienne (*fem.*)
tragic
   tragically
   tragicomedy
   tragicomic

trail
  trail-blazer
  trailer
train (railway)
train (of dress)
train (sequence of events)
train (to make efficient)
  trainee
  trainer
traipse
  traipsed
  traipsing
trait
traitor
  traitorous
  traitor's (of the traitor)
  traitors' (of the traitors)
  traitress (*fem.*)
trajectory
  trajectories (*pl.*)
tram
  tramcar
trammel
  trammelled
  trammeled
tramp
  tramp's (of the tramp)
  tramps' (of the tramps)
trample
  trampling
trampoline
trance
tranquil
  tranquillisation
  tranquilization
  tranquillise
  tranquilize
  tranquilliser
  tranquilizer
  tranquillising
  tranquilizing
  tranquillity
  tranquilly
transact
  transaction

transatlantic
transceiver
transcend
  transcendent
  transcendental
transcontinental
transcribe
  transcribing
  transcript
  transcription
transept
transfer
  transferable
  transference
  transferred
  transferring
  transfers
transfigure
  transfiguration
  transfiguring
transfix
transform
  transformation
  transformer
transfuse
  transfusing
  transfusion
transgress
  transgressing
  transgression
  transgressor
tranship
  transhipment
  transhipped
  transhipping
transient
  transience
transistor
  transistorisation
  transistorization
  transistorise
  transistorize
transit
  transition
  transitional

  transitorily
  transitory (temporary)
transitive (*grammar*)
translate
  translatable
  translating
  translation
  translator
  translator's
    (of the translator)
  translators'
    (of the translators)
transliterate
  transliterating
  transliteration
translucence
  translucent
transmigrate
  transmigrating
  transmigration
transmit
  transmission
  transmits
  transmitted
  transmitter
  transmitting
transmute
  transmutation
  transmuting
transoceanic
transom
transpacific
transparence
  transparency
  transparent
  transparently
transpire
  transpiration
  transpiring
transplant
  transplantation
transport
  transportable
  transportation
  transporter

transpose
  transposing
  transposition
transubstantiate
  transubstantiation
transverse
  transversely
transvestite
  transvestism
trap
  trapped
  trapper
  trapping
  traps
trapeze
  trapezium
trash
trauma
  traumas, traumata (*pl.*)
  traumatic
travail (painful effort)
travel
  travelled
  traveled
  traveller
  traveler
  traveller's
    (of the traveller)
  travellers'
    (of the travellers)
  travelling
  traveling
  travelogue
traverse
  traversing
travesty
  travesties (*pl.*)
  travestied
trawl
  trawler
  trawler's
    (of the trawler)
  trawlers'
    (of the trawlers)
tray

treachery
  treacherous
  treacherously
treacle
  treacly
tread
  treadle
  trod
  trodden
tread (of tyre)
treason
  treasonable
  treasonably
treasure
  treasurer
  treasuring
  Treasury
treat
  treatable
  treatment
treatise (literary article)
treaty
  treaties (*pl.*)
treble
  trebly
tree
  tree's (of the tree)
  trees' (of the trees)
trefoil
trek
  trekked
  trekker
  trekking
  treks (he, she)
trellis
tremble
  trembling
tremendous
  tremendously
tremolo (in music)
tremor
  tremulous
  tremulously
  tremulousness
trench

trenches (*pl.*)
trenchant
  trenchancy
  trenchantly
trencher
    (for serving food)
trend
  trendy
trepan
  trepanned
  trepanning
  trepans
trepidation
trespass
  trespassed
  trespasser
  trespasses
trestle
trial
triangle
  triangular
  triangulate
  triangulating
  triangulation
tribe
  tribal
  tribalism
tribulation (distress)
tribune
  tribunal
tributary
  tributaries (*pl.*)
tribute
trice
trick
  trickery
  trickier
  trickily
  trickster
  tricky
trickle
  trickling
tricycle
trident
tried (*from* try)

257

trier
triennial
trifle
 trifler
 trifling
trigger
 triggered
trigonometry
 trigonometric
 trigonometrical
trill
trilogy
trim
 trimmed
 trimmer
 trimming
Trinity
trinket
trio
triode
trip
 tripped
 tripper
 tripping
 trips
tripartite
tripe
triphthong
triple
 triplet
 triplicate
 triplicating
 triplication
 triply
tripod
 tripodal
tripos
triptych (picture)
triptyque
  (travel document)
trite
 tritely
triumph
 triumphal
 triumphant

triumphantly
triumvirate
trivial
 trivia
 trivialise
 trivialize
 trivialising
 trivializing
 triviality
 trivialities (*pl.*)
 trivially
trod (*from* tread)
 trodden
troll (giant)
troll (to sing)
trolley
 trolleys (*pl.*)
trollop
trombone
troop
 trooper
trophy
 trophies (*pl.*)
tropic
 tropical
tropism
troposphere
 tropospheric
trot
 trots
 trotted
 trotter
 trotting
troubadour
trouble
 troublesome
 troubling
trough
trounce
 trouncing
troupe (actors)
 trouper
trousers
trousseau
trout

trowel
truant
 truancy
truce
truck
truckle
 truckling
truculence
 truculent
 truculently
trudge
 trudging
true
 true-blue
 truer
 truism
 truly
truffle
trump
 trumped up
trumpery
trumpet
 trumpeter
 trumpeting
truncate
 truncating
 truncation
truncheon
trundle
 trundling
trunk
trunnion
truss
 trusses (*pl.*)
 trussed (tied up)
trust
 trustee
 trustee's (of the trustee)
 trustees'
  (of the trustees)
 trusteeship
 trustful
 trustfully
 trustworthiness
 trustworthy

truth
  truthful
  truthfully
  truthfulness
try
  tried
  trier
  tries
  trying
  try-out
try (in football)
  tries (pl.)
tryst
tsetse fly
tub
  tubbiness
  tubby
tuba (wind instrument)
  tubas (pl.)
tube
  tubing
  tubular
tuber (swelling)
  tubercle
  tubercular
  tuberculosis
  tuberculous
tuck
Tuesday
tuft
  tufted
tug
  tugged
  tugging
  tugs
tug (boat)
  tug's (of the tug)
  tugs' (of the tugs)
tuition
tulip
tumble
  tumbler
  tumbling
tumescent
  tumescence

tumour
  tumor
tumult
  tumultuous
tun (barrel)
tuna, tunny (fish)
  tuna, tunas, tunny,
            tunnies(pl.)
tundra
tune
  tuneful
  tunefully
  tunefulness
  tuner
  tune up
  tuning
tungsten
tunic
tunnel
  tunnelled
  tunneled
  tunneller
  tunneler
  tunnelling
  tunneling
  tunnels
tunny, tuna (fish)
  tunny, tunnies, tuna,
            tunas(pl.)
turban
  turbaned
turbid
  turbidity
turbine
turbo-alternator
turbo-generator
turbo-jet
turbo-prop
turbot
turbulence
  turbulent
tureen
turf
  turfs, turves (pl.)
  turfed

turgid
turkey
  turkeys (pl.)
  turkey's (of the turkey)
  turkeys' (of the turkeys)
turmeric
turmoil
turn
  turncoat
  turner
  turnstile
  turntable
turnip
turpentine, turps
turpitude (wickedness)
turquoise
turret
  turreted
turtle
tusk
tussle
  tussling
tussore, tussah, tusseh,
         tusser(fabric)
tutelage
  tutelary
tutor
  tutorial
  tutor's (of the tutor)
  tutors' (of the tutors)
tutti-frutti
tutu
tuxedo
  tuxedoes, tuxedos (pl.)
twaddle
twain
tweak
tweed
tweezers
twelve
  twelfth
twenty
  twenties (pl.)
  twentieth
twice

twiddle
  twiddling
twig
twilight
  twilighted
  twilit
twill (fabric)
'twill (it will)
twin
  twinned
  twinning
twine (thread)
twine (to twist)
  twining
twinge
twinkle
  twinkling
twirl
twist
  twister
twit (silly person)
twit (to jeer at)
  twits
  twitted
  twitting
twitch
twitter
  twittered
  twittering
  twitters
two
  twofold
tycoon
tying (*from* tie)
tyke, tike (dog)
tympanum (eardrum)
type
  typical
  typically
  typify
  typified
type
  typescript
  typewriter
  typewriting

typewritten
typing
typist
typist's (of the typist)
typists' (of the typists)
type-cast
  type-casting
typhoid
typhoon
typhus
typography
  typographic
tyrant
  tyrannical
  tyrannically
  tyrannise
  tyrannize
  tyranniser
  tyrannizer
  tyrannising
  tyrannizing
  tyrannous
  tyranny
tyre (on car)
  tire
tyro, tiro (beginner)
tzar, tsar, czar
tzigane (gipsy)

U

ubiquity
  ubiquitous
udder
ugly
  uglier
  ugliness
ukase (order)
ukulele
ulcer
  ulcerated
  ulceration

  ulcerous
ulster
ulterior
ultimate
  ultimately
ultimatum
  ultimatums,
          ultimata(*pl.*)
ultra- (beyond)
  ultra-conservative
  ultramarine
  ultramicroscopic
  ultra-modern
  ultrasonic
  ultraviolet
umber (colour)
umbilicus
  umbilical
umbrage
umbrella
umpire
  umpire's (of the umpire)
  umpires'
      (of the umpires)
  umpiring
umpteen
  umpteenth
unable
unabridged
unacceptable
unaccompanied
unaccountable
  unaccountably
unaccustomed
unacquainted
unaffected
unafraid
unalterable
un-American
unanimous
  unanimity
  unanimously
unanswerable
  unanswered
unapproachable

unarmed
unashamed
unasked
unassisted
unassuming
unattached
unattainable
unattended
unauthorised
unauthorized
unavailable
unavailing
unavoidable
unaware
unawares
unbalanced
unbearable
unbearably
unbeaten
unbeatable
unbecoming
unbeknown
unbelievable
unbelievably
unbeliever
unbend
unbent
unbiased, unbiassed
unbiased
unbidden
unblemished
unblushing
unborn
unbosom
unbounded
unbowed
unbroken
unburdened
unburied
unbuttoned
uncalled-for
uncanny
uncannily
uncanniness
uncared-for

unceremonious
uncertain
uncertainty
uncertainties (*pl.*)
unchangeable
uncharitable
uncharted
unchristian
uncivilised
uncivilized
unclaimed
uncle
uncle's (of the uncle)
uncles' (of the uncles)
unclean
uncomfortable
uncomfortably
uncommitted
uncommon
uncommonly
uncommunicative
uncompleted
uncompromising
unconcern
unconditional
unconditionally
unconfirmed
uncongenial
unconnected
unconquerable
unconscionable
unconscious
unconsciously
unconsciousness
unconstitutional
unconstitutionally
uncontrollable
uncontrollably
uncontrolled
unconventional
unconventionally
unco-operative
unco-ordinated
uncorroborated
uncouple

uncoupling
uncouth
uncouthly
uncouthness
uncover
uncovered
uncritical
uncritically
unction
unctuous
unctuously
unctuousness
uncultivated
undated
undaunted
undeceive
undeceived
undecided
undefended
undeniable
undeniably
under
underarm (bowling)
undercarriage
underclothes
underclothing
undercover
undercurrent
undercut
undercuts
undercutting
underdeveloped
underdog
underdone
undergo
undergoes
undergoing
undergone
underwent
undergraduate
undergraduate's
(of the undergraduate)
undergraduates'
(of the undergraduates)
underground

261

undergrowth
underhand
underlie
  underlay
  underlain
  underlies
  underlying
underline
  underlining
underling
undermanned
  undermanning
undermine
  undermining
underneath
undernourishment
  undernourished
underpass
underprivileged
underrate
  underrating
undersigned
understand
  understandable
  understanding
  understood
understatement
understrapper
understudy
  understudies (*pl.*)
  understudies
  understudied
  understudying
undertake
  undertaker
  undertaking
  undertook
underwater
underwear
underweight
underworld
underwrite
  underwriter
  underwriting
  underwritten

  underwrote
undeserved
undesirable
  undesirably
undetermined
undeterred
undigested
undignified
undisciplined
undo
  undoes
  undoing
  undone
undoubted
  undoubtedly
undress
  undressed
  undresses
  undressing
undue
  unduly
undulate
  undulating
  undulation
  undulatory
undying
unearned
unearth
  unearthly
  unearthing
uneasy
  uneasily
uneatable
uneconomic
  uneconomical
  uneconomically
uneducated
unemployed
  unemployable
  unemployment
unenterprising
unequal
  unequalled
  unequaled
  unequally

unerring
uneven
  unevenly
  unevenness
uneventful
unexceptionable
                (satisfactory)
unexpected
unfailing
unfair
  unfairly
  unfairness
unfaithful
  unfaithfully
  unfaithfulness
unfashionable
unfasten
  unfastened
unfavourable
  unfavorable
  unfavourably
  unfavorably
unfeeling
  unfeelingly
unfeigned
unfit
  unfitness
  unfitted
  unfitting
unfold
unforeseen
unforgettable
  unforgettably
unfortunate
  unfortunately
unfounded
unfriendly
  unfriendliness
unfurl
  unfurled
unfurnished
ungainly
ungodly
ungovernable
ungrammatical

ungrammatically
ungrateful
ungratefully
unguarded
unguent
unhappy
  unhappier
  unhappily
  unhappiness
unhealthy
unheard-of
unhinge
  unhinged
unhoped for
unicellular
unicorn
unidentified
  unidentifiable
uniform
  uniformity
  uniformly
unify
  unification
  unified
  unifying
unilateral
  unilaterally
unimpeachable
  unimpeachably
uninhabited
uninhibited
unintelligible
  unintelligibility
  unintelligibly
union
  unionisation
  unionization
  unionise
  unionize
  unionised
  unionized
  unionising
  unionizing
  unionism
  unionist

unique
  uniquely
  uniqueness
unison
unit
  unitary
  unit's (of the unit)
  units' (of the units)
unite
  united
  uniting
unity
  unities (*pl.*)
universe
  universal
  universality
  universally
  university
  universities (*pl.*)
unjust
unjustifiable
  unjustifiably
  unjustified
unkempt
unkind
  unkindly
  unkindness
unknowing
  unknown
unlawful
  unlawfully
unleavened
unless
unlettered
unlicensed
unlike
  unlikelihood
  unlikely
unlimited
unload
unlock
  unlocked
unlucky
  unluckier
  unluckily

unmanageable
unmarried
unmask
unmentionable
unmistakable
  unmistakably
unmitigated
unmoved
unnamed
unnatural
  unnaturally
unnecessary
  unnecessarily
unnerved
  unnerving
unnumbered
unobservant
unobtrusive
  unobtrusively
  unobtrusiveness
unoccupied
unofficial
  unofficially
unopened
unpack
  unpacked
unpaid
unparalleled
unparliamentary
unpleasant
  unpleasantly
  unpleasantness
unpractical
unprecedented
unprejudiced
unprepared
unprincipled
unprintable
unprofessional
  unprofessionally
unqualified
unquestionable
  unquestionably
unravel
  unravelled

unraveled
unravelling
unraveling
unravels
unreadable
unready
  unreadiness
unreal
  unrealistic
  unrealistically
unreasonable
  unreasonably
unrecognised
  unrecognized
  unrecognisable
  unrecognizable
unreliable
  unreliably
unreserved
  unreservedly
unresponsive
unrest
unrestrained
unrighteous
unripe
unrivalled
  unrivaled
unruffled
unruly
unsafe
unsaid
unsatisfactory
  unsatisfactorily
  unsatisfactoriness
unsatisfied
unsavoury
  unsavory
  unsavouriness
  unsavoriness
unscathed
unscientific
  unscientifically
unscrupulous
  unscrupulously
  unscrupulousness

unseasonable
  unseasonably
unseeing
unseen
unseemly
  unseemliness
unserviceable
unsettle
  unsettling
unsightly
  unsightliness
unskilled
unskilful
unskillful
unskilfully
unskillfully
unsociable
  unsociably
unsophisticated
unspeakable
  unspeakably
unspoiled
unstable
  unstably
unsteady
  unsteadily
  unsteadiness
unsubstantiated
unsuccessful
  unsuccessfully
unsuitable
  unsuitably
unsupported
unsurmountable
unsuspected
untactful
  untactfully
untenable
unthinkable
untidy
  untidier
  untidily
  untidiness
untie
  untied

unties
  untying
until
untimely
unto
untold
untouchable
untoward
untraceable
untrue
  untruth
  untruthful
  untruthfully
unusual
  unusually
unveil
  unveiled
unwanted
unwarranted
unwary
  unwarily
unwell
unwholesome
  unwholesomeness
unwieldy
  unwieldily
  unwieldiness
unwilling
  unwillingly
  unwillingness
unwind
  unwinding
  unwound
unwise
  unwisely
unwitting
  unwittingly
unwonted (unusual)
unworkable
unworldly
  unworldliness
unworthy
  unworthily
  unworthiness
unwrap

unwrapped
unwrapping
unwraps
unwritten
upbraid
upbringing
update
　updating
upheaval
uphill
uphold
　upheld
upholster
　upholstered
　upholsterer
　upholstering
　upholstery
upkeep
upon
upper
　uppermost
uppish
　uppishness
upright
　uprightness
uprising
uproar
　uproarious
upset
　upsets
　upsetting
upshot
upside
　upside-down
upstairs
upstart
uptight
up to date
upward
　upwards
uraemia
　uremia
uranium
urban (of a town)
urbane (polite)

urbanely
urbanity
urchin
urea
urge
　urgency
　urgent
　urgently
　urging
urine
　urinal
　urinary
　urinate
　urinated
　urinating
urn
urology
　urologist
use
　usable
　useable
　usage
　useful
　usefully
　usefulness
　useless
　uselessly
　uselessness
　user
　user's (of the user)
　users' (of the users)
　using
usher
　ushered
　usherette (*fem.*)
　ushering
　ushers
　usher's (of the usher)
　ushers' (of the ushers)
usual
　usually
usurp
　usurpation
　usurper
usury

usurer
usurious
utensil
uterus
　uterine
utilise
　utilize
　utilisable
　utilizable
　utilisation
　utilization
　utilising
　utilizing
　utility
utilitarian
utmost
Utopia
　Utopian
utter
　utterance
　uttered
　uttering
utterly
uttermost
uvula
　uvular
uxorious

V

vacant
　vacancy
　vacancies (*pl.*)
vacate
　vacating
　vacation (holiday)
vaccine
　vaccinate (to inoculate)
　vaccinating
　vaccination
vacillate (to hesitate)
　vacillating

vacillation
vacuole
vacuous
  vacuity
vacuum
  vacuums, vacua (*pl.*)
vade-mecum
vagabond
  vagabondage
vagary
  vagaries (*pl.*)
vagina
vagrant
  vagrancy
vague
  vaguely
  vagueness
  vaguer
vain (conceited)
  vainer
  vainglorious
  vainglory
vain (useless)
  vainly
valance (curtain)
vale (farewell)
vale (valley)
valediction
  valedictory
valence (*chem.*)
  valency
valentine
valerian
valet
  valeted
  valeting
  valet's (of the valet)
  valets' (of the valets)
valetudinarian
valiant
  valiantly
valid
  validity
validate
  validating

validation
valise
valley
  valleys (*pl.*)
valour
  valor
  valorous
value
  valuable
  valuation
  valueless
  valuer
  valuing
valve
  valve's (of the valve)
  valves' (of the valves)
  valvular
vamp
vampire
van
vandal
  vandalism
vandalise
  vandalize
  vandalised
  vandalized
  vandalising
  vandalizing
vane (weathercock)
vanguard
vanilla
vanish
vanity
vanquish
vantage
vapid
vapour
  vapor
  vaporisation
  vaporization
  vaporise
  vaporize
  vaporiser
  vaporizer
  vaporising

  vaporizing
vaporous
variable
  variability
  variance
  variant
  variation
varicoloured
  varicolored
varicose
  varicose veins
variegated
  variegation
varlet
varnish
varsity
vary
  varied
  varies
  variety
  various
  varying
vascular
vase
vaseline
vast
  vaster
  vastly
  vastness
vat (tank)
V.A.T., VAT
    (value-added tax)
vaudeville
vault (cellar)
vault (to jump)
vaunt (to boast)
veal
vector
  vectorial
veer
  veered
vegetable
vegetarian
  vegetarianism
vegetate

vegetating
vegetation
vegetative
vehemence
vehement
vehicle
vehicular
veil
veiled
veiling
vein (blood vessel)
venous
vein (manner)
vein (thin strip)
vellum
velocity
velocities (*pl.*)
velours, velour (fabric)
velvet
velveteen
velvety
venal (corrupt)
venality
venally
vend
vended
vendor (seller)
vender
vendor's (of the vendor)
vendors'
     (of the vendors)
vendetta
vendettas (*pl.*)
veneer
veneered
veneering
venerable
venerate
venerating
veneration
venereal (disease)
vengeance
vengeful
venial (pardonable)
venison

venom
venomous
venous (*from* vein)
vent
ventilate
ventilating
ventilation
ventilator
ventral
ventrally
ventricle
ventricular
ventriloquism
ventriloquist
venture
venturer
venturesome
venturing
venue
veracious
veracity (truthfulness)
veranda, verandah
verb
verbal
verbally
verbatim
verbiage
verbose
verbosity
verbalise
verbalize
verbalising
verbalizing
verbena
verdant
verdancy
verdict
verdigris
verdure
verdurous
verge
verging
verger
verify
verifiable

verification
verified
verifies
verifying
verily
verisimilitude
verity
verities (*pl.*)
veritable
veritably
vermicelli
vermilion
vermin
verminous
vermouth
vernacular
vernal (springlike)
vernier
veronal
versatile
versatility
verse
versed
versification
versified
versifies
versifier
versify
versifying
version
versus (against)
vertebra
vertebrae (*pl.*)
vertebral
vertebrate
vertex (highest point)
vertices, vertexes (*pl.*)
vertical
vertically
vertigo
vertiginous
verve
very
verily
vesper

vessel
vest
vestibule
vestige
  vestigial
vestment
  vesture
vestry
  vestries (*pl.*)
vet (to examine)
  vets
  vetted
  vetting
vetch
veteran (old soldier)
veterinary, vet
  veterinary surgeon
veto
  vetoes (*pl.*)
  vetoed
  vetoing
vex
  vexation
  vexatious
  vexed
via (by way of)
viable
  viability
viaduct
vial (small bottle)
viand
vibrate
  vibrant
  vibrating
  vibration
  vibrato (in music)
  vibrator
  vibratory
vicar
  vicarage
  vicar's (of the vicar)
  vicars' (of the vicars)
vicarious
  (on behalf of another)
vice (depravity)

vicious
viciously
viciousness
vice (tool)
  vise
vice- (in place of)
  vice-chancellor
  vice-president
  vice-presidential
  viceregal
  viceroy
  viceroyalty
  vice versa
vichyssoise
vicinity
vicious (*from* vice)
vicissitude
victim
  victimisation
  victimization
  victimise
  victimize
  victimising
  victimizing
  victim's (of the victim)
  victims' (of the victims)
victor
  victorious
  victory
  victories (*pl.*)
victual
  victuals (*pl.*)
  victualled
  victualed
  victualler
  victualer
  victualling
  victualing
video
  video-cassette
  video-disc
  video-frequency
  video-player
  video-recorder
  video-signal

  videotape
  videotext
    (TV plus telephone)
  Viewdata (UK version)
vie (to compete with)
  vied
  vies
  vying
view
  viewer
  viewpoint
vigil
  vigilance
  vigilant
  vigilante
  vigilantly
vignette
vigour
  vigor
  vigorous
  vigorously
  vigorousness
vile (very bad)
  vilely
  vileness
  viler
vilify
  vilification
  vilified
  vilifier
  vilifies
  vilifying
villa
village
  villager
villain (wrong-doer)
  villainous
  villainously
  villain's (of the villain)
  villains' (of the villains)
  villainy
villein (serf)
vim
vinaigrette
vindicate

vindicating
vindication
vindicator
vindictive
vindictively
vindictiveness
vine
vinery
vineyard
vinous
vinegar
vinegary
viniculture
vintage
vintner
vinyl
viol
viola
viola da gamba
violin
violinist
violinist's
   (of the violinist)
violinists'
   (of the violinists)
violoncello
violoncellos (*pl.*)
viola (flower)
violate
violating
violation
violator
violence
violent
violently
violet
V.I.P., VIP
(very important person)
viper
viper's (of the viper)
vipers' (of the vipers)
virago
viragos (*pl.*)
viragoes (*pl.*)
virgin

virginity
virgin's (of the virgin)
virgins' (of the virgins)
virginal (harpsichord)
virile
virility
virtu, vertu (love of art)
virtual
virtually
virtue (goodness)
virtuous
virtuously
virtuoso
virtuosi, virtuosos (*pl.*)
virtuosity
virulence
virulent
virulently
virus
viral
viruses (*pl.*)
visa
visas (*pl.*)
visa'd
visaed
visaing
visage
vis-à-vis
viscera
visceral
viscid
viscidity
viscosity
viscous
viscount
viscount's
   (of the viscount)
viscounts'
   (of the viscounts)
viscountess (*fem.*)
viscountesses (*pl.*)
viscountess's
   (of the viscountess)
viscountesses'
   (of the viscountesses)

visible
visibility
visibly
vision
visionary
visit
visitation
visited
visitor
visitor's (of the visitor)
visitors' (of the visitors)
visits
visor, vizor
vista
vistas (*pl.*)
visual
visualisation
visualization
visualise
visualize
visualising
visualizing
visually
vital
vitalisation
vitalization
vitalise
vitalize
vitalising
vitalizing
vitality
vitally
vitals
   (vital parts of body)
vitamin
vitiate
vitiating
vitiation
viticulture
vitreous
vitrify
vitrification
vitrified
vitriol
vitriolic

vituperate
  vituperating
  vituperation
  vituperative
vivace (lively music)
vivacity
  vivacious
viva voce
vivid
  vividly
  vividness
vivify
  vivified
  vivifying
viviparous
vivisect
  vivisection
  vivisector
vixen
vizier
vocabulary
  vocabularies (pl.)
vocal
  vocal cord
  vocalisation
  vocalization
  vocalise
  vocalize
  vocalising
  vocalizing
  vocalist
  vocalist's
      (of the vocalist)
  vocalists'
      (of the vocalists)
  vocally
vocation
  vocational
vocative (*grammar*)
vociferate
  vociferating
  vociferation
  vociferous
  vociferously
  vociferousness

vodka
vogue
voice
  voiceless
  voice-print
  voicing
void
  voidable
voilà
voile
volatile
  volatilise
  volatilize
  volatilising
  volatilizing
  volatility
vol-au-vent
volcano
  volcanoes, volcanos (pl.)
  volcanic
volition
volley
volley-ball
volt
  voltage
  voltaic
  voltmeter
volte-face
voluble
  volubility
  volubly
volume
  volumetric
  voluminous
voluntary
  voluntarily
  volunteer
  volunteered
  volunteering
  volunteers
voluptuary
  voluptuaries (pl.)
  voluptuous
  voluptuously
  voluptuousness

vomit
  vomited
  vomiting
voodoo
voracious
  voraciously
  voracity (greediness)
vortex (whirlwind)
  vortexes, vortices (pl.)
votary
  votaries (pl.)
vote
  voter
  voter's (of the voter)
  voters' (of the voters)
  voting
votive
vouch
  voucher
vouchsafe
  vouchsafing
vow
  vowed
vowel
voyage
  voyager
  voyaging
voyeur
vulcanise
  vulcanize
  vulcanisation
  vulcanization
  vulcanising
  vulcanizing
vulgar
  vulgarisation
  vulgarization
  vulgarise
  vulgarize
  vulgarising
  vulgarizing
  vulgarism
  vulgarity
vulnerable
  vulnerability

vulture
vulva
vying (*from* vie)

W

wad
  wadding
waddle
  waddling
wade
  wader
  wading
wafer
waffle
waft
wag
    (to move to and fro)
  wagged
  wagging
  wags
  wagtail
wag (joker)
  waggish
wage (war)
  waging
wage (pay)
  wages
wager (to bet)
  wagered
  wagering
  wagers
waggle
  waggling
wagon, waggon
  wagon
  wagoner
  waggoner
  wagonette, waggonette
  wagon-lit
waif
  waifs (*pl.*)

wail (to cry)
  wailing
wainscot
  wainscoting
waist (round the body)
  waistcoat
wait (to postpone)
wait (at table)
  waiter
  waiter's (of the waiter)
  waiters' (of the waiters)
  waitress (*fem.*)
  waitresses (*pl.*)
  waitress's
      (of the waitress)
  waitresses'
        (of the waitresses)
waits (street singers)
waive (to forgo)
  waiver
  waiving
wake
  wakeful
  wakefulness
  waking
  woke
  waked
  woken
  waked
wake (of ship)
wake
  (lamentation or holiday)
  wakes
walk
  walker
  walker's (of the walker)
  walkers'
        (of the walkers)
  walkie-talkie
  walking-stick
  walk-over
wall
  walled
  wallflower
  wallpaper

wallaby
  wallabies (*pl.*)
wallah, walla
wallet
wallop
  walloped
  walloping
wallow
walnut
walrus
  walruses (*pl.*)
waltz
wan
  wanness
wand
wander
  wandered
  wanderer
  wandering
  wanderlust
  wanders
wane
  waning
wangle
  wangler
  wangling
want
  wanting
wanton (free and easy)
  wantonly
  wantonness
war
  warfare
  warmonger
  warmongered
  warmongering
  warred
  warring
warble
  warbler
  warbling
ward (of hospital)
warder (of prison)
  wardress (*fem.*)
  wardresses (*pl.*)

ward (off)
warden (church, etc.)
  warden's
      (of the warden)
  wardens'
      (of the wardens)
wardrobe
ware (china, etc.)
warehouse
warm
  warmer
  warmth
  warm-hearted
  warmly
  warm-up
warn
  warning
warp
  warped
warrant
  warrant-officer
  warranty
  warranties (*pl.*)
warren
warrior
  warrior's
      (of the warrior)
  warriors'
      (of the warriors)
wart
wary
  warier
  warily
  wariness
wash
  washable
  washed out
  washed up
  washer
  washerwoman
  washerwomen (*pl.*)
  wash out
wasn't (was not)
wasp
  waspish

wassail (to make merry)
waste (to squander)
  wastage
  wasteful
  wastefully
  wastefulness
  waste-pipe
  waster
  wasting
  wastrel
watch (to look at)
  watcher
  watchful
  watchfully
  watchfulness
watch (for telling time)
  watchmaker
watch (sentry)
  watchword
water
  water-borne
  water-closet (W.C.)
  water-colour
  watercolor
  watercress
  watered
  waterfall
  watering
  waterlogged
  watermark
  waterproof
  water-ski
  water-skied
  water-skiing
  watertight
  waterworks
watt
  wattage
  wattmeter
wattle
wave
  waveform
  wavelength
  waving
  wavy

waver (to hesitate)
  wavered
  waverer
wax
  waxwork
wax (to grow)
way
  wayfare
  wayfarer
  wayfaring
  waylay
  waylaid
  waylays
  wayside
  wayward
  waywardness
we
  we'd (we had, would)
  we'll (we will)
  we're (we are)
  we've (we have)
weak (feeble)
  weakened
  weakening
  weaker
  weak-kneed
  weakling
  weakly
  weak-minded
  weakness
weal (scar)
weal (welfare)
weald (former forest)
wealth
  wealthier
  wealthy
wean
  weaned
weapon
  weaponry
wear (clothes)
  wearable
  wear and tear
  wore
  worn

worn-out
weary
  wearied
  wearier
  wearily
  weariness
  wearisome
weasel
weather
  weather-beaten
  weathercock
  weathered
  weathering
weave
  weaver
  weaving
  wove
  woven
web
  webbed
  webbing
  web-footed
wed
  wedded (married)
  wedding
  wedlock
  weds
wedge
  wedging
we'd (we had, would)
Wednesday
wee (tiny)
weed
week (seven days)
  weekday
  week-end
  weekly
  weeklies (*pl.*)
weep
  wept
weevil
weft
weigh
  weighbridge
  weighed

weight
  weightier
  weightily
  weightless
  weightlessness
  weighty
weir (across a river)
weird
  weirder
  weirdly
  weirdness
welcome
  welcoming
weld
  welder
welfare
welkin
well
  well-being
  well-born
  well-bred
  well-known
  well-made
  well-meant
  well-nigh
  well-read
  well-to-do
well (of water)
we'll (we will, shall)
  wellingtons
Welsh
  welsher
Welsh rabbit,
        Welsh rarebit
welt (of shoe)
welter (confusion)
welter-weight
wen (tumour)
wench
  wenches (*pl.*)
  wench's (of the wench)
  wenches'
        (of the wenches)
went (*from* go)
wept (*from* weep)

were (*pl.* of *was*)
  weren't (were not)
we're (we are)
werewolf
  werewolves (*pl.*)
west
  westerly
  western
  westernisation
  westernization
  westernise
  westernize
  westernising
  westernizing
  westward
wet
  wet blanket
  wetness
  wets
  wetted
wether (sheep)
whack
  whacked
whale
  whalebone
  whaler
  whaling
wharf
  wharfs, wharves (*pl.*)
  wharfage
  wharfinger
what
  whatever
  whatnot
  whatsoever
wheat
  wheaten
  wheatmeal
wheedle
  wheedling
wheel
  wheelbarrow
  wheelwright
wheeze
  wheezily

wheezing
whelk
whelp
when
  whenever
  whensoever
whence
where
  whereabouts
  whereas
  whereat
  wherefore
  whereupon
  wherever
  wherewithal
wherry
  wherries (*pl.*)
whet (to sharpen)
  whetstone
  whetted
  whetting
whether (...or)
whey (from milk)
which
  whichever
whiff
Whig
while
  whilst
while (away)
  whiling
whim
  whimsical
  whimsy
  whimsies (*pl.*)
whimper
  whimpered
  whimpering
  whimpers
whine (to cry)
  whining
whinny
  whinnied
  whinnies
  whinnying

whip
  whipcord
  whip-hand
  whipped
  whipping
whippet (dog)
whirl
  whirligig
  whirlpool
  whirlwind
whirr
  whir
whisk
whisker
  whiskered
whisky (Scotch)
whiskey (other makes)
  whiskeys, whiskies (*pl.*)
  whiskies (*pl.*)
whisper
  whispered
  whisperer
  whispering
whist
whistle
  whistler
  whistling
whit (small amount)
Whit
  Whitsun
white
  whitebait
  white-haired
  whiten
  whitened
  whitening
  whiter
  whitewash
whither (where to)
whiting (fish)
whitlow
whittle
  whittling
whizz, whiz
  whiz

whizzed
whizzes
whizzing
who
  whoever
  whom
  who's (who is *or* has)
  whose
whole
  whole-hearted
  wholesale
  wholesaler
  wholly
wholesome
  wholesomely
  wholesomeness
whoop (to shout)
  whoopee
  whooping-cough
whopper
whore
  whoremonger
  whoring
whorl
whortleberry
  whortleberries (*pl.*)
why
wick
wicked (bad)
  wickeder
  wickedly
  wickedness
wicker
  wickerwork
wicket (cricket)
  wicket-keeper
  wicket-keeper's
  (of the wicket-keeper)
  wicket-keepers'
  (of the wicket-keepers)
wide
  wide awake
  widely
  widen
  widened

wider
widespread
width
widow
widowed
widower
widower's
(of the widower)
widowers'
(of the widowers)
widow's (of the widow)
widows' (of the widows)
wield
wife
wives (pl.)
wifely
wife's (of the wife)
wives' (of the wives)
wig (false hair)
wig (to scold)
wigged
wigging
wiggle
wiggling
wigwam
wild
wildebeest
wilder
wildfire
wild-goose chase
wildly
wildness
wilderness
wildernesses (pl.)
wile (trick)
wiliness
wily
wilful
willful
wilfully
willfully
wilfulness
willfulness
will
willing

willingly
willingness
willpower
wilt (thou)
will-o'-the-wisp
willow
willowy
willy-nilly
wilt (to droop)
wimple
win
winner
winner's (of the winner)
winners'
(of the winners)
winning
wins
won
wince
wincing
winch
wind
windier
windfall
windless
windmill
windward
windy
wind (to twist)
winder
winding
windlass
wound
window
window-pane
window-shopping
window-sill
wine
wine-cellar
winy
wing
wing-span
wing-spread
wink
winkle

winkling
winner
winnow
winsome
winsomely
winsomeness
winter
wintered
wintering
wintry
wipe
wiping
wire
wireless
wiriness
wiring
wiry
wisdom
wise
wiseacre
wisely
wiser
wish
wishful
wishfully
wishy-washy
wisp
wistaria, wisteria (shrub)
wistful
wistfully
wistfulness
wit
witless
witticism
wittier
wittily
wittiness
witty
witch
witches (pl.)
witchcraft
witchery
witcheries (pl.)
witches' (of the witches)
witch's (of the witch)

with
  withal
withdraw
  withdrawal
  withdrawn
  withdrew
wither (to shrivel)
  withered
  withering
withers (of a horse)
withhold
  withheld
  withholding
within
without
withstand
  withstood
witness
  witnesses (*pl.*)
  witness-box
  witnessed
  witnessing
  witness's
        (of the witness)
  witnesses'
        (of the witnesses)
wizard
  wizardry
wizened
woad
wobble
  wobbling
woe
  woebegone
  woeful
  woefully
wold (open hilly country)
wolf
  wolves (*pl.*)
  wolf's (of the wolf)
  wolves' (of the wolves)
woman
  women (*pl.*)
  womankind
  womanly

womenfolk
womb
won (*from* win)
wonder
  wondered
  wonderful
  wonderfully
  wondering
  wondrous
wont (accustomed)
  wonted
won't (will not)
woo
  wooed
  wooer
  wooing
wood
  wooden
  woodenly
  woodenness
  woodland
wool
  woollen
  woolen
  woolliness
  woolly
word
  wordily
  wordy
wore (*from* wear)
work
  workable
  worker
  work.nan
  workmen (*pl.*)
  workman's
        (of the workman)
  workmanship
  workmen's
        (of the workmen)
  workshop
world
  worldliness
  worldly
  worldly-wise

world's (of the world)
world-wide
worm
  worm-eaten
worn (*from* wear)
  worn-out
worry
  worries (*pl.*)
  worried
  worrier
  worries
  worrying
worse
  worsen
  worsened
  worsening
  worst
worship
  worshipful
  worshipped
  worshiped
  worshipper
  worshiper
  worshipping
  worshiping
  worships
worst (to defeat)
  worsted
  worsted (cloth)
worth
  worthless
  worthwhile
worthy
  worthier
  worthily
would (*from* will)
  wouldn't
wound (to injure)
  wounded
wound (*from* wind)
  wound-up
wove (*from* weave)
  woven
wrack (seaweed)
wraith (ghost)

wrangle
 wrangler
 wrangling
wrap
 wraparound
 wrapped
 wrapper
 wrapping
 wraps
wrath (anger)
 wrathful
wreak (to inflict)
wreath (of flowers)
 wreaths (*pl.*)
wreathe (twist)
 wreathing
wreck
 wreckage
 wrecked
 wrecker
wren
wrench
wrest (to snatch)
 wrested
wrestle
 wrestler
 wrestler's
  (of the wrestler)
 wrestlers'
  (of the wrestlers)
 wrestling
wretch
 wretches (*pl.*)
 wretched
 wretchedly
 wretchedness
 wretch's (of the wretch)
 wretches'
  (of the wretches)
wrick, rick (to sprain)
wriggle
 wriggling
 wriggler
wring (to twist)
 wrung

wrinkle
 wrinkling
wrist
 wristband
 wristlet
 wrist-watch
writ (legal document)
write
 writer
 write-off (cancellation)
 write off (to cancel)
 writer's (of the writer)
 writers' (of the writers)
 write-up
 writing
 written
 wrote
writhe
 writhing
wrong
 wrongdoer
 wrongdoing
 wronged
 wrongful
 wrongfully
wrote (*from* write)
wrought (shaped)
wrung (*from* wring)
wry (twisted)
 wryly
 wryness

X

xeno- (foreign)
 xenophobia
  (dislike of foreigners)
 xenophobe
 xenophobic
Xerox
Xmas (Christmas)
X-ray

X-rayed
xylophone

Y

yacht
 yacht's (of the yacht)
 yachts' (of the yachts)
 yachtsman
 yachtsmen (*pl.*)
Yankee
yap
 yapped
yard (length)
 yardage
 yardstick
yard (enclosure)
yarn (story)
 yarned
yarn (thread)
yashmak
yawl (boat)
yawn
yea (yes)
year
 yearling
 year-long
 yearly
 year-round
 year's (of the year)
 years' (of the years)
yearn
yeast
yell
yellow
yelp
yen (longing)
yeoman
 yeomen (*pl.*)
 yeomanry
 yeoman's
  (of the yeoman)

yeomen's
    (of the yeomen)
yes
yesterday
  yesterday's
    (of yesterday)
yester-year
yet
yew (tree)
yield
yippie (American hippie)
yodel
  yodelled
  yodeled
  yodeller
  yodeler
  yodelling
  yodeling
  yodels
yoga (Hindu religion)
  yogi (person)
yogurt, yoghourt,
        yoghurt
yoke (fitted on neck)
yokel (peasant)
yolk (of egg)
yonder
yore (long ago)
you
  you'd (you had, would)
  you'll (you will)
  your
  you're (you are)
  yours
  yourself
  yourselves (*pl.*)
  you've (you have)
young
  younger
  youngest
  youngster
youth
  youths (*pl.*)
  youthful
  youth's (of the youth)

youths' (of the youths)
yowl
yo-yo
yule
  yuletide

Z

zany
  zanies (*pl.*)
zeal
  zealot
  zealous
zebra
  zebras (*pl.*)
  zebra crossing
zen
zenith
zephyr
  zephyrs (*pl.*)
zero
  zeros (*pl.*)
zest
  zestful
zigzag
  zigzagged
  zigzags
zinc
zinnia
Zion
  Zionism
  Zionist
zip
  zip fastener
  zipper
zither
zodiac
zombie
zone
  zonal
zoo- (animal)
  zoo (zoological gardens)

zoological
zoologist
zoology
zoom
  zoom lens